SOCIETY WITH TEARS

IRVING SARNOFF

SOCIETY
WITH
TEARS

THE CITADEL PRESS

NEW YORK

Contents

	Preface		9
CHAPTER	1	Aggrandizement versus Realization	15
CHAPTER	2	Images for the American Dream	34
CHAPTER	3	From Frontier to Oligarchy	57
CHAPTER	4	The Tyranny of Class and Caste	75
CHAPTER	5	The Conformity of Egoism	113
CHAPTER	6	Injustice, Crime, and Delinquency	158
CHAPTER	7	Sanity and Love Besieged	177
CHAPTER	8	Palliatives in Purgatory	193
CHAPTER	9	Musings on Utopia	220
CHAPTER	10	Society with Tears	255
	Notes		291
	Index		313

ACKNOWLEDGMENTS

My wife, Suzanne, read the various drafts of this book with love and concern, helping me to clarify obscure points, deal with neglected questions, and resolve subtle contradictions. Nor did she shrink from such dreary mechanics as typing, reading proofs, and checking each of the references. Truly, she made my challenge her challenge; and I wish to thank her for sharing the strains of bringing this work to light.

I should like to express my gratitude to each of the following publishers for granting me permission to quote their copyrighted materials: George Braziller, Inc. for W. Miller, *A New History of the United States*; Harper & Row, Publishers, for L. E. Lomax, *The Negro Revolt*, and S. L. Lubell, *Black and White: Test of a Nation*; International Publishers Co., Inc. for K. Marx, *Critique of the Gotha Programme*; John Wiley and Sons, Inc. for I. Sarnoff, *Personality Dynamics and Development*; Yale University Press for T. Dobzhansky, *Mankind Evolving*.

I.S.

Preface

SEVERAL YEARS AGO, a gracious, brilliant, and widely-traveled English visitor smiled pleasantly across our luncheon table and, in a voice at once confident and sympathetic, asked: "Why are Americans so unhappy?"

I was completely abashed, of course, and my first sputtering inclination was to defend us against such a sweeping charge. After all, what accusation could be more condemnatory? The very cornerstone of our political faith proclaims our inalienable right to the pursuit of happiness. Had we failed so abjectly, in our brief history, to maintain the birthright bequeathed to us by Jefferson and his optimistic cohorts?

In silent desperation, I sought to compile a mental inventory of people who might properly be described as more wretched than ourselves. I thought of the starving masses of India, where thousands upon thousands of families have no other bedrooms but the filthy streets. I recalled the tense stillness of East Berlin, where fearful, sullen, and lonely people are taunted on all sides by billboards celebrating a state of freedom that is grotesquely in contrast with the realities of their government's oppression.

So, I found it rather easy to regain some of my poise by calling forth these and other dreadful examples. But it soon became apparent that her inquiry rested upon tacit assumptions about the

9

well-being we ought to be enjoying in the light of our blessings. Given the abundance of our natural resources, the affluence we have produced, and our heritage of individual liberty, why do we nevertheless suffer as much as people who have been less favored by good fortune?

Seen in this context, her allegation was infinitely more difficult to refute. For even if we disregard the casual and highly subjective experiences of the tourist, and use, instead, the objective statistics of social pathology as our working definition of unhappiness, we find ourselves at or close to the top of the ignoble list on each unsavory item. But it is also apparent that we are far from unique among nations—in either the quantity or the quality of our symptoms. Therefore, while this books deals with the problem of unhappiness in modern America, its analysis and recommendations are appropriate to all societies in which conditions essentially similar to our own prevail.

After a dozen years of teaching and conducting psychological research, the traits of caution and precision—so vital to the scientific approach to knowledge—become a virtually reflexive part of one's personality. Consequently, I feel constrained to disavow any pretension to scientific rigor or empirical validity in the writing of this book. Most assuredly, the assertions and conclusions that fill these pages are not buttressed by evidence that I have obtained in the experimental laboratory or from carefully designed studies in the field. Of course, I shall have ample occasion to refer to the theories and findings of others; to acknowledge my intellectual debts and to marshal the wisdom of others in support of my contentions. But my principal aim has been to collect my own thoughts about the widespread distress of our society and to convey those thoughts as clearly and cogently as possible. In short, this is an essay—speculative, polemical, and utopian. And the weight of my argument must necessarily be borne entirely by the strength of my ideas. Yet I hazard to articulate them because of the encouraging reception they have evoked in discussions with colleagues and students. Indeed, I must confess to the belief that at least some of my views may illuminate the nature and origins of our collective dilemmas as well as the means by which we may set about resolving them.

To those unfamiliar with the culture of contemporary social science, my apologia may seem both puzzling and gratuitous. But the initiates—those whom, I suppose, I have especially sought to disarm—will appreciate how unusual it is, these days, for a specialist in a field of research to venture outside the narrow scope of his own investigations and, foregoing all the trappings, paraphernalia, and safety of his familiar mode of study, discuss so momentous an issue in such an opinionated manner.

Yes, most of my fellow laborers in the vineyards of social science still seem to be at peace with their society. True, many of them are as restive and distraught as the ordinary citizens who possess no technical training in or information about the social sciences. And it is equally true that social scientists may often be found in the forefront of organizations devoted to the amelioration of our most flagrant social ills. Nevertheless, most professional students of society (or of the individuals and groups that comprise it) busy themselves with the admittedly arduous task of becoming experts in circumscribed causes or consequences of their social order.

Naturally, this specialization is required by the complexity and fluidity of our subject matter. And, to utilize fully the logical power inherent in the scientific method, it is necessary to focus attention upon discrete aspects of the changing panorama, shunning problems that are too cumbersome for scientific containment. Moreover, insofar as the application of social science has been found useful to the conduct of practical matters, a growing number of social scientists are turning away from the timeless realm of pure scholarship in order to make a more immediate impact upon some segment of the workaday world.

Still, one cannot help but feel that many of one's colleagues have been too eager to immerse themselves exclusively in the imperatives of their scientific programs; too relieved at the prospect of spending all of their time in piling tiny blocks of data onto the edifices of theory they are seeking to build; too ardent to serve those emotionally crippled or crushed by their society rather than to treat the societal bases of that havoc; too willing to accept employment as technicians and consultants in military or industrial projects whose ultimate social effects may be damaging, repugnant, or horrifying to them.

But we shall scarcely be able to take comfort in any of these disparate endeavors if, while we have diligently worn our scientific and professional blinders in an effort to avoid distraction, the whole wellspring of our work—our society—goes dank and rancid. I am certain that thousands of my fellow social scientists are daily haunted by intimations of this, and some have already sounded the cry of alarm, offering their appraisals of our difficulties, their prescriptions for a more fulfilling and less debilitating society. Here, I am merely adding my own voice to what I fervently hope will become a swelling chorus of provocative questions and answers.

IRVING SARNOFF

New York City
November, 1965

SOCIETY WITH TEARS

I

Aggrandizement vs. Realization

CERTAIN HUMAN STRIVINGS have always appeared self-evident to those who have paused to ponder on the meaning of life. Hunger, thirst, and the goadings of sex, for example, seem to be so obviously intrinsic to man's biological make-up that the necessity of their appeasement presents no difficulty in comprehension. Nor is it difficult to understand how these needs of the flesh may be requited. Admittedly, human beings in different lands reveal an enormous variety of culturally conditioned tastes, appetites, and manners. But while a Chinese may prefer boiled rice eaten with chop-sticks, he would soon learn to eat blubber with his hands if he were marooned among the Polar Eskimos. Similarly, although various cultures have contrived differing postures for sexual intercourse, the orgasm is its consummation everywhere—for the Zulu as well as the New Zealander.

Essential to survival as the physiologically derived motives are—fascinating and exotic as may be the ways in which we gratify them—their actual indulgence occupies surprisingly little time among most people of the world. Even people in the least technologically advanced societies do not spend most of their waking moments in eating, drinking, and sexual activities. Instead, people in both modern and preliterate societies bend the bulk of their energies toward the attainment or expression of states of mind and qualities of experience that are not stirred by the innate imperatives of their biological functioning but, instead, by the values they have *learned* as members of their society.[1] And the really significant differences in behavior—not only between cultures but within cultures—stem from the differences in the values that people have acquired and to which they have committed their lives.

Because America is such a mosaic of classes, castes, and religious denominations, our composite set of values is neither monolithic nor given to easy description or classification. Acknowledging the heterogeneity of our existing values does not mean they cannot be sorted out in terms of their relative importance. On the contrary, taking, as our measure of importance, the amount of time and energy we expend on their behalf—the extent to which we mold our daily lives and plan our distant futures in their service—we can readily perceive a hierarchy of values. Without pretending to order that hierarchy with mathematical exactness, it does seem possible to set forth a fairly accurate twofold classification.[2]

The Values of Aggrandizement

In the first category, commanding the top of the hierarchy, are the *major* values of our society: the philistine triumvirate[3] of material wealth, prestige, and power, the *values of aggrandizement*. Motives based upon these values are directed toward augmenting the individual's conception of himself.

While material wealth still seems the ranking value of this cluster, the relative positions of prestige and power are more difficult to locate. Thus far in our national history, however, we have generally been more preoccupied with prestige than with power. On the other hand, pursuit of these three values usually occurs quite simultaneously. Certainly, wealth tends to bring the others almost irresistibly in its wake. Hence, persons accorded high prestige or holding positions of high power are likely to reap greater financial rewards than those who have either less social status or less power.

Wealth, as a value, may be defined as the desirability of acquiring the goods, services, and legal tender that represent the material resources of one's society. Prestige, on the other hand, stresses the worthiness of obtaining the respect and admiration of others. Finally, the goal of power is control over the actions and destinies of others.

The single-minded pursuit of one but not all of these values might involve somewhat different behavioral means. For example, an individual desirous only of amassing wealth might conceivably leave the company of others entirely, striking out for unexplored jungles in the hope of locating new reservoirs of oil. In contrast, persons primarily covetous of prestige or power may forsake highly remunerative occupations in favor of less lucrative positions that bring them more public recognition or more influence over the lives of others.

Although the major values of our society may thus exert differing behavioral pressures, their *common* behavioral implications are vastly more significant for both the individual and society. First, the pursuit of these values *requires* the individual to *take* things from his environment; and these "things" may be either tangible commodities or social responses. Nor does the individual motivated by these values have an option in regard to this acquisitive orientation: as long as he is committed to them, he *must* take whatever they predicate. Second, the individual's acquisitions— both material and interpersonal—have a common psychological result. They feed his conception of himself and increase his appetite for greater and greater acts of taking. Third, in his thrust for acquisition, the individual grows numb to the humanity of those from whom he must extract that which he prizes. His ends *demand* that he contrive means of inducing others to serve them. Clearly, in the case of prestige and power, it is of crucial importance to evoke the necessary responses from others. Yet this evocation cannot be effectively carried out unless the individual views others as prestige-giving or power-giving mechanisms rather than as unique persons with emotions and desires and minds of their own. But, in contemporary society, the acquisition of wealth almost certainly requires the manipulation and exploitation of others; and the individual who pursues this value is likely to regard others as wealth-giving instruments. In short, if an individual *has* to use others as a means of advancing his own ambitions, he cannot be expected to be overly considerate of their needs and woes, overly touched by their feelings. Too much empathy with others would impede or preclude their employment as tools of his ambitions. On the other hand, detachment from the core of others can be most effectively maintained—can be most invulnerable to detection and protest—when it is cloaked, as so often is the case today, under a mantle of manufactured cordiality.

Finally, the values of aggrandizement produce great sensitivity to and awareness of the *social* criteria that mark their attainment. For the values of wealth, prestige, and power, *all* of these criteria are ultimately social in nature. This is most readily seen in regard to the defining criteria of prestige and power. But even if the pursuit of wealth is undertaken by a miserly hermit, its success can only be gauged by the amount of money he accumulates. And since he necessarily utilizes the system of currency shared by others in his society, the miser, although he counts his money in the sanctuary of his private vault, is evaluating himself in accordance with a social standard.

The Values of Realization

The lower half of the hierarchy of American values contains the *values of realization*. In contrast to the values of aggrandizement, these values lead to the development and unfolding of our distinctive human capacities; and the individual who lives by them necessarily contributes to the flowering not only of his own humanity but also that of others. Whereas the values of aggrandizement can be expressed only through taking, the values of realization can be expressed only through *giving*.

The values of realization may be properly designated as the *minor* values of our society simply because we cherish them less than we do the values of aggrandizement. True, there is no dearth of lip-service given to them in the utterances of our citizenry. Still, whenever Americans have had to decide where to direct the preponderance of their daily energies, the majority has given preference to the values of aggrandizement.

In their conjectured order of adherence among our people, the values of realization are: humanitarian, equalitarian, intellectual, and esthetic—although the last two have generally been tied for last place.

Humanitarian values are those that advocate the worth of human life and that, in consequence, motivate us toward its preservation and betterment. Equalitarian values are similarly oriented toward human beings. However, they focus, in particular, upon the basic equivalence of every person, upon each person's equal standing as a member of our species. In seeking to express equalitarian values, therefore, an individual would be inclined to favor any program of legislation, political action, or institutional change that aims to eradicate any social arrangement under which some members of the human race are put in a position inferior to that of others. Typically, humanitarian and equalitarian values are found in the same people. For to be equalitarian almost assumes an allegiance to humanitarian values, since wanting all men equally to share the benefits of their common existence implies an attitude of consideration for others that is identical to the concern the individual has for his own welfare. But one can be strongly humanitarian without being as strongly equalitarian—as in the case of an industrialist who provides his employees with commodious housing and the best of medical care, but whose benevolence does not include the full sharing of his profits or the prerogatives of his ownership. Similarly, a white person living in a Northern city may be in favor of every form of integration between Negroes and whites in Birmingham, Alabama, yet he might be the first to move out of his own neighborhood if a Negro moved into it.

Esthetic values emphasize beauty and artistic creation. Individuals deeply committed to such values would be expected to give enthusiastic support to the arts, to make frequent contact with products of their preferred artistic media—music, painting, sculpture, or literature, for example—and to engage in creative activities themselves.

Intellectual values refer to the exercise of man's capacity for thought and reason. Persons adhering to these values would show a fondness for ideas and would indulge in cogitation and the incubation and articulation of ideas as special forms of delight. Such persons applaud educational movements and programs that promise to develop the intellect of the young and that provide tangible support to the media, such as books, through which the workings of the mind are communicated.

As in the case of humanitarian and equalitarian values, esthetic and intellectual values are often found grouped together. For example, the appreciation or creation of serious literature involves both esthetic and intellectual qualities. Still, it is possible to find extremely intellectual pedants who are quite indifferent to beauty; and, conversely, intellectual primitives who take up the study of fashion and décor.

When they are transformed into motives, the values of realization impel the individual to give rather than to grasp; to contribute rather than to take; to express rather than to evoke. Once it becomes the basis of a social motive, *every one* of these values requires the individual to do something that will: (1) directly enhance the well-being of others; (2) provide others with an artistic or intellectual product that some, at least, may find pleasurable or enlightening; or (3) liberate perceptions, feelings, and thoughts that may gratify the creating person and that cannot *per se*, no matter how destructive the impulse they express, inflict bodily injury upon or manipulate others. What are the reasons for each of these three constructive results?

The enhancement of the well-being of others is an *explicit* imperative of the humanitarian and equalitarian values. Literally, being helpful to others, working and caring for them, is unavoidable insofar as one's behavior is motivated by humanitarian and equalitarian values. The provision of others with works of beauty, thought, and reason follows from adherence to the esthetic and intellectual values—either as an outcome of the individual's own creative efforts or from the material and moral support he gives to individuals or organizations that bring esthetic and intellectual products to the public. Regarding the emotional liberation of a person who works in the domains of art and intellect, his inner gratification need not be attained at the expense of others. The release involved in such work is largely its own reward; and even if no one in the world appreciates his final product, the artist or intellectual will have gained fulfillment in the very process of its creation. And even if the subject matter of his product deals with the most violent of aggressive feelings, the *form* in which those feelings are manifested cannot—*as an object in its own right*—be harmful to others.

Perhaps it may be true, as the aphorism asserts, that the pen is mightier than the sword. But brandishing a pen across reams of paper—regardless of the wrath of the ideas that flow from its tip—culminates only in a collection of symbols. And while such symbols may be employed to incite people to destructive action, they are, objectively, far from lethal in their direct impact upon the reader—something that could hardly be said of a sword. Moreover, depending upon their backgrounds and personalities, those who are exposed to artistic and intellectual works may share the perceptual, emotional, and cognitive experiences of the artist or intellectual who created them. To be sure, the re-experiencing of and empathy with a given work may evoke feelings of pain as well as joy, sadness as well as exaltation. But the negative affects are as much a part of the spectrum of human emotion as the positive ones; and our exposure to a wide variety of artistic and intellectual works is likely to extend the range of our sensibilities and enrich our store of memories.

Selfhood and Transformation
of Values into Motives

Values can have little effect upon the behavior of an individual unless he makes them his own and feels obliged to live by them. But this process of making values one's own and of orienting one's life on the basis of them seems to depend upon the development of what is, perhaps, the most peculiarly human of all psychological aspects of our functioning, the self-concept.

The individual begins life with no such conception. But while he is under the influence of those who rear and educate him, he develops the ability to use symbols and to form ideas. As this intellectual development proceeds, he begins to abstract a concept of his own being, in the same manner as he abstracts other conceptions from other stimuli that he perceives. To a great extent, the individual's concept of self reflects the evaluations that others have expressed concerning his person and behavior—although, as he matures, and as his perceptual acuity increases, he is also able to draw some inferences of his own about himself.

The concept of self "refers to the entire range of attributes that he assumes for himself, to all the objects, thoughts, motives, emotions and behaviors to which he attaches the pronoun 'my' . . . Because it is fed by so many sources of information, the self-concept is likely to become increasingly complex as the individual develops, and also increasingly different from the individual's earliest awareness of it."[4] However, some of his earliest experiences, which have become incorporated in his self-concept, tend to persist for a lifetime. In many persons, these early components may serve as a center about which later components of the self-concept take shape.

Once the self-concept is formed, it establishes a foundation for an entirely new pattern of motives—motives that pertain to its protection and perpetuation. But why should the conception of self become the foundation for these new motives? "First, the self-concept helps us to function in social relations. The labels that we attach to our persons impart the impression of a continuity of individual existence, of an identifiable uniqueness distinguishing us from all others. Lacking such symbols of individuality, we might become confused with others. Second, by referring our needs to a symbol of our personal being, we can articulate those needs to others whose cooperation is indispensable if we are to be gratified. Third, our self-concept helps us to impose order upon the barrage of stimuli that impinge upon us from moment to moment. If we had no guiding conception permitting us to recognize our inner life as belonging to one and the same being in spite of constant changes in the sensations which run through our organism, we might well be overwhelmed by the chaos of our perceptions and reactions. In short, as negatively toned as our self-concept may be, it helps us to meet minimal biological needs and prevents inner chaos. Finally, our self-concept serves to evoke from others responses that we have learned to give our own beings. This learning takes place in earliest childhood and in the context of interaction with those who rear us. Thus, our self-concept is acquired, in part, in an attempt to minimize the implicit threat to our existence that is posed by our infantile dependence upon others. Having been thus acquired, the self-concept is invested with the same necessity for survival as we attach to our biological functioning. This investment, in turn, requires us to behave in such a way as to elicit the same attitude from others toward our being as we hold. Hence, when we succeed in getting others to form a notion of ourselves that coincides with our own, we re-create the conditions under which our parents satisfied our most vital needs."[5]

Inevitably, therefore, our concepts of self reflect the values to which we have been exposed—especially those taught informally by our parents and formally by our educators. Still, the task of learning about and choosing among these values is a gradual one. In relatively stable and homogeneous societies, this task is not as complex or conflictual as it is in our own. The simpler societies present the growing child not only with fewer possible goals of life but also with greater agreement among adults concerning the relative importance of those goals. In any event, the values selected by the child become fused with his increasing self-awareness and become a significant element in that abstraction which is the child's self. Hence, the child comes to *define himself* as a person who has a number of different goals.

After *any* individual of *any* culture has defined himself as a person with a particular set of values, he is automatically heir to a lasting state of tension. For, by committing himself to those values, he accepts the idea of himself as someone who represents and personifies them; and, unless he can maintain his belief in that idea, he runs the risk of undermining the vital basis of emotional security that the very formation of his self-concept was formed to insure.

The simplest and most satisfactory way for the individual to maintain his belief in his conception of himself is to translate it into action. Appropriate action is also the best means of conveying the truth of that belief to others, whose perception of and reaction to its behavioral translation reinforces the individual's own sense of its validity. On the other hand, failure to undertake action—or to act successfully—in accord with his values may throw the individual into a state of turmoil; and, in such a state, the individual may become so desperate as to attempt, through extreme perceptual distortion, to eliminate the painful discrepancy between his image of himself and his actual inability to verify it in reality.

Adding immensely to the tension that commitment to values necessarily involves is the notion of perfectibility that often accompanies their adoption. In our society in particular, the growing individual is usually enjoined by his preceptors not only to adhere to a set of values but also to improve continuously in his pursuit or expression of them. As a consequence, no matter what values an individual is seeking to maintain, he will usually feel constrained to demonstrate endless improvement in the extent to which he is able to translate those values into action.

Thus, both the values of aggrandizement and the values of realization are usually linked to the necessity for endless progress.[6] For example, the businessman may measure his progress by increases in his income, whereas for the artist, the criterion of his progress may be the increasing freedom of line that characterizes his painting. But it would be dangerous insensitivity to overlook the enormous differences in the results of the unremitting pressure for progress in actions inspired by each of these contrasting sets of values. Since the values of aggrandizement can only lead to taking things from others, action in the interest of these values becomes most menacing when the grasping individual feels it his highest moral obligation to take more and more and more. Adding the element of insatiability to values whose inherent qualities are avaricious can only produce greater and greater extravagances of rapacity; can only encourage greater and greater disregard for the rights and integrity of others; can only magnify the social problems the pursuit of such values inevitably causes. Yes, the unceasing acquisition of more wealth, more prestige, and more power creates a Moloch of egoism whose maw grows ever more bottomless, ever more merciless. As much as we get for it, as large as it becomes, that Moloch requires still more than it did before; and, in a futile effort to appease it, we are driven to greater and greater excesses of exploitation and manipulation of others.

Admittedly, striving for perfection in the expression of the values of realization can drive the individual to lacerate himself unsparingly in his efforts to fulfill more and more of his human capacities. And, insofar as the individual fails, albeit by standards he alone sets for himself, he is likely to suffer intensely from guilt, remorse, and depression. But regardless of how much personal torment the individual assumes for himself in seeking to improve endlessly in expressing the values of realization, his efforts are all socially constructive. Feeling obliged to give more and more aid to his fellow men, to do more and more to break down the barriers of inequality, to articulate greater and greater depths of emotion and insight in his artistic and intellectual work, the individual necessarily does more and more to make this world a better place in which to live.

Thus, whereas the fruits of limitless aggrandizement are bound to be increasingly harmful to society, those of limitless realization are bound to be increasingly beneficial to society. And while limitless strivings on behalf of the values of aggrandizement excite insatiable egoism, limitless efforts to express the values of realization tend to reduce egoism and to dissolve the boundaries that separate one being from another and the individual from the sources of his own humanity. Indeed, the very word "pursue" seems appropriate only in speaking of motives formed by the values of aggrandizement, for such motives require that the individual look outside his own being and chase and seize those things that are stipulated by the values of aggrandizement. But the values of realization lead, prototypically, not to *pursuit* of anything but to the *expression* of that which resides inwardly and constitutes our unique potentials as human beings.

The Child's Development and the Learning of Values

Strictly speaking, human beings never exist in a state of nature but always in a state of culture. No assumptions concerning the characteristics of our growth can ignore the fact that all of us are born into and mature within a specific cultural milieu, and that we are continually subject to its influence. Still, several universal features of ontogenetic development appear to make it possible for any child to learn and adopt the values of aggrandizement more easily than the values of realization. The very fact that most societies—certainly *all* modern societies—have opted so unequivocally for the values of aggrandizement suggests that the values of realization, despite their infinitely more constructive interpersonal consequences, may be much more difficult to cultivate.

Concerning the matter of intelligibility, the values of aggrandizement seem easier for a young child to understand. The values of wealth, prestige, and power rest upon a primitive conception of one's relation to the world: one takes things, one gets recognition, one lords it over others. In contrast, the humanitarian and equalitarian values involve quite complicated and sophisticated concepts of justice and reciprocity—moral conceptions which, even for children in Western society, undergo a long process of elaboration and generalization before they crystallize into their final and universally applicable forms.[7]

Motives based upon the values of aggrandizement do not require the child to have genuine empathy with others. Instead, he simply has to use them, and he can use them to his best advantage by tailoring his manipulative efforts to their individual predilections. But this radar-like[8] awareness of the reactions of others to oneself merely underscores the grasping individual's desire to insure that others will yield whatever he is determined to extract from them. By contrast, in order to appreciate and fulfill humanitarian and equalitarian values, a child must be able to transcend self-centeredness and put himself in the place of others, treating them as he would wish them to treat him. On this score, Freud[9] and Piaget,[10] two of the seminal theorists of psychological development, are agreed that the child only gradually and reluctantly gives up his initial and exclusive concern with his own self-centered view of the world; he only slowly and reluctantly becomes accessible to the views of others. According to Freud, this shift in orientation from the "pleasure principle" to the "reality principle" occurs primarily because the child learns that he must take into account the attitudes and motives of others in order to satisfy his own cravings; he must minimize the possibility of imposing those cravings upon others in a manner regarded as abhorrent by his culture, thus reducing his vulnerability to punishment. In fact, Freud holds that it is only after the child's conscience is fully developed that he is capable of truly moral behavior—the kind of behavior that would be consonant with the expression of humanitarian and equalitarian values. Yet even this development is postulated to be initially opposed by the child and effected largely by punishment or threats of punishment on the part of his caretakers.

In regard to the learning of esthetic and intellectual values, it is again possible to detect problems of complexity that do not exist for any of the values of aggrandizement. Undoubtedly, full and gratifying participation in artistic and intellectual activities depends upon the child's development of the motoric and conceptual skills that are utilized in such activities. In comparison with other pastimes, such activities are relatively passive and they require the individual to work alone. However, both of these requirements run counter to the young child's inclination to explore and interact with the concrete world about him. Before he can involve himself in artistic and intellectual creation, the child has to develop not only the ability to deal nimbly and joyfully with symbols but also the patience and self-reliance necessary to work in solitude.

Values and Attainment

In addition to their differences in cognitive complexity, the values of aggrandizement differ from those of realization in that their criteria of attainment are both more readily perceptible and more amendable to widespread consensus. For example, it is easy to define success in pursuing the values of aggrandizement by numerical quantities: wealth—the number of dollars or acres of land; prestige—the number of invitations one receives from prominent persons or one's ratings on a TV poll; power—the number of people one employs or the number of troops under one's command. Not all the criteria relevant to the pursuit of these values are so clear-cut, however. Prestige and power, in particular, are often reflected in the signs of deference and submission that people display toward each other; and these signs may be conveyed very subtly, or even unwittingly.

A person motivated by the values of realization may also refer to statistics in assessing the effectiveness of his efforts. For instance, he may evaluate himself in terms of the number of persons to whom he has given aid, the number of demonstrations he has joined in protest of racial segregation, the number of art galleries he has visited, or the number of books he has read. But whereas all of the criteria of success that pertain to the values of aggrandizement depend *without exception* upon the attainment of a commodity or a social reaction from one's environment, fulfillment of the values of realization is frequently independent of external response. The most ecstatic rewards of artistic and intellectual activity are entirely private and subjective, entirely contained within the being of the artist and the intellectual. It is their own inner promptings that such persons are uncovering and to which they are giving form and coherence; it is the intrinsic pleasure they derive from the *process* of their work that sustains them in its attendant rigors and agonies. The dedicated artist and intellectual sticks to his work *despite* its failure to bring him commercial success, *despite* its inability to gain him recognition, *despite* its lack of power to control the destiny of others and, indeed, *despite* the discrepancies between his finished products and the conceptions and visions that provoked him to their expression.

Similar subjective criteria are used by those who embrace artistic and intellectual values as viewers, readers, or listeners rather than as painters, authors, or composers. Can there be any more compelling evidence of the difficulties of attaining consensus upon the extent to which these values may have been realized than the disputes that occur—among lay persons as well as professional critics—about the nuances of feeling and meaning contained in and evoked by particular works of art and intellect?

As to the humanitarian and equalitarian values, actions undertaken to further them often have either unknown effects or effects that may not come to light within the individual's own lifetime. Thousands of people have been laboring to discover the cause and cure of cancer, for example, and they will continue their labors in spite of the fact that the disease persists as an intransigent killer against which all combative efforts have thus far failed. Similarly, political and social agitation aimed at providing equal civil rights to all segments of our population may take years and years before it yields results. Hence, the individual conducting such agitation must often sustain himself solely through the sincerity and fullness of his commitment.

Values and Innate Motives

Another difference between the values of aggrandizement and the values of realization concerns their psychological relationship to our innate sources of motivation: the values of aggrandizement seem more immediately reflective of our physiologically derived motives. The in-taking, acquisitive qualities of the pursuit of material things appear to be functionally akin to the infant's desire for food. And although the young child's needs for affection and mastery—reminiscent of the adult's desires for prestige and power —may not be innate, they are surely learned early in life and are unquestionably helpful to his survival.

Actually, it is theoretically possible to attribute various values of the adult individual to his particular history of learning in the ways of expressing implacable bodily processes. According to Freudian theory, for example, an adult's avidity for money may be indicative of his lingering and unconscious reaction to the manner in which he was toilet-trained.[11] Harsh and precipitous toilet-training is held to arouse the child's desire to retain his feces in opposition to the commands of his parents. This kind of treatment may cause the child to attach great value to his own excrement, a trait that is later consciously and symbolically manifested in his tendency to hoard money and to worry excessively over its loss or expenditure. Moreover, parents who are very strict in their methods of toilet-training are also likely to disapprove of the child's attempts to play with mud or anything suggestive of fecal matter; and this disapproval may induce in the child an enduring distaste for creative modes of expression that involve getting one's hands dirty.

Conversely, psychoanalytic theorists may be inclined to ascribe an adult's generosity with money to quite different childhood experiences of toilet-training. Specifically, permissive and gradual toilet-training may lead the child to associate the expulsion of his feces with enjoyment rather than deprivation. Hence, as an adult, he may unconsciously regard the spending of money as a pleasure instead of an odious capitulation to the unreasonable demands of others. Similarly, parental approval of the child's manual explorations with dirt and other plastic materials may favor the development of adult preferences for "messy" forms of artistic activity, such as sculpture. Indeed, Freud postulated[12] that such activities may function as disguised, unconscious, and socially acceptable means of fulfilling the same wish to smear his own feces that the individual had once consciously entertained much earlier in life.

Regardless of the scientific validity of this and similar theoretical accounts of the idiosyncratic child-rearing factors that may determine the selection of adult values, it seems safe to say that the values most strongly upheld by most of the people mirror the degree of support accorded to those values by their society. For the family exists as a small unit within the framework of a much larger social system; and the practices employed by parents to rear their young tend to reflect the values current in the society at large.

Values and the Basic Functions of All Societies

Compared with the values of realization, the values of economic gain, prestige, and power seem to bear more affinity to the basic functions that any social order must fulfill if it is to survive at all. Every society must provide its members with some mode of sustenance, a necessity that stimulates economic behavior and infuses it with value. In addition, *all* societies are characterized by formal and informal means of socialization and social control. Therefore, social approval and disapproval (associated with prestige) as well as social sanction and coercion (associated with power) may be considered unavoidable consequences of any society—however it is organized.

The values of realization do not seem to be as directly related to the social institutions that are essential to sheer survival. Logically, in fact, it would be possible for a society to subsist with little, if any, concern for humanitarian, equalitarian, intellectual, and esthetic values. But such a society would resemble a brutish jungle, dominated by an all-powerful elite who mercilessly exploited the slaves under their control.

Unfortunately, societies of that sort have shamed the history of man. Yet they are scarcely appealing models—devoid of the values that bring us dignity and delight, that earn for us whatever honor our species deserves. Indeed, insofar as we do not cultivate the values of realization, we fail to develop the capacities for civilization that we inherit with our neuroanatomical complexity. Certainly, only humans could become *consciously* concerned with the welfare of their species and the desirability of establishing equality in the relationships among them. Only humans, among all the species, have the capacities for expression and communication that are the bases of artistic and intellectual activity. But, regarding the phylogenetic implications of the values of *aggrandizement*, their absence, at least in their essential forms, is less certain among lower animals. Pecking orders and hierarchies of social dominance may be found among such diverse creatures as chickens and apes. Rooting pigs surely do not hesitate to shove each other aside in their gluttony, while squirrels appear to lay away their hoards of acorns without the slightest thought for others who might also use them for food. And roosters seem to experience no inhibition in strutting and crowing. True, in lower animals, these similarities to the pursuit of the values of aggrandizement are largely manifestations of biologically inherited traits. Yet it is just because the *learned* values of aggrandizement bear such striking resemblance to those pursued by lower animals that they fall so far short of the capacities that are a special part of our human endowment.

Values, Institutions, and Social Change

Important as a society's values are in determining the social motives and behavior of its citizens, they cannot and do not function in an institutional vacuum. For the institutions of a society not only reflect its values but also provide the concrete means by which they are inculcated and maintained. Yet both the values and the institutions of contemporaneous society reveal the stamp of those crucial historical trends that captivated the imagination and energy of previous generations of men, turning their hearts and minds in the present direction rather than in another.

Consequently, an understanding of our most significant social problems involves an appreciation of the historical sources of our principal values as well as their institutional manifestations and supports. And, although the immediate impact of such an analysis may be depressing, it has decidedly optimistic implications. Thus, by becoming vibrantly aware of the fact that we are not eternal slaves of unalterable biological forces, we are free to sever the psychological bonds of our cultural experience and embark upon a more promising societal course.

2

Images for the American Dream

IT IS NOT NECESSARY to dig cracked and faded documents out of dusty library shelves in order to piece together the classic drama of America. Slip invisibly into the darkened den of a contemporary suburban ranch house, silently draw up a plush lounge chair, and join an unwitting American male as he relaxes before the TV set, his half-glazed eyes fixed hypnotically upon the screen. There, shining forth with dazzling luminosity, sits the fabled, the deathless hero of our culture, astride a horse so vigorous that it chafes at its own repose. The lean horseman is starkly etched against the cloudless sky. Looking down from his hilly pedestal, his forthright eyes narrow ever so slightly as he surveys the sweep and fecundity of the land below. There it basks in its own lushness—the green, loamy, virgin land! Countless untrammeled acres of it—and all of it fated to become his own. Taking a deep breath and hunching up his tall shoulders, the exultant pioneer spurs his horse into a trot and rides off to stake his claim.

It matters little that the entranced viewer earns his livelihood within the beehive of a huge building, honeycombed with hundreds of offices exactly like his own, or that his place of work is a teeming, claustrophobic city. Nor is it disconcerting for him to learn, later on in the program, that the intrepid frontiersman has had to pay in blood for his pasture and his herd—fighting off the onslaughts of squatters and rustlers alike. The important thing is that the viewer is able again to be a witness to the great American dream of possession, again to experience vicariously the driving American fantasy to take the bounty of the earth and to build with it an infinitely growing monument to himself.

What is so singular about this spectacle—both the one on the screen and the one of the rapt onlooker—is that neither embarrassment nor shame is associated with the dramatization of the dream. Not at all. The electronic hero—alert and tense with wondrous anticipation—is pious and somber in his mien. It is almost as if he were about to partake in a holy sacrament rather than in a greedy act of appropriation. Does the slightest wave of consternation becloud his eyes, the outward ripple of an inner doubt about the implications of his behavior for himself and others? Far from it. Here is a man who is so much a personification of the guiding values of his culture that he is indeed a caricature. And what of the living man who is a voluntary spectator to this oft-repeated ritual of aggrandizement? Surely, one would have thought that a full-grown man might sometimes be moved to ask himself whether or not he could find a more humane goal for his life. But it is extraordinarily difficult for such a question to occur to a person who has matured in a society that upholds barely veiled megalomania as its most exalted ideal—a society that exhorts its citizens to spurn the fulfillment of their essential humanity and to crave, instead, superhuman glory. Yes, the most influential ideologies of American cultural history have offered us beguiling paths to delusion; beguiling because each has tendered its invitation to limitless egoism under the guise of a dedication to high social ideals.

Undeniably, the American Dream developed under conditions peculiar to this continent and to the ways in which our predecessors reacted to them. But this country was settled and built largely by Europeans, who stepped ashore in the New World with perspectives formed by the Old one. Thus, to appreciate the evolution of the American Dream, one must first consider the outlook that our forbears brought with them. It should also be admitted that many Americans may entertain a Dream that differs profoundly from the one characterized here—a vision of life devoted to the values of realization. In attempting to locate the spark behind that vision, we might well find that it was also struck in Europe.

But what were the ideas that kindled the American Dream of aggrandizement—a dream that is still more prevalent than any other in this land? Four major factors seem to have exerted the most influence. But their separate importance, formidable as it may be, is overshadowed by their combined force; for each of them tends to be in psychological harmony with the others, yielding an ideological network that is as compelling as it is dehumanizing.

Monotheism, Christianity, and Megalomania

Oddly enough, the invention of monotheism has been widely regarded as a sure step forward in man's attempt to civilize himself. Presumably, the polytheistic religions of the ancients were conceptually more primitive, tending to attribute separate deities to the various forces of nature. These personifications are analogous to the concrete, animistic modes of thought that may be found among young children everywhere; and to the forms of pagan religion that still prevail in the dwindling number of preliterate cultures of our contemporary world. Monotheism, then, is thought to represent a more advanced—because more abstract—stage in the development of human thought.[1] Second, monotheism has been credited with reducing man's egoism and inducing him to subordinate his own willfulness to the beneficent designs of a heavenly sovereign; a God at once loved, feared, and respected; an all-pervasive force for good, which man can serve rather than his own mean and petty appetites.[2] The third of the principal virtues accorded to monotheism is its supposedly unifying[3] effects upon its followers. For if everyone has faith in the same unitary abstraction—*the one and only God*—everyone should experience a profound sense of brotherhood with fellow believers; and this kinship should be basic enough to withstand divisive trends stemming from differences in the customs of worship evolved by various groups of people.

In evaluating these claims for monotheism, it may be instructive to note, first of all, that the Greeks of antiquity, whose thought and art are still deemed worthy of emulation, conceived a theology that abounds with gods and goddesses.[4] Certainly, this fountain-head of intellectual and esthetic inspiration cannot be aptly described as primitive. But even setting aside the Greeks as a special case, even agreeing that a people whose civilization is advanced in many respects may be backward in others, how *abstract*, really, is the image of God that presently engages the faith of the majority of religious Americans?

The Hebrews, it is true, rested their invention of monotheism upon a quite abstract concept of God. But they endowed Him with an awesome array of powers, before which mortal man appeared puny, trivial, and helpless. The very omniscience and omnipotence of God set Him so far above His earthly creatures that they could scarcely presume to conjure an appearance for Him, or to fathom His remote inscrutability; and the strict injunction against any attempt to portray God in works of art insured the perpetuation of His overwhelming and ethereal mysteriousness.

But even as they gave full voice to their fear and respect of God, singing His praises and beseeching His protection against their own insignificance, fallibility, and finitude, the Hebrews contrived to assume for themselves more than a little of His infinite power and glory. And they did it in a most ingenious and subtle manner. For while they diligently refrained from making God a superman, they succeeded in making every man a demi-God.

The Hebrews defined themselves as God's ultimate creation. Obviously, beings molded by God Himself, shaped by His hand, must necessarily reflect His spirit. Granting that all men were children of God, they reserved for themselves the fondest niche in His affections. For they perceived themselves as His Chosen People, the segment of mankind singled out by Him over all the rest, selected for His special favors, guided by a destiny uniquely given to them by Him. By seeing in their very beings and in all of their actions the revelation of God's will, they could conclude that they were *themselves* concrete manifestations of God, placed upon this earth as His most beloved offspring. In this way, the Hebrews became, paradoxically, living personifications of the God whose image they forbade themselves to depict.

It may well have been true, as the Biblical story has it, that monotheism cemented the unity of the tribes of Israel and elimi- nated the plethora of idols that competed for their allegiance. But if they gave up the worship of such deities as the Golden Calf, they began, unknowingly, to worship themselves. Hence, the be- ginning of monotheism also marks the origin of megalomaniacal religion—religion in which man elevates himself to godhood and single-mindedly pursues the deluded objective of transcending his own humanity.

In comparison with monotheism, religions that involve the worship of sun and moon, cats and eagles, wind and sea, are much more modest. For they implicitly acknowledge that men are de- pendent upon and inspired by many aspects of this universe. Each of the spirits is accorded a specific and limited role in the total tableau of life, and none of the deities can pre-empt all of the functions that the others are required to perform. Insofar as they are infra-human, the gods cannot readily be employed as vehicles for human megalomania.

From a psychological viewpoint, man uses the same process in attributing characteristics of personality to animals and natural events as he does to an abstract concept of God that is not given any figurative embodiment. The Hebrews did not hesitate to ascribe to their Jehovah various kinds of traits which, while fan- tastically in excess of those possessed by any actual person, re- ferred unmistakably to qualities of human motivation and ideation. In his well-known psychoanalytic treatise on the psychology of religion,[5] Sigmund Freud argued that God was, basically, an exaggerated projection of the father figure, a functional fiction, as it were, that helped men to deal with conflicts between their lustful desires and the paternal authority that had opposed their gratification. According to this view, God, the celestial Father, who looks down upon men with a blend of sternness and solicitude, is an omnipresent mental construction, constantly reinforcing the moral prohibitions of our society and, at the same time, promising us protection in return for our obedience.

Regardless of the merits of Freud's explanation, it cannot be denied that such prohibitions as are advocated, for example, in the Ten Commandments, have the intent of curbing human rapacity; and that, once adopted by believers, these moral strictures work to limit predatoriness among men and to support decency in their relationships. Despite the humane morality that accompanied it, however, the concept of monotheism encouraged men to place into an all-encompassing deity all of their vain desires to escape the boundaries of their mortality. From the outset, the grandiose powers concentrated in God were coveted by man; and they have since sought to take back those very powers that their own imagination permitted them to give to God. Thus, monotheism became the stimulus that has led generation after generation of men to aspire to a twisted kind of grandeur, an exaltation that comes not from actual efforts to fulfill their human capacities but, instead, from the false hope of denying them.

In due course, Christianity made it even simpler than Judaism for men to cultivate religious megalomania. For, in the figure of Christ, the apotheosis of the human-God, people were presented with as concrete a deity as ever characterized any polytheistic religion. It is quite true that Christianity endowed its epitome with qualities of gentleness, mercy, forgiveness, and tender love that tempered the implacability of the God of the Hebrews; and it is equally true that the vision of Christ dying on the Cross for the salvation of mankind stirs to the fullest the talents of men for

sacrifice, self-abnegation, and charity. But humble, meek, and loving as the portrait of Christ may be, its overall effect has been to
exacerbate the thirst for aggrandizement already whetted by the
Hebraic version of monotheism. For Christianity sets forth nothing less than the life, the attitudes, and the style of God's Own Son
as an exemplar to man. Thus, in the New Testament, believers are
repeatedly admonished to follow His direct example. Nor is the
way to Christ reserved for any elite persons or groups. Rather, it is
open to all—to the weak and the poor no less than to the strong
and the prosperous.

But it should not be overlooked that Christ was also portrayed
as a worker of miracles, whose ardent wishes were bound to materialize. Since miracles are the province of the superhuman, the
very aspiration to imitate Christ implies a presumption to assimilate His omnipotence. Consequently, far from calling man back to
himself, far from helping him to return to and accept his human
potentials and limitations, Christianity further unleashed his
megalomaniacal strivings. If any doubt exists concerning the extremities of this megalomania, one need only dwell upon the
abominations of torture and murder that Christians—nay, leaders
of the Christian clergy themselves—have, from time to time, per-
petrated upon heretics in the name of the Lamb of God. Nor has
the devastation in the name of Christ been restricted to groups
outside of the Christian faith. On the contrary, the bloody perse-
cutions inflicted by Christians upon each other in the cause of true
belief rival any that Christians have ever wrought upon non-Chris-
tians. Hence, it would appear that the madness inherent in the
desire for Christhood can readily destroy brotherhood in Christ.

It may be objected that Christ's teachings are not identical with
the Gospels, and that the Apostles and other transcribers of His
words may have somewhat corrupted them. One might also feel
sympathy with Kropotkin,[6] who implored us to differentiate between Christ and Church, holding the organized clergy of the
various denominations largely responsible for inducing flagrant
and pernicious deviations from the spirit of Christ and for sowing

dissension and rivalry throughout Christendom. And one may acknowledge that the State, by means of its coercive grasp on the daily life of men, has often enlisted reluctant Christians into its nefarious services, including the waging of war upon fellow Christians of other States.

But even admitting every one of these qualifications, the potentially destructive roots of delusion contained in the inducement of men toward godhood cannot be denied. Certainly, one may concur with Kropotkin that Christ, no less than Buddha, is an "ideal man-god"[7] if there ever was one. But it is just *because* the Christian image of God contains such discernible elements of humility that its implicit blandishment to grandiosity is obscured. Hence, it is possible for Christians to aspire to superhuman states of self-aggrandizement while feeling, at the same time, that they are but timid and kindly lambs in the flock of God.

Interestingly, in connection with the concretization of the concept of God introduced by the followers of Christ, the early Christians soon rejected the Hebraic injunctions against graven images. The depiction of Christ, Mary, Joseph, and the Apostles—all the leading sacred figures of the New Testament—became a virtual obsession with those who established the organized Church. This propensity toward the literal personification of Christ, His family, and His Apostles has continued to the present day. The Catholic Church has been in the forefront of this tendency, and the Vatican itself is a fantastic repository of the visual glorification of Christ.

Through the sacrament of communion, Catholics have preserved a ritual in which the faithful believe they are ingesting the body and blood of Christ; that He is, in effect, entering their beings and infusing them with His qualities. Is it possible to conceive of a more concrete definition of a deity's essence than that represented by the wafer and the wine? Is it possible to arrange a more straightforward transaction with God, a more literal acquisition of His magical powers? Here are found expressions of the very idolatry that Hebraic monotheism had prided itself upon banishing from religion. Whereas the idols of the pagans were often inhuman or inanimate, the idol of monotheism—in Christianity more clearly than in Judaism—turned out to be the wished-for superhumanity of man himself.

Although Protestant churches have generally been less concrete and literal in their forms of worship, they have, paradoxically, added even more fuel to the deluded wish for godhood that monotheism crystallized and fostered as a proper aspiration for men. Catholicism, despite its backhanded idolatry, imposed a stringent limitation upon man's pretensions to the boundless glory of God. For it stipulated that those pretensions must be formally mediated by a cadre of clergymen who possess the exclusive right to administer the sacraments. That clergy is organized in a hierarchy of spiritual power, running from the Pope, Christ's most intimate ally on earth, down through the Cardinals, Archbishops, Bishops, Monsignors, and parish priests. Important religious questions must be funnelled upward through this hierarchy; and, conversely, important answers funnelled downward through it.

All of this organized and systematic intercession between God and the men who are seeking to appropriate His qualities exacts disciplined obedience from the rank and file parishioners. In extending obedience to their clergy, Catholics accept a set of restrictions upon their strivings for godliness; they accept definite limitations upon the extent to which they—and they *alone*—can take God into themselves. These restrictions reduce the load of individual responsibility for insuring the success of *all* of one's God-seeking activities. In return for their obedience, the faithful can enjoy the reassurance of the highly structured rituals which, administered by a specially trained clergy, remove doubt about how godhood is to be attained. Some of the sacraments, notably that of confession, provide the additional comfort of restoring the sinner to the good graces of God—assuring the faithful that none of them need ever despair about straying irrevocably far from the path to everlasting glory.

But when Protestantism challenged the authority of the Catholic clergy and broke its grip upon the loyalty of all Christians, it vitiated the control of the aspiration to godhood that is implicit in the restraints of Catholicism. Thus, Protestantism was first acclaimed by its leaders and adherents for its liberating character. And it did free its followers from the enforced ministrations of a clerical hierarchy. But this heralded freedom proved to be a dubious blessing. For it cut Protestants off from the psychological security that the Catholic clergy and sacraments provided; and it permitted them to pursue their religious megalomania without surcease, without the external limits involved in the necessity of going through clerical channels.

The Protestant release of Christians from the traditional Catholic order of the Middle Ages favored the spread of capitalism, it has been held,[8] because the uncertainty of each man about his ultimate salvation—a perpetual anxiety induced by Calvinism in particular—stimulated economic activity to vouchsafe salvation through one's own efforts alone. True, according to the doctrine of predestination, the assignment of souls to Heaven or Hell was solely the expression of God's will—before which all the wishes and strivings of men were of no consequence. Yet men could not help but search for indications of their election for salvation, for earthly signs of God's intentions for them. An upright and successful career—as opposed to a dissolute life of failure—could be taken as such a sign. And the doing of "good works," of conveying Christian charity to those in need, required financial resources. The more such resources one acquired, the more charity one could dispense; and, through both financial success and dispensations, one not only avoided the scarlet sins of sloth and greed but one also attained further assurance of having been chosen by God for eternal bliss after death.

Valid as this psychological formulation may be, it seems to emphasize only one of the major results of the Reformation. For it lays all of its stress upon the God-fearing effects of Protestantism; upon unremitting anxiety over salvation as the motivation for achievement; upon the groveling attitude of men who, oppressed with the taint of original sin, lashed themselves mercilessly to greater and greater capitalistic endeavor in the futile attempt to reduce their anxieties, diminish their guilt, and avoid any stigma of worldly failure, which might have also connoted failure in the eyes of God.

But what seems to have been disregarded in this approach to the psychology of Protestantism is the grandiosity that it invited. For if men had to suffer hellish torments of doubt concerning their ultimate salvation, they could also aspire to godliness in every and any way they might imagine. And while capitalism encouraged them to go into business for themselves, Protestantism enabled them to undertake a private transaction with God. No longer answerable to an interceding clergy, the individual Protestant was able to define his relationship to God in an entirely personal fashion. Although that very freedom of definition may have been an onerous burden, it also offered untold possibilities for self-glorification and self-aggrandizement. For what was to prevent a person from interpreting his own behavior as holy? What was there to dissuade him from being his own Pope and raising himself to sainthood? What check was there upon the extravagance of his self-righteousness, upon his own supposed affinity to Christ?

Yes, by unfastening men from the anchorage of the Catholic Church, Protestantism set them adrift on a sea of their own fantasies, where the high tide of their own presumption could rise without limit and where the most ascetic and least flamboyant of Puritans could, at the helm of his own ship, set sail toward the incandescent shores of godhood.

The Renaissance and the Cult of Egoism

Although the Protestant Reformation opened up unlimited vistas for self-aggrandizement through the megalomaniacal pursuit of godhood, the Renaissance had already pointed the way toward the individualistic acquisition of unlimited secular power and fame. And the models of both personal despotism and creative accomplishment that emerged during the Renaissance—an epoch

running from the fourteenth through the sixteenth centuries—
have not yet been surpassed. In Italy of the fifteenth century,[9] for
example, the absolutism of the local Princes, such as the Dukes of
Milan, and the creations of the artists in their retinue, such as
Leonardo da Vinci, were so consummate as to rival those of a
deity.

In reviving the humanism of the ancient Greeks, the artistic
giants of the Renaissance were giving support to the values of
realization—if humanism is understood as the attitude that deems
the flowering of human capacities to be the most worthy goal of
life; and if it is distinguished from what may be called "super-
humanism," the attitude that regards man's humanity as an insufficient basis of his existence. Certainly, the creative triumphs of
the Renaissance can be counted among the milestones of human
realization. And all men can rejoice in the sublimity of the esthetic
experiences that those creations made available to us. In the stat-
uary of Florence, the frescoes of the Sistine Chapel, and the dialogue of *Hamlet*, the expressive potentials of our wayward species
are evident.

However, as the artists of the Renaissance were creating works
of stunning and transporting genius, they began to be set apart
from other men—not only because of their special talents but also
because of the high esteem and tangible rewards that they received. Their worldly success could scarcely fail to stimulate those
less gifted to curry prestige and fortune through the individualistic
application of their own abilities. The artistic activity of the Middle Ages was largely anonymous and ancillary to the work and
mission of the Catholic Church.[10] The individual artist functioning as an entrepreneur on his own behalf was then a meaningless
and unknown activity. But as the spirit of entrepreneurship began
to flourish in Europe, the artistic vocation could be established as
an individualistic and identifiable enterprise in its own right. The
artist could not only receive due recognition for his own work but
he could also be paid for it.

Even after the Renaissance was fully launched, the Catholic

Church—especially through the person of the Pope[11]—continued to be a leading patron of the arts. Indeed, the sale of indulgences by Pope Leo X to raise money for the construction of St. Peter's in Rome was an "investment in culture"[12] that helped to provoke the Reformation. But the secular Princes of Europe also brought artists into their employ, subsidizing them in return for their products and services. This arrangement put the artist in a dependent position; and he often had to create in accordance with the requirements of his patron rather than exclusively in terms of his personal inspirations. Artists were commissioned to compose this piece of music or paint that portrait in honor of someone whom the patron wished to flatter; or to satisfy one of the patron's passing whims or fancies. Thus, although he may have had considerable leeway in matters of style, the artist usually had to work on specific projects requested by his patron.

Still, the artist of the Renaissance functioned artistically as a unique person rather than as a medieval monk whose creations merged with those of an anonymous ecclesiastical team. No matter how dependent he may have been at the start of his career, he sometimes attained a public stature that equalled that of his patron;[13] and he could, in such instances, assert a great measure of independence in the matter of accepting commissions and in obtaining financial support for whatever he personally wished to create. Similar developments of individualism also took place in the lesser arts and crafts; the outstanding goldsmiths, silversmiths, and potters of the era could aspire to fame for their products, for recognition and reward for their esthetic signatures.[14] Eventually, the quest for aggrandizement through social acclaim accorded to individualistic expression became not only morally acceptable but also most ardently desired. The vitally humanistic function of art —its expression of human emotion and thought as an end in itself—was gradually undermined, and artistic activity was put to use for superhumanistic ends. For the individualism involved in self-aggrandizement does not connote the fuller and fuller expression of the individual's capacities as its prime object—although that may well be a partial by-product. Instead, it employs individual talent and skill as a means to social rewards which, in turn, have the effect of causing the person to seem greater and greater in his own eyes, and to feel that he should become still greater and greater. Ultimately, the egoism that is generated becomes insatiable, and the individual is driven toward the construction of his own glorious images. Since the self-concept is capable of infinite expansion, the individual who is caught up in its aggrandizement may come to view himself not as the mortal he started out to be but as a kind of superman whose godliness is worthy of his own worship. Seen in this light, the self-centeredness instigated by the art of the Renaissance may well have opposed the spirit of humanism as much as or more than it gave it encouragement.

The artists of the Renaissance were not the only ones who set the pace for our modern cult of egoism. On the contrary, although their names are the first to leap to our minds when we think of the pre-eminent individuals of the Renaissance, they were far from the only group to pursue aggrandizement through the secular manifestations of their uniqueness. After all, most of those artists worked in the employ of powerful patrons—who were inclined to regard such employees as mere instruments of their own will, and who used the exquisite creations of the artists to aggrandize themselves and to advertise their own superior estate. In addition to their self-aggrandizing roles as patrons of the arts, the European nobility of the Renaissance period cultivated the arts of political manipulation. The loathsome treachery and the heinous crimes committed to advance their secular powers reflect the exorbitance of their dedication to their personal omnipotence. Protestantism itself was brought to England by the incomparable pique of Henry VIII, who would brook no opposition—spiritual or temporal—to his whims.

But what example of restraint did the churches set for monarch and subject alike? Surely, the Princes of the Catholic Church pursued conspicuous modes of aggrandizement as assiduously as the Princes of commerce and the State: architecture, painting, sculpture, interior decoration, furniture, jewelry, and dress. It may be argued that all of these things are necessary to fill the minds of men with the glories of God; and that, in effect, the whole gaudy catalogue of ceremonies, habits, and possessions represents so many props in the enactment of a drama whose sole aim is to turn the attention of men away from their petty affairs and to focus their souls upon God. But the apparatus is so breathtaking in its sensuous impact that even the most devout are likely to be impressed with the privileges and powers enjoyed by those who rule the Church in the name of Christ. Although the Pope is repeatedly confronted in the course of his coronation procession with the sobering aphorism *sic transit gloria mundi,* the pomp with which he is surrounded would seem to deafen both him and his parishioners to the import of that reminder. For how can people put the glories of the world in the true perspective of their transience when they are bedazzled by them? How can the faithful keep before their mind's eye the image of the impoverished and impaled Savior, when His living proxy is borne aloft on a resplendent throne, draped from head to toe in finery and installed in a palace whose luxury and magnificence would be the envy of an Oriental potentate?

The Protestant clergy, vocally outraged by the blatant vanity of their Catholic counterparts, cannot be said to have cloaked themselves in sackcloth and ashes—nor to have housed their congregations in lowly hovels rather than in splendid churches. But if the Protestant clergy were less openly indulgent of the temptation to display their newly acquired authority through opulence, they did not shrink from other means of demonstrating and exercising their coveted superhumanity. Like the Catholic Inquisitors who had condemned heretics to death, Protestant clergymen showed no hesitation to assume the God-like authority of judging who shall live and who shall die. And when they, too, burned alleged witches at the stake, they gave all of their parishioners clear notice of the magnitude of their presumption. In carrying out these quintessential acts of personal willfulness, the Church joined the State in the cultivation of unbridled egoism.

The Megalomania of Nationalism

Of all the virulent types of insanity, nationalism is, perhaps, the most perfidious. On the surface, it seems almost inherently noble —almost "natural"—to favor one's homeland over all others, to work toward its growing stature in the community of nations, and to protect it against the competition of rivals. But the moment one peeks beneath the surface of this doctrine, one is appalled by a famished demon of megalomania whose hunger for superhuman aggrandizement is as ravenous as that of monotheism. Far from doing honor to man, far from helping him to realize his human capacities, nationalism, like monotheistic religion, only succeeds in further alienating him from himself.

But one would have supposed that such irrational feelings of superiority might be the earmark of primitive cultures; that literate and technologically sophisticated societies might have become enlightened enough to see through the falsity of such beliefs; that modern men could recognize the dangers which must inevitably arise when groups become convinced of their superiority over each other and feel it their moral duty to assert this conviction at the cost of their own lives as well as the lives of those who have the temerity to question it.

Unfortunately, the history of our modern era has, if anything, revealed a steady growth in the disease of nationalism. Both the Renaissance[15] and the Reformation[16] produced a notable excrescence of that malignancy. Successfully challenging the power of Rome, the self-aggrandizing monarchs of Europe began to consolidate their own powers and impose them on the provinces and peoples in their region. Within a particular geographical area, such as that encompassed by England, Scotland, and Wales, rival monarchs struggled unto death in nationalistic wars, dragging large segments of their populations into the grave with them. Between geographical entities, such as England and France or England and Spain, both Catholic and Protestant sovereigns contested to expand the boundaries of their national power.

During this time, the ordinary inhabitants of these competing

States were led to identify themselves increasingly *not* with the visible fields and villages of their localities, *not* with their flesh-and-blood neighbors, friends, and relatives, *not* even with the concrete realities of the rolling hills that ran beyond the limits of their sight to the remotest part of the kingdom. Instead, the peoples of Europe were asked to identify themselves with a pure abstraction—the State—and to equate their powers with its powers, their grandeur with its grandeur, their aggrandizement with its expansion. In general, they responded affirmatively to this mad call to unending greatness—much to their misery and ours.

It is true that the monarchs themselves stood as the concrete representatives of the abstraction; and that the State was widely symbolized in flags, maces, palaces, armies, uniforms, and countless other trappings. Still, it was the concept of the State itself that required and received the devotion of men; that came to be employed by them as an instrument of their personal glorification. As France and England grew, so blossomed the self-concepts of Frenchmen and Englishmen; as Spain increased her dominions, so grew the deluded pride of Spaniards; as tiny Holland reached out to the New World, so did the hearts of Dutchmen overflow their dikes and wash across the Atlantic. In every case, the people could feel personally magnified by the advances of "their" nation; they could congratulate themselves for the influence that "their" nation exerted in the affairs of the world.

Christians had long since been taught that people should render no less obedience to Caesar than to God. And the Catholic Church, with the exception of rear-guard skirmishes initiated by especially recalcitrant Popes, developed a congenial rapprochement with the reigning monarchs of those nations in which Catholicism continued to be the dominant religion following the Reformation. But, as exemplified by the Church of England, the newly established Protestant Churches were brazenly used by monarchs to sanctify their authority and, simultaneously, the concept of the State. The Reformation produced the institution of State religion—the religion that the ruling monarch designated should henceforth be the official theology of his realm. Under this arrangement, the newly established clergy were dedicated to minister to the royal family and to put their moral weight behind the monarch. But both Catholic and Protestant Churches sanctioned the doctrine of the "divine right" of kings to rule their subjects.

Much later, when that "divine right" was disputed and smashed, when the powers of the State were wrested away from absolute monarchs and taken over by democratically elected governments, one might have expected the concept of nationalism to lose some of its grip over men. But no such development has occurred. On the contrary, the introduction of representative government—whether by evolutionary means, as in Great Britain, or revolutionary means, as in France—simply resulted in a different basis for perpetuating and furthering the fortunes of the State. Moreover, the struggles for republican forms of government were often wedded—as in the case of America—to aspirations for national independence. And it is an ironic note that the very success of those struggles to end the absolutism of monarchs entrenched the psychological tyranny of nationalism. For if the people created "their" State with "their" own hands, if *they themselves* ousted the formerly reigning despot, how much more identified must they have become with "their" State?

So, the victory of democracy over autocracy was not accompanied by a reduction of nationalistic fervor. The subsequent emergence of totalitarianism—in both its fascistic and communistic varieties—brought nationalism to its diabolical zenith, filling the throats of Germans, Italians, Japanese, Russians, Chinese, and others with hysterical cries of fatherland, motherland, or whatever superhuman personification they may have learned to use to symbolize their State. And it was nationalism that provoked them, like frenzied lunatics, to snuff out the lives of "enemies" of "their" State, to sacrifice their own lives in countless numbers so that "their" State might triumph over others. Thus did that dizzying idea narcotize its believers to extremities of barbarism and suicide; thus did it estrange them from their own humanity and the humanity of those whose heads were turned by other concepts of State; thus did they condone and perpetrate dehumanizing oppression and wholesale slaughter in pursuit of aggrandizement.

Aggrandizement and the Economy of Capitalism

That anyone in the world could have swallowed, even in a fleeting moment of intellectual weakness, the philosophical rationale for capitalism put forward by its early proponents, is surely a testimony to human vulnerability to delusion. Yet many people evidently thought it logical to conclude, with Adam Smith,[17] that each man's diligent efforts to enhance his own material estate would result in the greatest possible social good; and that, by looking out exclusively for his own economic interests and attempting increasingly to maximize his own financial gains, every man would be necessarily making his fullest possible contribution to the welfare of all.

Admittedly, in developing his line of reasoning, Smith obscures its absurdity somewhat by advising all entrepreneurs to realize that it may well be in their best economic interests to show some restraint in the extent to which they exploit the resources of the land and the people on it.[18] Even so, the expectation that an entirely self-centered system of economics would be the best guarantee of the general welfare of society seems ludicrously contradictory. It can only be assumed, today, that its promulgation has been more effective as a means of justifying *de facto* economic practices than as a program that could ever be taken seriously by those interested in a social philosophy truly concerned with insuring the common social good.

At any rate, no matter how contradictory and absurd it was as a social philosophy, capitalism flourished as an economic practice. Reasons for its initially enthusiastic reception are not difficult to find. Like the Reformation, capitalism promised to free men from their fetters in a hardened social order, fetters that held them fast to the material and social stations of life into which they were born, fetters that kept them tied to field, hoe, and hut, that confined them within the walls of the manor and bound them to their lords. It is not surprising that men should have welcomed the opportunity—now blessed by both Church and State—to escape their traditional confinements and to seek, through the application of their wits and energies, to sample fresh experiences and amenities.

In the early stages of capitalism, the neophyte entrepreneur faced the pleasant prospect of setting up his enterprise with little competition in sight. True, even the most enterprising trader had to contend with such dangers as stormy seas, impassable terrain, and highwaymen. But he also had before him the incentive of an open field of economic activity in whatever he chose to do. On the other hand, even in the beginnings of capitalism, many business ventures required greater financial backing than most potential entrepreneurs had at their disposal, and companies had to be formed to underwrite the businesses that needed large-scale investment. But certainly, in comparison to later developments, the first generations of capitalists could not have perceived competitors to pre-empt the fields of economic activity in which they hoped to augment their fortunes.

The existing opportunities and the temptation to break with tradition were not the only forces promoting the spread of capitalism. Another most important psychological consideration was the fact that private enterprise offered a secular road to glory that every man could strive to travel. And since the leaders of both Church and State had set the style in grandiosity—had shown the way to subjects and parishioners—they led the population to search for means of pursuing their own self-aggrandizement. However, the powers of the state were monopolized by the hereditary nobility and the few commoners who were sufficiently educated to serve as their lackeys. And the ranks of the clergy could not possibly absorb all of those who were hoping to aggrandize themselves. Thus, the economy was the principal means by which persons neither noble nor high-born—neither aristocratic nor off-spring of the influential clergy—could seek to acquire the criteria of aggrandizement. With a sufficient accumulation of wealth per-mitting contributions to both crown and mitre, a commoner of lowly parentage might attain not only knighthood but also the prayers of his Church. And even if he were but a middling success who never rose to such heights, the entrepreneur could reward himself with the universally accepted indications of his presumed grandeur—feathering his nest and adorning himself and his family with the appurtenances and plumage of peacocks rather than of sparrows.

It was in this manner that the aspirations of Western man for superhuman aggrandizement became attached to economic activ-ity. Such activity was the channel most accessible to all, since it presented the fewest barriers of birth, talent, and education. Hence, for most people, it held the greatest possibility of success-fully pursuing—*through the accumulation and deployment of wealth*—the egoistic glories of godhood, artistic fame, and politi-cal might.

Capitalism translated the drive for personal aggrandizement into very elementary terms, which even the most sluggish mental-ity could understand. Quite simply, as Pirenne puts it, one had only to learn the principle of "buying cheap and selling dear."[19] The resulting profits could then be put to the uses of aggrandize-ment, including investment that produced or acquired more com-modities for sale in order to make more profits. Obviously, the more things one sells at a profit, the more one gains for oneself; and, the greater the gap between the cost of an item and the price at which it is sold, the higher the range of profit one makes.

Assuming that an entrepreneur has found a profitable market for his goods, why should he persist in selling them after he al-ready has on hand sufficient profits to meet his physical needs for the rest of his life? Why should he not typically retire and desist from economic activity as soon as his own basic security is guar-anteed? Why, even if he can accept the exploitative nature of capitalistic commerce, would he not wish to put every superfluous penny of his profits to uses that benefit others?

The answers to these questions lie in the thrust to aggrandizement that is the impetus to entrepreneurial activity, that blunts the entrepreneur—as it blunted the Chief Inquisitor—to the extremity of megalomania involved in the use of others as instruments of one's own aggrandizement. For the spirit of capitalism is neither modest nor socially constructive. Instead, it is grandiose and egoistic—depending for its success entirely upon the willingness of the entrepreneur to regard the acquisition of profits as the guiding principle in his interactions with the fellow creatures who are his customers. Certainly, capitalism requires the entrepreneur systematically to violate the humanitarian constraints of the Golden Rule. Clearly, the entrepreneur has no wish to be treated by his customers as he treats them, since such a commitment to reciprocity would bankrupt him and undermine the whole exploitative goal of the transaction. And yet, if he can bring himself to make a single profitable sale, why should he find the second more repugnant? On the contrary, the more profit he makes, the more he reinforces the aggrandizement that led him into entrepreneurial activity in the first place.

As his profits pile up, the entrepreneur's image of himself balloons in like proportion. Because there are no imaginable limits to the size of this image, it offers no brake for the cessation of profitable activity. Indeed, since the individual tends to adapt rather quickly to increments in his self-image, and since the possibilities for self-aggrandizement are infinite, each new economic conquest arouses the capitalist's desire for another and greater one. And insofar as the accumulation of wealth is revealed in tangible objects, an individual's affluence may be put on display. Each person may then gauge the financial condition of his fellows in their dress, their place and type of residence, their mode of transportation, and the ways in which they take their leisure.

Wealth also buys power in society, for he who possesses its material resources often, through his ownership of the very land

and equipment that produces them, controls the economic fate of those who work for him. He can also spend some of his money for the purpose of manipulating public opinion and influencing the course of political action that is undertaken by members of government. Thus, in both its direct and indirect potentials for social influence, wealth can serve as a chief source of social distinction, elevating its possessor above the ranks of those who are less affluent. Undoubtedly, the psychological implication of capitalism that is of the greatest historical importance concerns its widespread facilitation of self-aggrandizement. Through its auspices every citizen of a nation in which it blossomed could entertain a dream of transcendent glorification that depended upon neither noble nor clerical station in life. Instead, by descending, as it were, to the mundane machinations of the marketplace, every man could attempt to use the economy of capitalism as a pulley that would hoist his ego to superhuman heights.

3

From Frontier to Oligarchy

As EUROPE STIRRED and shook itself loose from the binding traditions of the Middle Ages, the sprawling American continent—wide, wild, and bursting with untapped riches—lay invitingly beyond the western horizon of the Atlantic. Initially, only a few exceptionally venturesome explorers—frenzied by loot, gain, and power, subsidized by their sovereigns and blessed by their Church—set out to brave the hazards of the crossing and the unknown dangers of the interior. Next came organized clumps of more commonplace souls, bound together by spartan religious ideologies that helped them to endure the rigors of their new settlements along the Eastern seaboard. Soon, the uninhabited West attracted those discontented with their restricted lot in the settled and already appropriated areas of the East; and they pushed forward in the face of unimaginable hardship, visions of their ultimate glory sustaining their travail. Finally, the boundaries of the New World were breached in wholesale fashion, as wave after wave of immigrants rippled over the broad reaches of the country—a veritable flood of individuals, each motivated by his personal fantasies of milk and honey, gold and silver; each feeling righteous in taking for himself as much of the resources of the country as his talents and energies allowed; each fleeing from places where there existed no such chance endlessly to augment his personal wealth.

The land was so bountiful that, for some time, it was possible for many newcomers to put the American Dream into practice without blatantly frustrating or depriving others who were also driven by it. True, from the very outset, it was necessary for the settlers to fight war after war—with the French, the English, and the Indians—in order to safeguard their newly acquired lands or to wrest them away from those already settled upon them. But it was far from a rare experience for an immigrant to locate and take over land that was unsettled or unclaimed by anyone else; to uncover mines or forests that became his simply for the asking; to establish small businesses that were the only ones of their kind for miles and miles around.

Frontiersmanship and the Functional
Virtues of Rugged Individualism

Our huge and untamed continent could not be settled and culti-vated by people who were too effete to get their hands dirty, work up a sweat, or sleep in the woods. Pioneering was uncouth; to do it with a zest, one could not be too squeamish about its physical rigors. If one was already used to physical hardship, if one was already accustomed to privation and the barrenness of poverty, if one was also fleeing intolerance, persecution, or imprisonment—one might be favorably disposed toward hacking a life out of the forest. And if one's vision of that life was filled with the glories it promised to deliver, one was superbly conditioned for a bout not only with the wilderness but also with one's own frailties.

Seen in this perspective, it is not surprising that the call of the American wilds failed to evoke an avid response among the aris-tocracy of Europe. Why, after all, would they have wished to leave the affluence and power, the comfort and status that they enjoyed in their native lands? A few noblemen came over to lead expeditions or to serve as representatives of their sovereigns; and some educated members of the new European middle class arrived as commercial agents for European trading companies or to take important positions—in government, education, or religion—for which there existed an extreme shortage of qualified personnel. Essentially, however, America was inhabited by Europeans who had much to gain and little to lose by cutting their ties to the Old World.[1]

Not every immigrant departed voluntarily from Europe with the sole purpose of improving his material circumstances in America. Certainly, many of the thousands of refugees who fled Europe to escape religious, political, or social persecution would not have come over of their own accord, much less for economic reasons. Nevertheless, from the Colonial days onward, America has attracted, primarily, those who perceived themselves as economically dispossessed in Europe; or who felt so confident that their fortunes would increase in this country that they were willing to give up whatever stake they had in their homelands.

So, the ax and plow and hammer of America—its peddler's sack and its flint rifles—were taken up by European hands that were generally well prepared for calluses. But as ready as the early immigrants from Europe may have been to commit themselves to toil and effort, they could scarcely have anticipated all of the hardships and dangers that were latent in an entirely uncultivated land; a land without roads, trails, or the amenities of a village—let alone a city; a land without books, without art, without fashion; without diversions or graces to counter the bleakness of unending work.

And it was a hard, bleak life for the early settlers; a life in which they could hardly maintain whatever niceties of manner or subtleties of esthetic taste they may have developed in Europe. In the rough wilds of America, the stark practicalities of life counted most: the trees to be cleared, the water to be found and drawn, the hut to be built and secured against the encroachments of men and beasts, the seed to be sown, the clothes and candles to be made.

In such an elemental environment, success went to the man who set aside all other concerns and devoted himself unsparingly to combat with intransigent nature. In this combat, an American pioneer needed all the luck he could get from the accidents of discovery and the vicissitudes of climate and terrain. But he could not afford to rely heavily upon the favors of chance. Instead, to insure his progress, to keep nature from getting the upper hand, he had to develop reliance upon his own physical prowess, his own cunning intuition, his own practical ingenuity. He had to be quick to perceive opportunities to advance his cause and just as quick to take advantage of them. Toughness, decisiveness, courage, foresight, perseverance—these were the traits of character that primeval America demanded of those who would use her resources to pursue their dreams of glory. And, if those who first left Europe to meet her challenge did not have the demanded traits, they were soon obliged to develop them or they lost the fight.

Brought to our shores by the early settlers, the Protestant Ethic —with its implicit requirement that the individual work mightily and ceaselessly to insure his own salvation—was a perfect complement to the demands of nature, providing a spiritual incentive to the development of the very traits that practicality also dictated. In addition to its principal stress on self-reliance and endless work, the Puritan version of Protestantism elevated frugality and asceticism to high virtues.[2] By strict adherence to proscriptions against waste, idleness, and indulgence of the pleasures of the flesh, a Colonist would, instead, be inclined to keep his "nose to the grindstone"—assuring, thereby, a more rapid accumulation of wealth than would be possible otherwise.

But even after the European immigrants began to represent other varieties of monotheism—Catholicism and Judaism—they showed no reduction of initiative, frugality, or willingness to immolate themselves upon the altar of work. America became a veritable charnel house of labor, into which millions upon millions of men almost passionately threw themselves, the drunkenness of their ambitions blinding them to the price of admission.

In the single-minded pursuit of aggrandizement through the continual accumulation of wealth, there was little time for expressing the values of realization. Certainly, most of those striving without surcease to improve their economic conditions must have seen no practical (that is, financial) use for esthetic activity—unless such activity happened to be their business. As for intellectual values, the pragmatic skills that were most effective in the hand-to-hand struggle with the frontier were not those that taxed one's intelligence. The impractical dreamer and intellectual—the five-thumbed genius with words or the artistic soul who was slow on the draw—were not only earmarked for failure but were potential objects of ridicule.

The prototypical story of success in the economy of early America was one in which a stalwart and practical-minded person literally carved out his individual piece of the continent, imposing the will of his individualistic ambitions upon the dumb but often brutal mindlessness of nature. And if many of those who engaged in the struggle fell, they could not blame others for their defeat. Nor, conversely, did the successful ones feel compelled to share credit for their accomplishments with others. On the contrary, the successful "rugged individualist" of the frontier could often quite appropriately feel that he—and he alone—was responsible for his own aggrandizement. While the failure could hardly take comfort in a similar sense of personal responsibility for his own undoing, he could at least salvage some self-esteem in the thought that he had done his best; and he could continue to uphold the virtues of rugged individualism by perceiving his failure not as a result of unequal opportunity but as a result of the inherent difficulties of the material environment.

Any exclusively self-centered use of wealth implicitly deprives others with whom it could be shared. Still, even persons occasionally troubled by such a thought could honestly believe, in the early days of our nation, that hard work was the faithful handmaiden of good fortune. While they settled upon sizeable tracts of land or established flourishing businesses, prospering individuals could sincerely feel that they were in no way pre-empting the chances of their fellow citizens to do the same. The landless had only to move beyond the next range of mountains to find arable acreage of their own; the aspiring merchant needed only to open his shop in the next county seat in order to find trade for his goods. Thus, a man's success need not have been attained at the expense of others—whether or not they were potential competitors.

This principle of equal opportunity to pursue the values of aggrandizement has always contained striking mythological features. For the social realities of class and caste have, from the first days of the Republic, enhanced the opportunities of some groups in our population while decreasing those of others. Nevertheless, while the open frontier was still an existential fact—although one quite outside the daily existence of slaves and indentured servants —the actuality of opportunity was great enough to warrant widespread belief.

But this apparent freedom to expand one's own fortunes without crimping those of others eventually did become a popular myth rather than an economic reality. For the land was finally settled and parcelled. Even the frantic largess of the Homestead Act of 1862, by which the government gave away millions upon millions of acres, proved to be exhaustible. In due course, too, the available mines were discovered and claimed, while the forests were possessed for the sale of timber.

Keeping pace with the movements of our population, business enterprises fanned out from the East into every corner of the nation, creating more competition with each other, making it more and more difficult for each of them to enjoy the confident prospect of financial success. Consequently, those entrepreneurs who most avidly wished to aggrandize themselves were faced with the necessity of applying their shrewdness, tenacity, and hardness toward the elimination of flesh-and-blood competitors rather than toward the conquest of impersonal nature.

The ruthlessness with which competitors were often dispatched was equalled only by the sense of purpose on the part of the dispatcher.[3] Generally, they were not stalked and put to death, as Daniel Boone might have trailed and shot down a bear that threatened his encampment. But while competitors may have shown deference to the Biblical injunction against murder, they were much less averse to using all kinds of economic devices and chicanery in their efforts to wipe each other out. Even so, it might be said that a conflict between entrepreneurs is still individualism in practice—with each contending party having an opportunity to beat his rivals. And it was often possible, in battles that were joined between single entrepreneurs or those who controlled a given company, to discern opportunities that might exist for each in equal number; opportunities which went to the quicker, the more ingenious, the tougher of the competitors. But equality of opportunity also depends upon the financial reserves available to each in conducting the fight. Thus, vast reserves of capital did permit some of the combatants to absorb drastically lower prices, thereby driving less affluent competitors to ruin.

Economic Consolidation and the Bureaucratic Organization of Work

Paralleling these mercantile developments was the growth of industrial production, which became more and more mechanized as well as more and more specialized. To exploit the economic possibilities of the proliferating inventions and techniques of engineering, it was necessary to build larger and larger factories and to divide the tasks of labor within them. Moreover, the principle of the rational application of technology to production dovetailed with the acquisitive motives of those who owned and managed the budding industrial empires. For if the endless making of continually rising profits is the aim of one's enterprise, it is eminently reasonable to adopt those procedures that seem most likely to promote that end. The fact that the assembly line and the table of organization might have adverse effects upon employees assigned to slots within them could hardly have impeded the industrial application of these devices. Given their greater adherence to the value of wealth than to humanitarian and equalitarian values, our pioneers of industry were eager to make use of any technique that might guarantee steadily mounting profits. Certainly, most of the entrepreneurs who introduced the dehumanizing and invidious modes of organizing industrial production would have been loath to renounce their use—if the alternative were a sacrifice of profit or the risk of bankruptcy.

Competition grew to be as keen among enterprises of distribution—wholesalers and retailers—as it was among productive industries. The distributors, for their part, found it increasingly profitable to adapt to their own purposes the organizational principles and methods that industry had been developing in the interest of its financial benefit; from an organizational standpoint, in terms of both size and bureaucratic structure, these two arms of our economy began to resemble each other.

As the fierceness of competition waxed and considerations of efficiency pointed to the economic advantages of centralized ownership and coordination of the component organizations involved in the production and distribution of a given product, the consolidation of business into monopolistic or quasi-monopolistic behemoths began to be a salient fact of American economic life.[4] Nor were the banking and investment firms of the nation mere bystanders to this development. On the contrary, they often provided the capital necessary to effect mergers, permitting one set of contestants to swallow up their antagonists.[5]

The huge profit-making organizations that resulted from the consolidation of competing businesses gradually eliminated more and more "middle men"—the jobbers and retailers through whom products had been channeled from manufacturer to consumer; more and more of the specialized and independent suppliers of the materials used in the manufacturing process; more and more of the incipient titans who had also aspired to gigantic stature but who failed to make the grade.

The enormous concerns that weathered the most severe period of attrition began to appreciate the felicity of a mutually profitable coexistence with the remaining competitors in their field as an alternative to incredibly costly battles that might be harmful to all of them and beneficial to none. So, they started to enter into collusion with each other—not only for the purpose of fixing prices but also to regulate the production and distribution of their similar products and services.[6] The apparently pristine separateness of these entities often obscured the fact that they were ruled by many of the same directors[7]—an arrangement that permitted easy coordination of the policies and practices of the organizations involved.

Various administrations of our government have been cognizant of the potential public danger inherent in these concentrations of wealth and productive capacity. For such organizations can keep the price of their goods or services at exorbitant levels, violating the so-called classical economic law of supply and demand with impunity. The directors of these organizations can also put their corporate wealth to use as a political instrument, thereby wielding power greatly in excess of that which can be mobilized by any like number of less affluent citizens.

Functioning in the field of mass information and entertainment —newspapers, magazines, radio, television, and films—these engulfing enterprises can, by means of propaganda that they pour into their media, directly impress their political objectives upon the minds of their audience. In this way, a virtually totalitarian, albeit subtle, screen may be placed over the purportedly unbiased dissemination of news, limiting the degree of freedom with which the public can form its political opinions.

Since the Federal government has had a little success in anti-monopoly legislation and litigation, it may now be *literally* correct to assert that, apart from the public utilities, the *bald* and *absolute* monopoly of any market by a single firm no longer exists. However, what cannot be denied, and what no less a proponent of the economic status quo than Galbraith freely admits,[8] is the fact that our economy has jelled into a rather stable pattern of *oligopoly* or *crypto-monopoly*. Although a particular market may not be the exclusive domain of one seller, the relatively *few* sellers that have survived to share it among themselves protect themselves by the practice of "price-making."[9]

The trend toward bigness, oligopoly, and the bureaucratic structure of work was by no means confined to the economics of industrial production, marketing, and communications. Agriculture, which began with the solitary farmer tilling his own acres, also started to be organized[10] on a large scale—demanding considerable outlays of capital investment—as the blights of drought, pestilence, and depression made it impossible for many small farmers to retain title to their land. At the same time, the burgeoning industrial and commercial cities drained manpower from the farms; greater and greater numbers of people left the countryside for the enticement of urban life. Finally, as the technology of farming grew more and more efficient—yielding larger and larger crops for less and less human labor—it became feasible for fewer men to run bigger farms.

Thus, farming and ranching also began to reflect the pressures toward economic consolidation. Sharecroppers, tenant farmers, and itinerant laborers—sometimes imported temporarily from Mexico and other Latin American countries—began to work on the land as employees. Frequently, their employer was not even an observable owner who resided on his own holdings but, instead, an impersonal corporation, such as an insurance company, that sent its hired managers and foremen out to run the agrarian branch of its economic empire.

But what of the millions of people upon whose labor all of these large-scale organizations depend for their operation? What happened to American labor while American business was coalescing into its present vastness? In the earliest days of the Republic, labor was in scarce supply. Since one's own land was readily attainable, there was little incentive to work for others. Therefore, the earliest freemen who sold their labor could demand and get a very good price for it—so good that many decided to take employment until they could amass a tidy sum with which to launch their own careers as independent farmers or merchants.[11]

But freemen did not remain the only available source of labor. On the contrary, the spirit of entrepreneurship that animated the capitalists of the Colonial era soon led them to import laborers who were distinctly not free—white indentured servants[12] and Negro slaves. Since the slaves were cheaper and their possession permanent, they quickly outnumbered the indentured servants.

But even before the Negroes were freed, and thus added to the available pool of men who worked for wages, American labor had known some hard times. Following the financial panic of 1837, for example, unemployment was widespread, and so clearly discerned abroad that, for a while, immigration slowed to a trickle. In spite of the continued expansion of industry and commerce, as well as the spread of our population to areas of new land and previously untapped natural resources, the country experienced a series of crises that dramatically underscored the damaging economics of the "business cycle" and the vulnerability of workers to its caprice. The depression of 1857 was so shocking that it brought into question the value of liberty—for workers who were free to starve. Thus, "the *New York Herald* took advantage of the crisis to dwell upon the blessings of slavery, alleging that, while 200,000 workers had lost employment in the North and a million persons were threatened with starvation, the South had no need for soup kitchens. The slaves would be fed."[13]

The depressions of 1837-43 and 1857-59 were followed by those of 1882-86 and 1893-97. Yet none of these matched the economic holocaust that was to come during the 1930's: in 1933, the legions of the unemployed numbered 13 million.[14] It was in the periods of acute unemployment, when the supply of labor far exceeded the demand of employers for it, that the inequality of the relationship between employee and employer became most apparent. Even when there exists a marked scarcity of labor, the individual worker *must* sell his labor for wages if he is to subsist.

While he can command a much higher wage under those circumstances than when labor is in abundant supply, he cannot, lacking savings or any potential source of capital other than his own labor, remain idle for long. Granted that he can shop about briefly for the best rates in the vicinity, he is obliged to arrive promptly at an agreement concerning his wages.

The employer, on the other hand, eager to see his enterprise go forward, may pay much more for scarce labor than pleases him. But since he owns the plant, equipment, and land that comprise his business, he has a potential source of capital of which he can avail himself to ride out economic squalls, including that needed for recruiting and bargaining with employees who may prove willing to work for a price he deems appropriate to the amount of profit he wants to make. The owner can, in a pinch, obtain a mortgage on his property; or, if sufficiently depleted, sell it or, perhaps, rent it out. In short, ownership simply gives one access to capital that is otherwise unavailable.

An employer may take many risks in conducting his business, including that of bankruptcy. Certainly, the severity of competition and the economic depressions that our country has suffered did drive thousands of entrepreneurs out of business. But the individual owner—be it of a farm, industrial plant, or shop—generally had more economic resources at hand than the individual worker who negotiated with him for employment. This inequality of resources, favoring the employer, implicitly gave him the upper hand in any one-to-one negotiations with individual employees.

If the individual entrepreneur had always dealt with the individual worker from a position of financial strength, how much stronger still was the negotiating stance of the corporation? As American business was transformed from individual to corporate ownership—from small, individually owned enterprises to great, corporate oligopolies—the bargaining power of the individual worker precipitously declined. For he had to confront not merely a self-employed entrepreneur who needed extra hands to build his business but, rather, a corporation, usually capitalized by the public sale of stock and run by an oligarchical clique. These corporations often had such resources and reserves of capital at their disposal that they could actually use the suspension of their operations as a threat or weapon against recalcitrant employees. So, the lockout became one of the commonplace features of disputes between owners and employees. It was understood by both parties that the individual workers were singularly unprepared to withstand long periods of enforced unemployment and that they would, in the face of a lockout, be inclined to accept lower salaries or poorer conditions of work than they had requested or desired.

In time, American workers set about to balance the distribution of power involved in their negotiations with employers. The device they used, of course, was the formation of unions. It was through such organizations that the workers sought—by the solidarity of their coordinated actions and the establishment of funds based upon their combined dues—to offset the power and resources of their corporate employers. The unions could use the strike as a counterpoise[15] to the lockout. And they could use their savings to sustain striking members, thus rendering all of them less susceptible to quick and disadvantageous settlements with their employers.

Theoretically, American workers might have sought a more radical solution to the inequities inherent in their economic position. Specifically, they might have espoused Marxism, combining their numerical strength to replace our capitalistic economy with a socialistic one. But most American workers have never been sufficiently disaffected from the ideology of capitalism to give their endorsement[16] to the Socialist or Communist parties. They have never even united to form a nationally effective equivalent of the British Labour Party, which might have provided them with an ongoing channel—independent of both the Republican and Democratic parties—for pressing the objectives of a socialistic economy.

So, Samuel Gompers has proven to be "the true prophet of

American labor."[17] It is his conception of labor-capital relationships that still guides the policies of our present unions. Gompers neither questioned nor fundamentally challenged the capitalistic system. Instead, accepting the legitimacy of that form of economy, he regarded the labor of his membership as a commodity. In his negotiations with employers, he simply strove to obtain as high a price for that commodity as the traffic would bear—or, to put it more precisely, as the various considerations attendant upon the negotiation of a particular contract appeared to permit.

American unions, having begun, like American businesses, on a small scale, steadily expanded—again like their protagonists of business—into mammoth organizations. Bigness appeared to hold forth similar desiderata to labor. The size of the union treasury was proportional to its membership; the larger that treasury, the better prepared the union to absorb the ravages of a strike. Union dues could be invested, and the proceeds applied to the provision of such necessities as medical care; the money could also be used to promote legislation and political candidates amicable to the economic interests of the union. In addition, union funds could be used to organize new branches of the union in previously non-union shops, adding to the union's size and financial resources.

The depression of the 1930's convinced even the least socialistic of workers that it was economically prudent to band together for mutual support in wresting higher salaries and better conditions of work from reluctant employers. But, like their rivals in commerce, the growing unions began to compete with each other for membership and jurisdiction. They, too, eventually perceived the sagacity of consolidation. With the merger of the AFL-CIO, the unions finally consummated a consolidation that, in its own way, was as encompassing as any effected in industry. By 1960, 15 million of the national total of 18 million unionized workers were affiliated with the AFL-CIO.[18] Nevertheless, a number of unions—the Teamsters most prominently, perhaps—still function outside the AFL-CIO. And, within the AFL-CIO, the affiliated unions still retain their separate staffs and organizational structure. However, the field of union organization may be described as an oligopoly, in which only a few organizations represent the majority of unionized workers.

Together with their evolution to bigness,[19] American unions have adopted other characteristics of the bureaucratization that typifies American economic life. Internally, they are pyramidal in structure.[20] Unions themselves employ clerical and other types of workers to carry out their affairs; and they place their own employees within the same hierarchical table of organization as may be found in an industrial concern. Moreover, the oligarchs who run the unions seem to possess interminable authority. Gompers, for example, was president of the AFL for thirty-eight years. Succeeding him in 1924, William Green held office for nearly thirty years. After heading the Carpenters for over three decades, Hutcheson retired and was replaced by his son.[21] Finally, insofar as unions rigidly restrict the quota of workers who shall be admitted to their membership—sometimes even descending to racial discrimination[22]—they exclude from access to their economic advantages the very class of people on whose behalf unions were originally organized.

But what happened in the organization of business and labor also took place in other American institutions of work. Relentlessly, bigness and bureaucracy, the specialization of work and the oligarchical control of organizations of work, have come to characterize every conceivable way in which Americans might seek to earn a living. Today, it matters little, in regard to those conditions of work, whether a person sets out to make his livelihood in industry, government, merchandising, communications, or agriculture. No matter what occupations they choose, the overwhelming majority of Americans will wind up as employees of an organization. Even the criminal underworld has kept pace with this trend. Crime itself has now become largely organized along bureaucratic and oligarchical lines. Nor, evidently, can the most willing of potential hoodlums look forward to a viable career in that organization unless he is selected by it for membership and successfully passes a rather demanding apprenticeship in its lowest rank.[23]

By the middle of this century, eighty-five per cent of American breadwinners could already be classified as employees, half of whom worked for organizations so large that they "prevent face-to-face interpersonal relations among most of their members."[24] In 1960, approximately 11 million Americans were "public servants, civilian and military, in local, state, and federal governments"; while about 9 million worked "for our 500 largest industrial corporations, eleven of which have over 100,000."[25] Impressive examples of these concentrations of manpower in various types of oligarchies included: American Telephone and Telegraph, 745,-000; General Motors, 625,000; and Sears, Roebuck, 185,000.[26]

We still have with us a goodly number of professionals[27] in private practice—doctors, lawyers, dentists, architects, and others. But increasing proportions of them are functioning as employees of organizations. Naturally, too, one can still point to small and thriving shops that have been started and are being run by lone entrepreneurs. But with the phenomenal growth of chain stores and nationwide discount houses, such individual successes are much more the exception than the rule; they may soon become as rare and fragile as antique automobiles. Yes, we have become a nation of organizations and employees; and all present indications point to the likelihood that, in the years to come, our organizations will become even larger, and fewer, and even more of us will work for them.

This change from a frontier society to an organizational society has taken place with such startling alacrity that many Americans have yet to assimilate it. Nor do the TV Westerns or the homey commercials of the mammoth corporations help us to confront this reality. Like it or not, the fact is that very, very few of us can now function economically with the independence and autonomy that was commonplace in the first century of our national life. On the contrary, virtually all of us who work for a living are now employed as members of an organizational team. And while contemporary Americans still seek ways of pursuing their dominant values, they are now increasingly pitted not against the forces of nature but against each other; not against unpredictable shifts in

the wind or weather but against the calculated plans of their superiors in the organization; not against the wrath of strange animals
but against colleagues and associates who have ambitions identical
to their own.

Thus, the most pronounced change in the tactics of aggrandizement has been necessitated by the bureaucratization of work itself.
For, within a modern bureaucracy of work, *literally nothing can
be accomplished by anyone on his own.* True, an individual may
still often be in a position within such an organization to initiate
action. But his initiative counts for nothing unless others carry it
out wholeheartedly. Similarly, an individual may be eager to do
whatever he can to implement a policy. But his eagerness is wasted
unless someone else puts that policy forward or is persuaded by
the individual in question to put it forward.

Whether he is placed high or low in the organization, whether
he is classified as management or labor, no individual can get what
he wants, can advance his aggrandizing motives, simply by going
out and acting upon them with straightforward, individual effort.
On the contrary, everything necessary to advance his personal
ambitions—every possible means of pursuing his self-aggrandizing
ends—must be mediated through the acquiescence, compliance,
collusion, or cooperation of others.

What are the social implications of this state of affairs? Organizationally speaking, the individual is truly a member of a team.
No semblance of common purpose, no ultimate product or service
—car, washing machine, telephone call, or pair of shoes—can be
yielded by the organization unless everyone in it is willing to play
his assigned role in the division of labor. But, although he may be
a member of the team, the American employee's own self-aggrandizing motives, essentially unaltered since Colonial times, demand
that he regard the organization as a vehicle for their pursuit. Since
the organization is entirely social in its composition, and since the
individual can only pursue his ambitions through the behavior of
others, each member of the team is induced to regard all of the
others as objects to be manipulated in the interest of his personal

advancement. It is to everyone's best interest to manipulate the rest, setting himself apart from them psychologically even as he works in their midst; even as he smiles at his associates and hands them the instructions or equipment necessary for each to perform his particular role in the ensemble of work. With each person so similarly oriented toward his teammates, each contributes to the playing out of a curious game—a game in which a seething and carefully dissimulated competitiveness underlies the cooperative behavior of every member of the team. It is as if, while they cheerfully pass the ball to each other—which their organization pays them to do—they are secretly hoping it will be fumbled by a teammate, implicitly revealing his gracelessness in comparison with their agility; or hoping, at least, that, somehow, their way of passing the ball will be noticed, approved, and specially rewarded by the captain of the team.

This state of affairs is most poignantly relevant to those categories of employees for whom upward economic mobility is based upon individual promotion. But even those routine clerical or "blue collar" workers who have almost no chance of advancement on an individual basis feel obliged to work well enough on the job to avoid being discharged. Yet they may begrudge the obvious advantage that their employers have over them; and they may perform minimally rather than maximally, seeing in their very withholding of effort a competitive gain for themselves and a vicarious triumph over their economic superiors, whose own financial interests would be best served if each employee worked as effectively as it was physically possible for him to do.[28]

4

The Tyranny of Class and Caste

THERE ARE ONLY two ways in which the individual can assess his progress in self-aggrandizement, and both of them involve reference to external criteria. First, he can compare his attainments and station in life with those of his own past. For example, he can compare his current income with the amount of money he made last year and the year before; or he can compare his present position in a table of organization with the position he occupied at an earlier point in his career. The second method of assessing one's progress in aggrandizement, however, takes the behavior and status of other persons as points of reference, permitting the individual to compare his fortunes with theirs. In this case, the relativity of self-evaluation—implicit in both methods of assessing aggrandizement—has a decidedly social focus; and the individual may become preoccupied not only with adding increments to his own history of accomplishment, but also with overcoming the discrepancies he perceives between his own level of aggrandizement and that connoted by the greater affluence, prestige, or power of others.

Theoretically, in an economically "open" society—one characterized by equally unlimited opportunities for all to pursue self-

75

aggrandizement—every individual might be so successful in promoting his own amibitions that he would be little disposed to concern himself with the attainments and social position of others. Let others stand higher, for the moment, in the permeable socio-economic structure of society. No matter. In time, one would attain just as desirable a place and then continue to press upward from there. In such a hypothetical society, people would generally be quite free of resentment toward those whom they perceive, at any moment of self-assessment, to be in a more advantageous position than their own.

But as a society becomes economically "closed," offering statistically few opportunities for endless self-aggrandizement to all who wish to pursue it, everyone's socio-economic position becomes more enduringly frozen into the slot that he is presently occupying. Consequently, an individual's position *relative to others* in the social pyramid may assume greater significance in the estimation of his degree of aggrandizement than his *own past position.* And, despite the fact that the entire society may increasingly prosper—each segment in its own niche, in its own way—the individual may still feel hemmed in and resentful insofar as he continues to occupy the same *relatively inferior* position that he did during the society's leaner years.

Socio-economic Class and Social Reality in American Life

There really was a far-off time when "perhaps four-fifths of the free, white population were in one sense or another independent proprietors."[1] But America has never for a moment been the classless haven of our cultural myths. We have always had a laboring class and a class of owners of land and the means of production. We have always had classes of work and classes of leisure. And the closing of our geographical and industrial frontiers, as well as the bureaucratic organization of our economy, has simply had the effect of solidifying the differences between our social classes. Quite simply, the basic implications of these differences are: socially, people fraternize by class and live their day-to-day lives within the confines[2] of their economic stratum of society; economically, the lower one's class of birth, the less one's chances of rising[3] in the socio-economic ladder—which is to say, the less one's chances are of successfully pursuing the values of aggrandizement.

But why is the outlook so dismal for persons in the lower classes? First, lacking the money, they are less able to get the kind of education that would eventually lead to their economic advancement. The necessities of life force them more frequently than their more economically advantaged counterparts of higher classes to withdraw from school and enter the labor market with an absence of special skills that, in turn, assures their tenure in the lowest ranks of manual or semi-skilled workers. Second, because of their poverty, they cannot afford the nourishment and medical care that would provide them with the health and vitality required for the fullest exercise of their capacities. Indeed, mortality rates[4] of persons in the lowest class are significantly greater than those of persons born into the highest class. Third, because they are locked within a quite impermeable sphere of social life that precludes their acquaintanceship—and certainly, close friendship—with members of more favored classes, persons of the lower classes can benefit very little from the economic help that persons of the more prosperous classes can and do often give each other through recommendations for jobs and business ventures. Fourth, owing to their economically segregated places of residence—as well as the patterns of speech, dress, and manners that they develop through exclusive association with their own economic peers—members of the lower classes are readily identified and discriminated against by those above them in the socio-economic hierarchy.

In a society stratified by economic position and boiling with limitless aspirations for personal aggrandizement, class membership becomes an important basis for invidious distinction. Through the imputation of inferiority to those of low class and superiority to those of high class, persons who occupy any position in the overall hierarchy of invidiousness can gauge their grandeur by reference to their position. And while those who are low in the hierarchy may look "upward" with hatred for their purported superiors (and "inward" toward themselves, with self-hatred for their own purported inferiority), those more highly placed may look "downward" at persons "beneath" them with condescension and self-congratulation.

Insofar as those "above" can derive some sense of aggrandizement from keeping those "below" in their "place," they develop a psychological need for institutionalized inequality. While those in the socially designated positions of inferiority are led implicitly to oppose the class system because it limits their possibilities for self-aggrandizement, those in the more socially desirable positions are just as strongly induced to favor the class system, since it automatically provides them with a considerable degree of aggrandizement.

It must be stressed that invidious distinctions of socio-economic class can arise under any economic system, socialism included, in which various groups of people are systematically given differential degrees of external reward—money, titles, or other perquisites—that are explicitly denied to others; and that are understood to connote a greater social contribution to and higher social status in the total society. It is just these kinds of differential and external rewards that legitimize the psychology of invidious distinction where a class system already exists, and that create such a psychology wherever they are introduced.

Before the industrial revolution, class lines were drawn at the boundaries of one's property, and the ownership of land was the chief barrier that divided the economically privileged from the economically deprived. Subsequently, ownership of the means of industrial production and commercial distribution of goods augmented the ancient notion of property, which arose when direct cultivation of the land was the principal instrumentality of wealth. In our present epoch, the oligarchs who control our private corporations comprise the highest echelon of the class system. Since we have virtually become a society of employees, most Americans derive their class position—that is, their source of wealth—from their occupations. Their savings accounts, houses, automobiles, stocks and bonds, pension plans, and personal possessions notwithstanding, most Americans are ultimately dependent upon their *jobs* not only for their subsistence but also for the attainment of the crucial criteria of aggrandizement.

Viewing our present organizations of work in purely material terms, one is justified in concluding that *the majority* of Americans now spend their lives in occupational positions that *automatically preclude* as much access to the chief vehicle of aggrandizement—money—as is available to a very small number of their occupational superiors. This inequitable distribution of wealth, enforced through the institutionalized practice of unequal wages for different categories of employees, seems to have settled down into quite a stable pattern. Upward movement from one class to another appears to be a rather infrequent, although not yet extinct, phenomenon. It has for some time been true, in blatant contradiction of those fantasies which would have it otherwise, that an American son is more likely to remain in the socioeconomic class of his father than to rise above it. Or, to put it more forcefully, the class into which a person is born is an excellent indicator of the class in which he will die.[5]

Sociologists have tended to differ considerably in their preferred definitions of class.[6] Nor do the categories used here pretend to reflect a technical consensus on this matter. Still, linking class primarily to organizational rank, the rationale for which, as we have seen, emerges from the present facts of our economic life, the following classes, which appear to cover the totality of our economy, can be delineated.

Within our bureaucratic organizations of work, three classes have crystallized. In the descending order of their income, power, and prestige—but inversely proportional to their numbers—these classes are: the oligarchs, the managers, and the workers. And, the underlying basis of this ordering of invidious distinction concerns the relationship of these classes to the proprietorship of the organization.

But while it is very reasonable to regard the class of most Americans as a function of their position within a bureaucratic organization, some people cannot be so categorized, since they are not members of such organizations. The definition of two distinct classes—the idle rich and the unemployed poor—hinges largely upon the fact that they *lack* a status of work. Then, there are the self-employed persons—professionals in private practice and other entrepreneurs—whose income is gained through their solitary economic activities: persons who neither employ nor are employed by others.

Some people may qualify for dual classification—as in the case of an employee, such as an accountant, who supplements his regular salary by taking on private clients. Similarly, in the class of workers there are many who are not employed in large-scale industrial organizations and who do not belong to unions—itinerant agricultural laborers, domestic workers, and others. For their part, housewives can be properly categorized in accordance with the class membership of their husbands. Theoretically, wives who earn money qualify for membership in whatever class is appropriate to the character of their employment. It is possible for a woman to be in a class that is higher or lower than that of her husband. However, owing to the long-standing adherence of our culture to male chauvinism, even employed wives are customarily assigned to the class defined by the occupations of their husbands.

It seems fair to say, in summary, that economic life in America is divided along six lines of class. Inside our organizations of work, which now contain 85 per cent of all Americans who work, we find that the workers occupy about 90 per cent of the positions.[7] The bulk of the remaining 10 per cent are filled by the managers, the oligarchs themselves holding only a minute but preeminent fraction of the positions. Outside our organizations of work—the 15 per cent of American breadwinners who do not earn a living as employees—we find the self-employed profession-als and entrepreneurs.

Apart from the classes that comprise those actively engaged in work, unemployed workers form the larger of the two remaining socio-economic classes. Subsisting on doles received from the State, unemployed workers have for some time represented about 5 to 6 per cent of the potential labor force.[8] Finally, a tiny group of people in our society live entirely upon inherited wealth, engaging themselves in no paid employment at all.

The Socio-economic Classes of Our Bureaucracies of Work

I. THE OLIGARCHS

Properly speaking, the oligarchs are not employees. They are, instead, the active proprietors of our economic organizations, who may own all or large parts of the organizations that they control. However, because of the public sale of stock in private corporations, it often happens that an oligarch actually owns little of the resources he is empowered to deploy. Whether they own much or little of the organizations they direct, corporate oligarchs are likely to draw the highest salaries in the land—and to supplement those salaries with personal expense accounts, bonuses of stock in their company, and options to purchase the company's stock at a price much lower than its price in the public market.

Principally, oligarchs are those who rule in the corporate domain. As Mills has pointed out,[9] this class might well include the individuals who make the basic decisions of policy in our officially non-commercial organizations—particularly governmental and military ones; and who, coincidentally, are the most economically rewarded members of those organizations. Certainly, in the light of the enormity of our governmental budgets and the impressive size of our current military expenditures, governmental and military oligarchs control sums of money and material resources that often exceed those controlled by their counterparts in purely profit-making organizations. Similarly, the oligarchs of the labor unions may be included under this category.[10] They appear to qualify not only in regard to the power they wield within their own organizations, but also in regard to the financial resources at their disposal. While their salaries are generally not equivalent to those of corporate oligarchs, they are impressively in excess of any earned by members of their unions.

II. THE MANAGERS

The *managers* are the people who implement the policies of the oligarchs. Prototypically, the managers also provide the oligarchs with information that they can take into account in arriving at their decisions. Not that managers have no discretion in making myriad decisions. On the contrary, depending upon their rank, their discretionary powers may be very great. But the decisions they make are restricted to matters of method and strategy. True, the managers frequently decide how best to pursue the objectives that are handed down to them from above. Yet it is the oligarch— and not the manager, however highly placed—who defines the basic objectives of the organization; and even if the command of the oligarch is simply the most general one—"Make more money for us!"—the manager will find his job at peril if he does not heed it. Should he fail to show the way toward higher profits, he is very apt to be replaced by another manager who has the temerity to take the job. Therefore, although they may glory in such honorific titles as Vice President in Charge of Production, Director of Research, or Assistant to the President, managers are employees whose connection with the organization may be severed by the wishes of the oligarchy. In fact, regarding the permanence of their jobs, managers often enjoy less security, in spite of their vastly higher salaries, than unionized workers who have seniority.

The category of manager is much larger than that of oligarch. It includes all of the executive and technical personnel who owe their allegiance directly to the oligarchs; and that allegiance is mediated through a hierarchical chain of command. Within the rubric of corporate management, for example, one might include the grades of employees that fan downward from president through foreman; from the head of sales in the central office to the regional director of the smallest marketing outlet for the company.

Although it may be couched in polite rhetoric, the loyalty that corporate oligarchs require of their managers—and that the managers, for their part, feel they owe to the oligarchs—refers to the continuation and enhancement of the proprietorship of the oligarchy. That is, the managers are expected to extract the greatest possible returns from the property—all of the land, equipment and capital—that the oligarchs hire them to superintend. And the managers, in turn, commit themselves to being the guardians and champions of the oligarchy's material resources. Hence, both the explicit function and implicit orientation of the managers lead them to identify themselves with the oligarchs and their property. Moreover, as both Mills[11] and Presthus[12] have noted, the extent of this identification probably plays a vital role in determining whom, among the highest group of managers, the oligarchs will ultimately co-opt for admission to their privileged circle. For even oligarchs die, necessitating the occasional elevation of a manager to their Olympus.

III. THE WORKERS

The *workers* perform the routine tasks of industrial production, marketing, and record-keeping; they are the men on the assembly lines, the file clerks, the salesgirls.

In an economic sense, the workers also function like managers, their labor implementing the proprietary and profit-seeking objectives of the corporate oligarchy. Yet, it is understood by all concerned that the workers do not *owe* allegiance to the oligarchy in the same way as the managers. Indeed, this understanding of a sharp cleavage of basic identification is reflected in the formal practices that define the relationships among oligarchs, managers, and workers. In negotiating rates of pay, for instance, oligarchs deal with workers *en masse*, through negotiations with representatives of the unions. But managers are not permitted to join the unions to which the workers belong. The oligarchy relates itself personally and individually to its immediate lieutenants in management—directly discussing with them the terms of their employment; personally dispensing to them special rewards or bonuses; personally communicating news of their promotion, transfer, or discharge. Similarly, each of the highest managers conducts personal negotiations with his immediate assistants—and so it goes downward through the managerial hierarchy.

But this chain of personal responsibility and loyalty to the reigning oligarchy stops abruptly at the level of the worker. Thus, it is virtually acknowledged that his economic fate is sealed by the very character of his job; that his stereotyped activities, however essential to the economic functioning of the organization, render him more like a simple tool than a sentient being whose capacity for thought must—as in the case of managers—be personally engaged and nurtured by the oligarchs in order to vouchsafe its application on their behalf.

Certainly, many persons in managerial positions experience special rewards for their work, in addition to the financial ones. Frequently, their jobs are inherently interesting and varied. Typically, they work in quite pleasant surroundings and are able to exercise initiative and inventiveness in the specific tasks assigned to them. The workers, by contrast, are typically obliged to cope with activities that are much more stultifying. Often, they work in distasteful physical circumstances: the pit of a mine, the clanging cavern of an automotive assembly line, or the relentless clatter of a corps of typists seated side by side in a secretarial pool. Adding implicit injury to economic insult, the mass media of information and entertainment are much more likely to glorify managers than workers.

The Socio-economic Classes Outside
Our Bureaucracies of Work

While the hierarchical structure of our organizations of work is a neat manifestation of the hierarchy of invidious distinction that envelops all persons in our society, the criteria of the values of aggrandizement can readily serve as a guide for the assignment of invidious distinction to persons who are not so assigned by virtue of their position in a bureaucracy. If we merely determine the size of a person's income, we have a quite reliable basis for placing him in his proper class. Thus, for persons not employed in organizations, their classes are arranged in this descending order of imputed distinction: the idle rich, the self-employed, and the unemployed worker.

I. THE IDLE RICH

The *idle rich* are persons of affluence whose source of income is inherited wealth. They do no productive labor themselves; nor do they occupy any salaried position in an organization. They may function as passive oligarchs owning a large portion of a particular business. But they do not become actively involved in the conduct of any commercial enterprise, including the ones in which they may have their capital. Turning such control over to active oligarchs, whose financial investment in the business may be much smaller, the idle rich devote themselves to pastimes of leisure and consumption, to philanthropy, or to some other avocation.

However, as Mills has observed,[13] the complexities of modern corporate intrigue may be making absentee ownership an uneasy condition of life; and persons with inherited wealth may feel increasingly compelled to participate in directing the organizations in which they have a proprietary interest. Otherwise, the financial value of their holdings might be jeopardized by the machinations of those who would necessarily fill the vacuum of authority.

II. THE SELF-EMPLOYED PERSON

Although reduced to a mere shadow of its former relative size, the group of self-employed persons is still an important force in our society. Many professionals in private practice earn more than highly placed and grandly titled managers; and their personal prestige, if not their power, may eclipse that of many oligarchs. For example, our leading singers, writers, or comedians—all in business for themselves—may be household luminaries to tens of millions of Americans, who would be at a loss to identify the Chairman of the Board of Directors of such multi-billion-dollar corporations as the Metropolitan Life Insurance Company or the Standard Oil Company of New Jersey.

But most self-employed persons are far from illustrious. Instead, they are likely to be decidedly local figures—the neighborhood grocer, the dentist on the corner of Elm and Oak, the lady who sells her bayberry candles at a roadside stand; and their success in the pursuit of the values of aggrandizement is likely to be more solid than spectacular. In fact, many claim that their experience of independence—of freedom from the coils of bureaucracy—is one of the principal motives for their economic mode. Professionals in private practice often feel that the autonomous exercise of their talents is the best of all the rewards of their work. At any rate, this socio-economic group does seem to uphold values of initiative and assertiveness that are less prevalent in the managerial class.[14]

III. THE UNEMPLOYED WORKER

The class of Americans least likely to be mentioned in the society columns of our newspapers is composed of unemployed workers. These are the men and women who are willing and able to work, but who cannot find jobs. Thus, their condition is more wretched[15] than that of the other classes. Clearly, they are the poorest class, being obliged to subsist on minimal payments from the State. Their morale is further undermined because their idleness is involuntary; they are subjected to poverty, social impotence, and boredom. In addition to this crushing psychological load, the unemployed worker must shoulder the humiliation of being considered socially inferior to everyone who has a job.

Socio-economic Class and the Societal Hierarchy of Invidious Distinction

Adding the three classes outside our bureaucracies to the three that were derived from organizational position completes a rough but reliable picture of our national hierarchy of invidious distinction. At the top are the oligarchs and the idle rich, who could become active oligarchs if they wished to exercise the prerogatives of ownership. The managers and the self-employed persons fall next in line, overlapping to a great extent—depending upon their particular incomes. True, the self-employed entrepreneur may own considerable property, giving him a base of capital that is unavailable to the manager, whose yearly salary is equal to the yearly earnings of the entrepreneur. On the other hand, the salary of a highly placed manager may dwarf the annual income of a private practitioner who may have no source of capital save the furniture in his office. The workers form the populous base of the hierarchy of invidious distinction, having only the unemployed worker to stand between themselves and the very earth itself.

Regarding upward mobility in the hierarchy, none of our socio-economic classes is easy to enter from the one below it. Undoubtedly, a good deal of upward mobility is still possible *within* the organizational groupings below the class of oligarch. *Within* the class of managers, a person may well be able to advance from lesser to higher managerial positions during the span of his career. Similarly, *within* the class of workers, a man may progress from the stage of apprentice, let us say, to that of master machinist. But, exceedingly few managers are ever taken into the enclave of the oligarchs. And, for the workers, foreman is the highest managerial position to which any of them is likely to be promoted. Indeed, it is the very rarity of upward mobility between worker and manager, on the one hand, and manager and oligarch, on the other hand, that permits us to regard these classes as stable and crystallized.

The prospects of a worker becoming a self-employed entrepreneur seem even more remote than his chances of moving into a managerial position. For where would he obtain the capital necessary to begin a business of his own? Entrepreneurs conducting their own businesses are presently finding it extremely difficult—often impossible—to muster the capital required to market goods at prices that can compete with those of corporate organizations. But capital is also needed to establish the independent practice of a profession, and where is a worker to obtain the financial backing needed to carry him through the long years of professional education? Hence, the class of the professional and the entrepreneur can be entered most readily by the children of those already in the class or by those of the classes of oligarch, idle rich, or managers —children whose parents can subsidize the pursuit of their professional or entrepreneurial aspirations.

Paradoxically, it is becoming as difficult for an unemployed worker to enter the class of workers as it is for a worker to become a manager. Not too long ago in our history, an unemployed worker could take heart in the belief that his situation was merely temporary; that he would be summoned back to work with the next upswing of the business cycle. But the increasing application of automation is rapidly depriving the unemployed worker of hope for his future. For if automation has thrown him out of work, it is difficult for him to believe that its wider and wider application will create more jobs than it eliminates.

The Strait Jacket of Caste

CASTE, RACE, AND RACISM

For tens of millions of Americans, the thwarting effects of lowly class are unbearably aggravated by the claustrophobia and humiliation of lowly caste. A child born of parents of lowly caste enters a social stockade from which he cannot escape. Even if he subsequently manages to acquire wealth in impressive abundance, he is given to understand that he is *inherently* unworthy of membership in the caste that excludes him. Conversely, while a child of high caste may be placed by poverty in a position of low class, he is free to engage his society in any way he wishes if his economic fortunes should later improve; and even if he has to spend a lifetime in a lowly class, his awareness of his caste membership allows him to feel *inherently* superior to more affluent members of a lower caste.

Neither in America nor elsewhere have differences in caste always been defined by physical differences. In ancient Greece, slaves and their masters were physically indistinguishable. In our own and more recent past, many Colonists did not hesitate to import fellow countrymen from their European homelands as indentured servants. And it has been estimated that "at least four thousand Negroes owned slaves as of 1860."[16]

But the evolution of our caste system has implacably drawn the boundaries of caste about genetic differences in physical appearance. Actually, there are no "pure" races in the family of mankind, the long history of human mating having thoroughly mixed the genes of all people. "Civilization causes race convergence, due to gene exchange, to outrun race divergence. In this sense, human races are relics of the precultural stage of evolution."[17] However, accidents of location and barriers of religion, custom, and discrimination have led to the relatively protracted in-breeding of various physical characteristics, on the basis of which one may attempt to classify physical differences between groups of people.

Among all the conceivable genetically-based physical differences, the color of his skin has become the most crucial determinant of an American's caste. But texture of hair, fullness of lips, drape of eyelids, shape of nose, and thrust of jaw may also be singled out as salient features in the determination of caste. In any event, most Americans have a configuration of physical traits that permits them to be classified as "whites," and that designation automatically entitles them to admission in the most favored caste of our society. All other Americans are regarded as "non-whites," and they are automatically relegated to a number of less favored castes, such as Mexicans and American Indians. And, since the social favor or disfavor of a caste is reflected in its possession of and access to commodities and conditions cherished by the whole society, the white caste not only possesses but also has a better chance to acquire more wealth, power, and prestige than the non-white.

Hypothetically, the American system of caste *could* have been based, with equal illogic, upon other physical characteristics. For example, height or weight might have been just as arbitrarily employed as the decisive stigmata of caste. Under those circumstances, both "whites" and "non-whites" of the same stature or girth would have been consigned to the same caste; and the "thins" or the "stouts," the "talls" or the "shorts," would have included individuals who varied along the entire spectrum of pigmentation. Or, given skin color as the defining criterion of caste, the most disadvantaged caste in our society might have been the fairest rather than the darkest of our inhabitants—exactly the lot that befell the light-skinned Ainu people of Japan.

Plainly, the historical and contemporaneous significance of our caste system is not to be found in anatomical imperatives. Instead, that system represents a crystallization of invidious socio-economic distinctions established in the earliest days of our society. Ever since those days, the preponderance of this country's wealth and power has been held by persons of European ancestry, and a numerical majority of our population has always consisted of descendants of Europeans.

As for the white indentured servants, they rapidly merged with the caste of their former masters. For the length of their service was limited by contractual agreement; and if they became too discontent, they could break their contracts by running away, their physical traits giving them every reasonable hope of being accepted as equals by whites in other localities. Besides, their caste was never so low as that of the African slaves upon whom enterprising whites eventually strapped the whole onus of compulsory and degrading servility.

Thus, while whites were consolidating their caste position, Negro slaves were pushed into the lowest of social and economic positions, their descendants constituting the largest non-white caste. Other non-whites included, principally, descendants of conquered Indians and laborers from Latin America and Asia. Taken together, all non-white persons today comprise a greatly outnumbered minority of the American population.

It is evident, therefore, that the American caste system evolved as an articulation and glorification of physical differences long associated with socio-economic differences. Insofar as they have actively endorsed this development, white Americans have conferred the special prestige of highest caste upon themselves, extolling themselves above and beyond whatever aggrandizement they may have attained through competitive struggles with members of their own caste. And the fact that non-whites can usually be identified quickly, makes it easy for whites to swing the gates of social and economic exclusion against them.

It is true that the lines of class overlap those of caste, and that the American caste system is not now so rigidly enforced as to ensure that *every* member of the white caste will have more wealth and power than *every* member of a non-white caste. However, the actual differences in wealth and power between white and non-white castes are enormous, the class level of the non-white caste being far below that of the white caste. For example: "More than 75 percent of all Negro workers are found in the three lowest occupational categories—service workers, semiskilled, and unskilled laborers and farm workers, whereas less than 39 percent of all white workers are in those categories."[18] "The unemployment rate is twice as high among Negroes as among whites; median family income is about half as much."[19] But even the poorest of whites can, owing to the irrationality fostered by the psychology of caste, regard the wealthiest of non-whites as his social inferior. Indeed, in many parts of the country, such whites, counting upon the complicity of the local police, daily exercise their feelings of superiority by subjecting non-whites of all classes to a veritable gantlet of indignity.

All members of the dominant white caste are, in fact, insidiously exposed to the temptation to maintain their entirely gratuitous position of social favor. To the extent to which they have adopted the values of aggrandizement, whites have a strong vested interest in perpetuating whatever extra advantages accrue to them through the sheer accident of birth. Yet their rearing in the rudiments of democracy makes it difficult for them to reconcile the glaring inequities of caste with the minimal requirements of justice. Besides, the resentments of non-whites can only be stifled with efficient ruthlessness if members of the white caste are profoundly convinced that they have a moral right to be socially supreme.

Seen in this light, spurious doctrines of racial superiority offer members of the white caste a means of resolving their ideological conflicts in such a way as to preserve their social supremacy without suffering qualms of conscience. These doctrines help whites not only to make a virtue of injustice but also to feel completely righteous about whatever coercive measures they may have to take to keep resentful non-whites penned within the prison of their caste. Yes, while color is the stamp of caste in America, racism is its ultimate guardian.

Quite simply, the mythology of racial superiority ascribes innate and immutable differences in emotional and intellectual functioning to persons who exhibit the superficial differences in physical appearance by which the myth-makers establish distinctions in caste. In essence, these purported psychological concomitants of physical differences are such as to aggrandize one group and denigrate all others. Viewed in terms of traits esteemed by our society, whites are presumed, among many other things, to be biologically more gifted with intelligence, creativity, initiative, sensitivity, and refinement. Indeed, the most presumptuous tenets of racism would virtually pre-empt the honorific status of human beings for whites, lumping all non-whites into infra-human species.

The weight of scientific evidence offers no support to these assumptions of racial superiority. Certainly, "no genetic linkage has been found between such a racially-designating physical trait as skin color and such capacities as intelligence."[20] And the vast majority of scientists would agree that "educability, the capacity to learn and profit from experience, is not concentrated in any one caste or class. It is not concentrated in any one race either."[21] Because human plasticity is common to all men, and because the interactions between men and their environments are so manifold and complex, any allegation that differences in culturally valued behavior between racially different groups are influenced by genetics alone is totally unwarranted.

But the advocate of white supremacy is not likely to be deterred by scientific evidence and opinion: his completely false biological conceptions help him to legitimize his illegitimate social prerogatives and arm him with a marvelous set of justifications for keeping non-whites in an unending state of subordination.

At his most benign, when non-whites are making no demands for social equality, the racist may regard his caste subordinates with sympathetic condescension, may even permit himself to be sufficiently moved by their quiet wretchedness to toss them a few additional scraps from his exclusive table. At his worst, however, when non-whites are insisting upon an end to the caste system, the threatened racist may display the fullness of his contempt. It is then that the false notions of racial superiority serve not only as rationalizations for the maintenance of injustice but also as the emotional fuel for perpetuating the cruelties required to keep the despised non-whites "in their place." And if all other measures of oppression should fail to quell the cry for justice, the racist can invoke the most extreme of his doctrines in an effort to silence the protesting voices altogether. For if he believes deeply that non-whites are not really human beings, he can kill them with impunity, feeling no more empathy with their death throes and no more remorse for his murderous actions than he might in slaughtering a chicken or a pig.

Turned in upon himself—hated, segregated, and discriminated against by the dominant caste—the non-white sometimes begins to show the very modes of behavior in which the white racist reads the imprint of biological inheritance. Deprived of educational incentives and opportunities, his intellectual performance may fall below that of whites. Regarded as unworthy of respect by whites, he may begin to lapse into apathy and despair. His life implicitly menaced by any demonstration of equalitarian assertiveness in the face of white domination, the non-white may seek solace and, perhaps, a pathetically devious kind of freedom in passive withdrawal from the world of work, upon which our society tends to place so much emphasis in judging the worth of a man.

Our caste system is thus a self-perpetuating social and psychological monstrosity. It creates the very differences in behavior that its apologists put forth to justify its existence. And its existence prevents its non-white victims from taking effective steps to wipe out these differences. But our caste system also victimizes the members of the white caste—brutalizing them, cutting them off from potentially enriching experience with a large segment of their compatriots, and undermining the possibility of removing the values and institutions of aggrandizement from which they, like Americans of every class and color, are bitterly suffering.

Of all non-white castes in America, Negroes are the largest and least favored. They now number about 20,000,000 people and represent 92 per cent of all Americans classified as non-white.[22] Consequently, although many of the problems of Negroes may equally beset similar groups in our society, it is fitting to focus upon the Negro in analyzing the effects and prospects of caste in American life.

THE NEGRO CASTE AND ITS SUFFERING

Before the Civil War, Negroes were explicitly denied the rights of American citizenship. Their subservient exclusion from the rest

of society was enforced by the institution of slavery[23] and con-
doned by the highest law of the land.[24] Regarded as chattel—
bred, bought, and sold like so many heads of beef—Negroes were
commanded by the white caste to provide brute labor and to obey
without complaint or opposition.

By the time Lincoln issued the Emancipation Proclamation, the
subordination of the Negro caste had been firmly buttressed by
socio-economic realities. Most of the prevailing material resources
of the nation were already in white hands. Blocked by discrimination as well as their own poverty, the overwhelming majority of
freed Negroes could not obtain the jobs or education required for
movement upward in the American hierarchy of class. Instead,
with but a very few exceptions, Negroes could continue to subsist
only by accepting the least remunerative kinds of employment, by
doing the same sort of menial work for whites that they had done
as slaves. Economically squelched, Negroes were also socially besieged by the hardened prejudices of whites, who used terror and
harassment to maintain the supremacy of their caste. And the
political advances made by Southern Negroes in the beginning of
the Reconstruction were pitilessly erased by Southern whites when
they regained their former monopoly of power. Nor were all the
legal yokes of caste broken with the abolition of slavery. On the
contrary, laws flagrantly demeaning to Negroes, such as those
forbidding their intermarriage with whites, are still standing in
many States. And even the Federal government, as recently as in
its Civil Rights Act of 1964, has balked at legally condemning the
existence of *all* instances of caste discrimination. Sadly, too,
some Negroes who attained national prominence have failed to
put their potential influence to use in uncompromising opposition
to the continuance of the caste system. For example, Booker T.
Washington, an ex-slave, not only implored Negroes to accept
social apartheid but also advised them to rest their economic
aspirations upon training in handicrafts, although the industriali-
zation of the American economy was well under way.[25]

So, the end of the Civil War left the Negro physically free but economically, socially, and politically tormented. Released from the crudities of slavery, he was still clamped in the ambiguous bondage of caste. Told that he was, at last, an American citizen, he was nevertheless treated by whites as an alien inferior. Invited by the impassioned rhetoric of Presidential speeches to embrace the values of our society, he encountered almost universal frustration in attempting to act upon those values. Urged to better himself economically, he was virtually shorn of genuine opportunities to do so. Congratulated on the attainment of equality, he was blandly ignored in his pleas for justice by those who could give it to him.

This kind of "welcome" into American society was certain to have a profoundly deleterious impact upon the Negro in every facet of life valued by our culture. Regarding the pursuit of aggrandizement, the limiting effects of the Negro's caste position have been suggested in the previously cited figures comparing types of employment, rates of unemployment, and income for Negroes and whites. Without question, Negroes are less able than whites to aggrandize themselves via the acquisition and consumption of material goods or the attainment of positions of high status and power. But the economic disparities between Negroes and whites also severely limit the extent to which Negroes can fulfill the values of *realization*. For example, Negroes are less able than whites to live in esthetically pleasing surroundings. And the housing that they can afford is often insufficient unto the basic humanitarian ideal of preserving life. "In 1960 one out of six nonwhite dwelling units—houses, apartments, duplexes—was dilapidated (i.e., a danger to the health or safety of its occupants), compared with one out of thirty-two white dwellings. Another 29 percent were deteriorating compared with 12 percent for white housing."[26] And, among Negroes, an average of four persons is obliged to share a single dwelling, whereas the average for whites is only three.[27]

However, the full extent of the inroads of caste upon the humanity of Negroes can only be appreciated by an examination of the statistics of mortality. Thus, "the life expectancy at birth of a Negro girl baby in the United States is 66 years; for a white baby girl it is 74 years. For a Negro baby boy the expectancy is 61 years and for the white baby boy it is 67 years. . . . In most of the nation, the infant mortality rate among nonwhites is roughly double that among whites." Moreover, as of 1958, the non-white maternal mortality rate was "nearly four times as high as the white rate."[28]

But if caste destroys life itself, it can scarcely be expected to spare the subtle and tender offshoots of growth and vitality. Admittedly, an assessment of the psychological ravages of caste on Negroes is fraught with more complexities than are involved in the compilation of mortality rates. Nevertheless, the available evidence indicates that Negroes have fewer chances than whites to develop their intellectual capacities and creative talents. Surely, such a conclusion is not too rash to draw from the following facts alone: "A Negro has about half the chance to complete high school as a white boy; one third as much to complete college or become a professional man";[29] and, considering even the lowest levels of elementary education, 22.1 percent of non-white adults 25 years or older have had less than 5 years of formal schooling, whereas only 6.2 percent of whites of the same age have been so educationally deprived.[30]

The Negro child is also more likely than the white child to suffer from fundamental social deprivations: the condition of being born out of wedlock or totally orphaned, the absence of a father from the home, or the lack of maternal attention. All of these factors tend to restrict the range of possibilities for a child's psychological development. Once again, material privation is as crucial in producing these forms of familial dislocation as it is in putting the Negro child at an educational disadvantage. Thus, according to the official census data of 1960: many more non-white than white mothers with children under the age of six have jobs—34.3 percent versus 19.5 percent; husband and wife are present in only three-fourths of all non-white families, whereas both parents are present in nine-tenths of all white families; and, "only two-thirds (66.3 per cent) of non-whites under eighteen years of age live with both of their parents as compared with nine-tenths (90.2 percent) of such whites."[31]

It is little wonder, therefore, that psychological studies[32] have reported a variety of ways in which caste may have scarred many Negroes by dampening their emotional spontaneity and zest for living; by generating feelings of self-hatred, inadequacy, and helplessness; by sapping hope and confidence; by making it difficult to formulate and retain a clear and positive sense of personal identity; by posing such threats to the expression of justifiable anger as to induce withdrawal into a state of numb aimlessness.

In general, these studies document many of the qualities of misery reported from first-hand experience by such sensitive Negro authors as Richard Wright, Ralph Ellison, and James Baldwin. Certainly, these studies can be interpreted as providing some empirical substantiation to the distress caste has caused among Negroes, and as illustrating the specific ways in which caste may undermine the development of human capacities and the enjoyment of life. But the results of these studies cannot and should not be put forth as a psychological portrait of *the* Negro in America, for the samples studied have often been far from representative of the nation's population of Negroes, and the methods of investigation have varied from highly subjective clinical interviews to fairly reliable objective tests. But even the findings yielded by comparatively objective measures must be viewed with great caution, since the caste of the examiner may well affect the way a Negro subject responds to a test; and much of the behavior of the respondent may merely indicate his transient feelings toward the tester and the context of testing rather than his relatively enduring and unique traits of personality.

From a scientific standpoint, it would thus be capricious folly for anyone now to speak definitively of *the* personality of *the* American Negro, as if it were a thoroughly established psychological entity. And one would be adding social mischief to scientific foolishness if one asserted not only that the encrustations of this "personality" were "holding Negroes back" from worldly success but that Negroes first had to undergo drastic changes in personality and behavior before they could presume to "make it" in American society.

Unfortunately, a number of evidently sympathetic commentators—both white and Negro—have given Negroes exactly this charge: "shape up or risk staying down." True, these writers deplore discrimination and prejudice on the part of whites; and they implore whites to take all necessary steps to admit Negroes to an equal footing in American society. However, in demonstrating their hardheaded judiciousness, in seeking to balance their heartfelt emotions with dispassionate reason, these commentators unwittingly call upon Negroes to pay a behavioral ransom for their freedom from the degradation of caste. Thus, Louis Lomax advises fellow Negroes to join him in dividing "our time between fighting for our rights and helping the masses of our people to become first-class citizens of the Republic." And he goes on to admonish: "The Negro crime rate is too high; Negro relief chiselers are an abomination and an embarrassment; the unthought-out migration of Negroes into major cities of the North, Midwest and Far West is creating problems that need not exist in a civilized society."[33] But if Lomax is displeased at the high rate of activity involved in the movement of Negroes into urban areas, he is equally critical of "the apathy and preachments of futility" among Negro college students, accusing them of having "no personal drive."[34]

Whitney Young, Executive Director of the Urban League, takes a similar position, although his indignation is more modulated. Thus, he chastises Negro professionals for having failed, in the past, to set their ambitions and their standards of excellence high enough—that is, for relying primarily upon other Negroes in the same field for their occupational frame of reference. Similarly, Young warns that Negro parents must raise their sights in regard to both child-rearing and participation in the affairs of the schools attended by their children.[35] Like Lomax, Young emphasizes the necessity for Negroes to "drive for first-class citizenship,"[36] the clear implication being that such citizenship presently character- izes the condition of the white caste and that Negroes should strive to shed whatever attitudes and behavior may have formerly prevented them from emulating whites.

As to white preceptors, there is no scarcity of persons who have the temerity to counsel Negroes against their purported shortcom- ings. Nathan Glazer, for example, virtually clucks his tongue in ominous disappointment at the "failure" of Negroes to have fewer miseries than now beset them: ". . . I think it is pointless to ignore the fact that the concentration of problems in the Negro commu- nity *is* exceptional, and that prejudice, low income, poor education explain only so much."[37] How much about the behavior of Ne- groes those factors might theoretically be expected to explain, Glazer does not tell us. However, he leaves no doubt, in discussing the future for Negroes in the North, that "a new phase in Negro leadership must begin";[38] and Glazer exhorts this leadership to devote itself, among other things, to the reduction of juvenile delinquency and family disruption among Negroes.

Glazer does have some vague awareness of the fact that caste has operated as a kind of social constraint *qualitatively* different for Negroes from that imposed upon various white minorities, who have had much greater success in eating from, if not melting into, the American pot. However, in shaking his head in puzzle- ment over the magnitude of the suffering still experienced by Ne- groes, Glazer seems to assume that the contemptuous barriers of caste are only *somewhat* more restrictive than the ethnic preju- dices which European immigrants, such as the Jews and the Irish, have largely surmounted within the past fifty years.

It is not difficult to agree with Glazer about the positive effects that fraternal organizations of self-help—and a long and rich cul- tural, religious, and linguistic heritage—have exerted among the Jews, for example. But how effectively would those organizations have functioned—and, indeed, how many of them would even have been formed—if American Jews had encountered the vicious depths of hatred and the granite exclusion that has been the Negro's destiny in this country? If Jews had been as vigilantly barred from the economy? If Jews had not been permitted, *by the leave and the patronage of other whites,* to obtain from that economy the wherewithal to conduct their fraternal organizations at an effective level of operation?

Jews have undeniably suffered from economic and social discrimination. But ugly and depressing as that prejudice has been, and continues to be, it does not, and never did, read Jews outside the pale of the *American*[39] white caste. And as long as they remain within that caste, Jews will generally have access to the concomitants of its socially favored position, although they may be disliked, snubbed, or even discriminated against by some of their caste peers.

Samuel Lubell warmly cites Glazer's conclusions: "Through the whole of Negro living there is also a desperate need for more energetic efforts by Negroes themselves to correct many of the ills that plague them."[40] Lubell, echoing Glazer, obliquely acknowledges the special destructiveness and intractability of caste, noting that "Negroes differ in their problems from old-time immigrant groups,"[41] yet he also argues that "after allowance is made for these differences . . . there is no question that Negroes and their leaders have not done as much as they could to help themselves."[42]

Taking up this theme, albeit with greater subtlety and sophistication, other white observers have advised Negroes to shake off their presumed apathy and mobilize the power of their numbers for circumscribed programs of political self-aid. With disarming enthusiasm and concern, these advisers contend that Negroes can and should do much to better the condition of their lives—even as they remain locked, on a societal basis, within the jail of caste. For example, both Charles Silberman[43] and Nat Hentoff[44] give glowing accounts of the work done in Chicago by a community organizer, Saul Alinsky, who has developed special techniques of enlisting the militant participation of downtrodden people in programs aimed at improving life in their neighborhoods. These programs have apparently resulted in such changes as new housing for the neighborhood and a decrease in the frequency with which local merchants seek to cheat residents of the area. And many participants in these programs are reported to experience a marked rise in self-respect and general morale.

Undoubtedly, all the writers just mentioned are well-intentioned men. But the flaw common to their seemingly "realistic" advice lies in their very willingness to discuss how *Negroes* should or should not behave *within the context of the caste system*. Discussing questions of *societal* change within an intellectual framework that implicitly assumes the indefinite continuation of the caste system, one cannot help but arrive at recommendations that shift some of the responsibility for change from those who maintain the system to the persons oppressed by it. But to demand as a condition for the granting of social justice the disappearance of *all traces* of the toll caste may have taken on the personalities of Negroes is to compound brazen injury with insufferable presumption. However sincerely proposed, it is similar to striking an innocent person and then informing him, with the utmost gravity, that his swelling offends your sensibilities and that he had better rid himself of it if he wants to stop getting hit.

Admittedly, as Robert Penn Warren[45] has pointed out, it is illogical to blame the present generation of whites for the sins of their fathers, grandfathers, and great-grandfathers, and to insist, as Martin Luther King[46] has done, that the existing white caste has inherited an accumulated debt of conscience, which they should now discharge by giving preferential treatment to Negroes in disbursing the resources of America. But it is just as unreasonable to expect contemporary Negroes to tolerate the continuation of caste simply because *their* fathers, grandfathers, and great-grandfathers suffered from it. No, there is no need for anyone to invoke the behavior of past generations in assessing and rectifying the present damages of caste. The evils of the caste system are plain enough for all living Americans to see and to condemn. But while whites and Negroes may be equally vociferous in denouncing that system, whites must bear the *full* responsibility for every moment it continues to prevail. For the ultimate power to end the American caste system is held by whites and not by Negroes.

FUTURE PROSPECTS FOR THE NEGRO CASTE IN AMERICA

But the white majority has conspicuously failed to exercise the power it has to eradicate the blight of caste from America. One may argue, it is true, that the years following World War II have produced some notable instances of anti-caste legislation and judicial rulings. Yet even the most sweeping of these measures, the Supreme Court's order against segregation in the public schools, has received very restricted application since its issuance in 1954. After a full decade, the figures on integration in public education bespeak, at best, only the most grudging and minimal sort of compliance with the Court's edict. "In the South as a whole, only 30,798 Negro students, or 1.06 per cent of all Negro students, were attending school with whites—and nearly half of this total was in Texas."[47] And, in the North, segregated patterns of housing have perpetuated *de facto* segregation in the schools. In fact, in some areas of the North, the growing influx of Negroes into the older sections of cities and the simultaneous exodus of whites from those sections to the suburbs have resulted in an *increase* of school segregation. Between 1957/58 and 1963/64, for example, the number of New York elementary and junior high schools "containing 90 per cent or more Negro and/or Puerto Rican students"[48] increased more than twofold.

Progress toward integrated housing has been similarly discouraging to Negroes. Despite the passage of numerous laws and ordinances outlawing discriminatory practices in many categories of housing, such as Federal housing projects, resistance on the part of whites to living in the same neighborhood as Negroes has baldly or subtly conspired to keep Negroes crowded together in residential ghettos—in North and South alike.

Because such confinement leads to a scarcity of accommodations, Negroes are often obliged to pay more for their housing than whites pay—and frequently for worse housing, too. On the other hand, Negroes are by and large less able than whites to afford whatever housing they can find.[49]

The dreary effects of caste on income, employment, health, family structure, and morale have already been amply illustrated; the studies quoted are recent enough to demonstrate the continuing reluctance of whites to let Negroes share equally in everything deemed important to life in our society.

Confronted by this stark and excruciating reluctance, many Negroes still attempt to adapt without protest to the liabilities of their caste position, living out their lives as best they can. Others, out of the maddening depths of their despair for the good will of their white countrymen, have succumbed to the chauvinistic appeals of the Black Muslims,[50] responding to a new brand of racism in which the "black" man (Black Muslims shun the word "Negro" as pejorative) is proclaimed inherently superior to the "white" man. Ingeniously, this doctrine reverses the psychology of the white racist by asserting the innate superiority of his traditional victim. More, the Black Muslims have devised a new theology in which God and His Chosen People are black, the Devil and his earthly agents, white. And, like white racists, the Black Muslims are vigorously opposed to integration, repelled by the mere thought of associating with persons they regard as inferior beings.

Consistent with their dogma, the Black Muslims would handle the abominations of caste by withdrawing from American society and forming a totally separate and self-contained nation of black men. Presumably, this black society would be a capitalistic theocracy with strong Puritan overtones. And, although they openly express contempt for Christians, whom they accuse of being among the chief corrupters of the black man, their Black Muslim State, if it were to materialize, might be very similar to Calvin's Geneva.

Some Negroes have channeled their resentments into political parties which hold that the obliteration of caste can only take place under one version of Marxism or another. But most Negroes who have decided to take action aimed at tearing down the walls of caste are giving their support to one or more of the organizations[51] involved in what has been called the Negro Revolution or the Civil Rights Movement.

Actually, the major spokesmen of this "revolution" or "movement" have not asked for anything more revolutionary than the total admission of Negroes into the existing society. They simply wish Negroes to have the same rights, amenities, power, opportunities, and respect—and to shoulder the same civic responsibilities —as whites. Apart from chastising whites for their caste-preserving practices and attitudes, leading representatives of the "movement" have voiced no essential quarrel with the basic values and institutions now accepted by most Americans. Repeatedly, these leaders have emphasized that Negroes, being American, merely desire to pursue what all Americans have learned to regard as the "good life."[52]

Because of their thoroughly conventional outlook, the spearheads of the Negro Revolution are likely to formulate and press the Negro's claim to justice within a perspective defined by the dominant values and institutions of aggrandizement.[53] Accordingly, they stress the desirability of distributing wealth, power, and prestige as equitably among Negroes as among whites. And, to redress past and present inequities in the apportionment of those commodities and conditions of aggrandizement, they have urged the country to endorse the kind of proposals Whitney Young has put forth[54] for a "special effort" or a "domestic Marshall plan." Under these proposals, public funds would be utilized in "crash programs" to improve the standard of living among Negroes and to raise Negroes as quickly as possible to the same levels of affluence, power, and prestige as whites.

Undoubtedly, such massive apportionments of the nation's resources and perquisites among Negroes would produce—indeed, necessitate—a drastic diminution, if not a complete eradication, of caste distinctions: it would require the same proportion of Negroes and whites at every level of employment, housing, education, and other realms of activity valued by the society as a whole. Obviously, to meet such a requirement, the presently unfair advantage that whites have over Negroes in all the relevant vehicles of aggrandizement would have to disappear. And, having proportionately equal material resources and access to the means of sustaining and enhancing life, Negroes would be just as able as whites to fulfill the values of realization. To be sure, voluntary segregation in purely personal relationships, such as friendship and marriage, might yet prevail to a considerable degree. But with whites and Negroes proportionately represented and integrated as equals at every level in the economy, in housing, in education, and in government, the two groups would have an infinitely greater possibility for intimate social interaction than they do today.

The matter of giving Negroes preferential treatment until such time as they attain the same proportional representation in all facets of society as whites poses problems of equity for other deprived minorities. Americans of Mexican and Puerto Rican ancestry, for instance, are not currently represented in proportion to their numbers in all levels of occupation and income. But let us assume that an equitable method of representation could be worked out for all caste and ethnic groups in society that are now disproportionately represented on the lower rungs of the socioeconomic ladder. And let us also assume that the white population, called upon to approve and implement this method of equalization, would voluntarily accept Negroes into preserves of aggrandizement from which they were formerly excluded (e.g., in the private sector of the economy, whites would willingly hire as many Negro executives and welcome as many Negro neighbors as would be required to make the principle of proportional representation a reality). Under such ideal circumstances, surely, the leash of caste would have been effectively removed from Negroes, and the Negro Revolution would, presumably, have come to a successful conclusion.

But while the successful Negro Revolution might eliminate caste from the American scene, it would leave intact the *class* hierarchy of invidious distinction as well as all representations of that hierarchy within our organizations of work. The Negro Revolution would not do away with the oligarchical character of those organizations or the prominence of the values of aggrandizement in American life. Nor would it lessen the pernicious influences of property, religion, and the State as media of aggrandizement.

Thus, if the Negro Revolution were successful, Negroes would find themselves occupying the same proportion of *class* positions as whites. In other words, like most whites, most Negroes would necessarily be relegated to low positions in the socio-economic hierarchy, there to languish with many of the same sources of discontent as lower-class Negroes and whites presently experience. A caste-free but class-centered society would still be poisoned by the injustice of invidious distinctions stemming from differences in socio-economic position, notwithstanding the fact that color would no longer be used to measure human worth. Thus, class would become the exclusive bulwark of social inequality, rather than class-plus-caste, as is now the case. At the same time, the destructive psychology of invidious distinction would continue to obtain reinforcement from the megalomania intrinsic to property, religion, and the State. And since our organizations of work would retain their bureaucratic and totalitarian character following the completion of the Negro Revolution, personal freedom for both Negroes and whites would still be sorely limited. Finally, the elevation of some Negroes into higher positions of class would involve their trading the obvious handicaps of poverty for the less obvious but tormenting problems aroused by the stimulation of insatiable desires for self-aggrandizement.

Still, the banishment of caste, even without any other changes in our society, would mean a definite advance in humanity for all citizens, both Negroes and whites. Among many millions of white Americans, it would herald a greater commitment to humanitarian and equalitarian values than they have ever before manifested.

For they will have had to become quite cleansed of racism and megalomania to volunteer the generosity and fellow-feeling needed to destroy caste while the rest of our social order remained unaltered. And the destruction of caste, with its accompanying attenuation of racism, would prevent a great deal of suffering that now results from the acute material privation and personal humiliation of millions of Negro citizens.

In any case, many proponents of "Freedom and Equality Now!" seem content to settle for a society whose fundamental institutions would still uphold subservience and inequality—providing the distinctions of caste alone disappear. Yet it appears that many whites do not want Negroes to have freedom and equality now (or ever) —even the limited freedom to be equally enslaved by class and the oligarchies of work; to be equally harassed and deranged by the pursuit of the values of aggrandizement.

Results of recently-taken public opinion polls testify to the rising antagonism of many whites to the Negro "movement." This mounting opposition is charged with intense feeling and prevails in both North and South, although sometimes focused about different concrete issues. "Resistance to living near Negroes seems to pack the same emotional equivalent for Northerners that school integration does for Southerners."[55]

In view of this so-called "white backlash," Negro leaders of the civil rights movement may well be thrust into a quandary of shocked chagrin. After all, they see themselves as asking only for the merest kind of decency, demanding only that Negroes be treated as individuals rather than as a group judged inherently inferior to whites. They have never expressed the slightest desire to overthrow the established economic and political foundations of our present society. And they have always advocated the use of only peaceful means of advancing their aims.

Yet many whites have begun to react as if the Negro's nonviolent request for an end to caste and racism were hurled down as an explosive threat to the very heart of our social order; as if Martin Luther King and his cohorts were inflamed radicals bent upon smashing the whole American way of life, rather than peaceful petitioners for entrance into that way of life.

But the heated and incipiently violent reactions of many whites to the civil rights movement becomes comprehensible when one considers the function that the maintenance of the Negro caste performs in flattering the egos of the white majority. Many, many whites have come to depend upon the existence of at least one group in the society whom they can dominate socially, if not economically, and in comparison with whom they can feel unquestionably superior. Yes, the awful paradox facing the Negro "revolutionaries" is that they are vehemently opposed by psychological forces spawned by the basic values and institutions of the very society they wish more fully to embrace: the values and institutions of aggrandizement. And when whites, already stimulated to megalomania by those values and institutions, are further demented by the hatred of racism, they are scarcely disposed to give up voluntarily any prerogative that helps them to maintain their feelings of superiority over Negroes. Nor does it matter to many whites *what* they are asked to share with Negroes—schools, neighborhoods, or jobs. Admittedly, the emotional impact of raw competition for the sheerest necessities of life is likely to intensify resentments between Negroes and whites. But our land is so abundant and our productive capacities are so great that the vital needs of every American could be readily satisfied if all of us felt it vitally important to satisfy them. And nobody *has* to be sacrificed or stupefied by the automation of industry, if we have the will and the wits to employ our technology in a humane fashion.[56] But certainly, quite apart from the fearful aspects of potential material privation and technological unemployment, the psychological essence of the threat many whites perceive when asked to share *anything* of social value with Negroes lies in the tendency of such sharing to equalize conditions between whites and Negroes. As a result, it is more difficult for whites to extract egoistic advantage from their social position with respect to Negroes.

Viewed in these terms, we may better understand why many

whites feel that the civil rights movement has been going "too far" or "too fast." For every palpable advance made by Negroes in lowering the barriers of caste may be seen by such whites as an implicit "lowering" of themselves—the worst possible fate in a society devoted to the limitless pursuit of self-aggrandizing motives. So, if their peaceful demonstrations and petitions, their boycotts and their ballots, begin to move Negroes up and out of their present confines, many whites may feel impelled to use forcible means of "keeping them down." And the warped tenets of racism may prompt those whites to instigate and justify (to themselves) the use of force. Conversely, if many Negroes, passionately aspiring to act upon the dictates of the American Dream, feel themselves too restrained and too despised, they may be provoked to express their own anger in violence, however much they are outnumbered.

Yes, the streets of America are staged for a bloody eruption of hostilities between Negroes and whites. Whether or not such an eruption occurs is contingent upon many imponderables. How deep, for example, does racist feeling actually run in the white population? How strongly is the white majority addicted to the psychology of megalomania? What degree of commitment do white Americans have to democratic ideals, political processes, and government? What are the outer limits of patience and self-control among the Negro population? And how constant will be the impartiality of police assigned to preside at face-to-face confrontations between Negro demonstrators and white antagonists?

Given the courage and resolve already displayed by members of the Negro Revolution, it is hardly to be doubted that they will go on protesting against caste in the future. And given the gathering of the white backlash, the Negro Revolution may yet encounter harsher opposition than it has in the past. But it is to be hoped that both whites and Negroes will soon acknowledge and permanently renounce the insanity of shedding blood in the interest of getting or retaining prerogatives which reflect an inhumane and megalomaniacal set of values and institutions; and that all Americans will sense the horrors in store for their offspring as long as aggrandizement continues to be taught and rewarded as the proper basis for assessing the meaning of existence.

Of course, the civil rights organizations should persist unflinchingly, yet peacefully, in demanding an end to the caste system. Of course, whites should take every initiative necessary to end it— without waiting to be prodded, cajoled, or shamed into doing what is right and good. But both Negroes and whites should consider the desirability of making the abolition of caste part of a larger and an even more ennobling objective: the creation of a society that has *genuine* equality—uncontaminated by the invidious distinctions of either caste *or* class; that is *genuinely* free[57] of the shackles of caste and class *as well as* those found in totalitarian oligarchies of work and in the workings of property, religion, and State.

Perhaps the *practicality* of viewing the elimination of caste as an integral part of such a program of societal change will become apparent to those in the Negro Revolution before anyone else. Thus, Negroes struggling to attain freedom from caste may eventually be unable to escape the realization that the American caste system, having emerged historically from the hardening of class positions, is going to be exceedingly difficult to abolish without the simultaneous abolition of class; and that whites lowest in the hierarchy of class have been psychologically conditioned to regard the Negro caste as occupying, in effect, a still lower position of invidious distinction. In fact, such white persons are likely to be more adamant[58] than whites of higher class in opposing the disappearance of the caste system; since they comprise a majority of the white population, whites in the classes of workers and unemployed may be able to insist, successfully, that Negroes remain "in their place" for the foreseeable future.

Objectively, however, lowly placed and economically dispossessed whites[59] have as much to gain from an end to the class system as have their Negro counterparts. And one hopeful possibility for the future of Negroes in America consists of an alliance with such whites, who would work with them to do away with the hideousness of class altogether—and not merely to obtain an improved class position. For we have seen that *all* persons of *all* classes suffer, although somewhat differently, from the socio-economic structure of our society and from the values represented by and pursued within that structure. Yes, *everyone* in our society has an equal, if yet unrecognized, stake in replacing our dominant values and institutions of aggrandizement with those of realization. For social justice and personal liberty are largely chimerical in our present society, and no Americans, Negro or white, will be truly able to enjoy those blessings until they have built another and better way of life.

5

The Conformity of Egoism

WITHIN THE SHORT SPAN of less than two hundred years, almost everything has changed in this nation except the content of the American Dream. Although the economic and social conditions available for the enactment of that Dream have become confined and crowded, the values of aggrandizement continue to receive passionate support from parents, educators, and the mass media of information and entertainment; from failures who impose their throttled fantasies upon their children; from the dramatic examples of those few who manage to rise from the bottom to the top of the hierarchy of invidious distinction. But it is now patently impossible for Americans to use the same means as their forebears in pursuing their Dream; the confinement of our present society requires their grasping to be severely modulated. The current barriers against soaring ambitions have become interpersonal rather than impersonal. Thus, masses and masses of individuals, all motivated by self-aggrandizement, confront the challenge of extracting what they want from each other.

Under such circumstances, one would expect people ultimately to lose patience with subtlety, and, when their ambitions have been frustrated beyond the limits of their tolerance, to turn upon each other like starving beasts in a common cage. That is exactly what has begun to happen, especially in regard to interracial hatreds, crime, and delinquency. For those to whom violence is too repugnant, such alternatives as drug addiction and insanity may be utilized as channels for taking out their disgruntlement upon themselves.

But the wonder of our era, thus far, has been the extent to which people have adjusted to the fundamentally untenable situation that arises from the interaction between their egoistic strivings and the social obstacles to their pursuit. From this point of view, the source of puzzlement lies not in our high rates of social pathology but in the fact that they are not enormously higher. Not that we can find any reason to be pleased with our statistics of human devastation. It is merely that, considering the explosive potentials of our situation, the American people have shown much restraint, have put up with much manipulation, guile, humiliation, and exploitation—and many trampled aspirations.

Still, such widespread public passivity in the face of the ravaging stresses of our social order does not result *only* from our national sense of humor or from an attitude of unquenchable optimism that is rooted in historical reality. Certainly, both of these factors may help to explain our resistance to even greater bouts of violence and despair than we have known. But, apart from the traits of character that permit forbearance in the face of adversity, it is possible to point to several important factors that have kept Americans "in line" during the transition from the days of Horatio Alger to those of the corporate oligarchy; factors that help to shape the individualistic ambitions of Americans to fit the societal mold into which they have been cast since the expansive days of the frontier.

How the Oligarchs Cultivate National Homage to Their Organization

The most certain means of safeguarding the permanence of an organization is to convince all persons of its indispensable role as

a surrogate of their general welfare. The oligarchies of our corporate world undertake to convey precisely that message to the citizenry of this nation. In the propaganda they disseminate, the
oligarchs attempt to legitimize their organizations by implying that
they exist solely for the implementation of the loftiest social objectives; and that it is *just because* they are so keen on helping society
to realize those objectives that their enterprises are required to do
things exactly the way they are doing them and to be organized
exactly in accordance with their present hierarchical structure.
One of our leading industrial corporations proclaims that "progress" (presumably that of the whole society) is its "business,"
while another assures us that its purpose is to provide all of us
with "better things for better living through chemistry."

Pronouncements of this kind appear regularly on radio and
television, in newspapers, magazines, and the intramural "house
organs" that the oligarchies distribute to their own employees.
Every conceivable medium is utilized for reaching not only the
publics outside the organization but also the microcosm within it.
Both customers and employees of the organization are regularly
briefed on the latest "contributions" that it is making to science,
health, education, or national defense. New products or services
offered for sale by corporations are emphasized in their propaganda, as are the processes, personnel, and facilities that gave rise
to them. In this regard, the propagandist has considerable opportunity to assert that the heralded marvels could only have come
about through the pooled efforts of a gigantic, smoothly functioning team, backed up by the enormous reservoir of capital and experience that the Big Organization alone has at its disposal.

There is a good deal of truth in the assertion that the mass
production of the manufactured articles that we have come to
regard as essential to our comfort or well-being requires the interlocking cooperation of myriads of people. And the same could be
said of the provision of such vital services as transportation and
telephone communication. But because organization is undeniably
involved in such matters, it does not follow, necessarily, that the
type of organization sponsoring the advertisement is the *only* one

capable of bringing forth the product or service in question. Far from it. Yet that is the very conclusion that the corporate "message in the interest of the public" would have the public draw.[1]

If an oligarchy can persuade the nation that it represents the best of all possible organizations, everyone will be inclined to endorse its proprietorship; and many people may, indeed, extend their heartfelt gratitude to it. Disarmed in this manner, neither its customers nor its employees are likely to think of or propose any fundamental changes in the way in which the corporation is organized, much less to question the right of the oligarchy to control it. An employee who is convinced of the necessity and virtue of the organizational status quo will strive to play out the imperatives of his personal amibition within the ground rules laid down by his occupational superiors. And, when his ambitions are frustrated— an inevitability for most employees—he will be less disposed to put the blame for his failure upon anyone in his organization than to take it upon himself.

The last point applies most often, perhaps, to managerial employees. For the workers, the chances of upward mobility into higher and higher positions of management are so slim that the effect of organizational propaganda upon them must be primarily one of cementing passive resignation to their lowly and stationary status within the organization. Surely, most individuals in the rank and file of labor must soon realize,[2] if they do not realize beforehand, that there is little realistic hope of going from their bench on the assembly line to a place behind an executive's desk; and the same could be said for a typist or any other ordinary clerical worker. These workers require much more powerful constraints to "go along" with the organization than the blandishments of propaganda. Nor are the managers so dim-witted that their compliance with the oligarch's wishes is effected merely by verbal manipulation. On the contrary, their docility and loyalty are also largely a function of the direct incentives and coercions that bear upon the extent to which they can personally pursue their needs for aggrandizement.

Still, it can scarcely be doubted that oligarchies rely heavily upon propaganda as a means of evoking universal approval of the reality of their control over their organizations. And, they must regard as especially notable any propagandistic headway that they make among their employees, without whose immediate compliance their power could not be put into effect.

How the Oligarchs Incarcerate Themselves

It may seem strange to think of oligarchs as being prey to forces that confine them within the narrow limits of their class and that vitiate their possibilities for happiness. For oligarchs are the ultimate proprietors of their organizations; it is they who contrive the choreography which their network of hirelings dance. Yet no class of men in our society is free from the destructive effects of our values of aggrandizement and the system of invidious distinction that mirrors them. In fact, there exists no more damning indictment of those values and that system than the harm they have brought, without exception, to all of our social groupings.

The manifestations of our societal desolation differ markedly from class to class and from caste to caste; and some strata of our society are smitten by torments that are unknown to others. But to assume that a particular social group has avoided the plague that infects all of us is to deny reality and to blink at sufferings whose quality may be dissimilar to our own. We have all been lacerated by the same scourge; and to imagine that others have escaped its dehumanizing sting is to live in as fanciful a world as do those who fail to perceive the existence of our distinctions of class and caste.

Oddly, even those repelled by capitalism have sometimes treated the oligarch as if he were miraculously immune[3] to the degradation that has the rest of society in its thrall; as if the most effective exploiter of the labor of others were, somehow, protected from the consequences of his exploitation. By naïvely simplifying the psychological condition of the oligarch, the opponent of capitalism unwittingly sets him up as an ideal toward whose blissful state all workers and managers might do well to aspire. For if, by becoming oligarchs, they would enter the Elysian fields, every worker and manager in society might conclude that the existence of such earthly paradise excuses all the evils of their society; that it is not the very fabric of their social order that is rotten, but only their present circumstances that separate them from the unparalleled joy awaiting those who scramble and fight their way to the high plateau. Thus, in implicitly glorifying the life of the oligarch, some social critics have not only depicted him as the most enviable person in his society but have also lent moral support, however backhanded, to the very system against which they railed. In this way, too, those critics have concocted a psychological balm for the oligarch who, in the midst of the hideousness of his actual condition, could feel that his presumed detractors—of all people —found reason to be covetous of him.

It is no doubt true, as Mills has asserted,[4] that the rich have, by virtue of their wealth, greater freedom of choice than the poor. And quite apart from the amenities, experiences, and education that money can buy, the most affluent class of our society is destined to live longer than the least affluent class. Certainly, here is the most monstrous of all inequities that result from our class system. But having denounced these injustices in the name of humanity, one should not overlook the problems of the oligarch, including the limitations upon the freedom with which he can exercise the potentials for choice that are granted to him by his access to wealth alone. In scrutinizing the dilemmas of the idle rich, on the other hand, the psychological constraints that stem, paradoxically, from a surfeit of choice will become apparent.

But if we admit that the oligarch is human, we must take as much care not to exaggerate his foibles as to extol his blessings. In the past, leading adversaries of this especially privileged class of society have written as if oligarchs were not men at all, but the personifications of consummate wickedness;[5] and if proponents of change vehemently disputed the oligarch's qualifications for an angelic place in heaven, they were tempted to attribute to him the superhuman malevolence of a Lucifer.

Yet, if we are ever to visualize—let alone create—a society that is more humane than the one we have, it is necessary to see how the swinishness of our social order adversely affects *all* who dwell within it. It must be said, in truth, that the situation of the oligarch is pitiable in several important respects; and that he merits the attentive commiseration of all who would call themselves humanitarians.

First of all, the oligarch has his hands on the wheel—property —that steers the entire society on its careening course to misery. He possesses, in an abundance greater than all others in society, those things which all have learned to desire as the criteria of superhumanity. Accordingly, he may perceive himself—and, certainly, be perceived by others—as the grandest of all men, the man who has come the closest to shedding his humanity altogether. But therein also lies a source of his pathos. For to the extent that he has attained aggrandizement, to that same extent he is concerned about losing it; and to the extent that his proprietorship has propelled him toward godliness, to that same extent must he guard himself from a fall from financial grace. Oligarchs are, therefore, obliged to be exceedingly vigilant toward their competing socio-economic peers and to exercise the greatest possible caution about whom they admit to membership in their own class.

The psychology of invidious distinction leads members of every class to safeguard whatever advantage in aggrandizement they perceive themselves to have over those in lower classes. But the oligarch's case is extreme, since his active proprietorship of the country's corporate wealth gives him an opportunity to aggrandize himself at the expense of every other class in society, including the idle rich. Consequently, oligarchs are faced with the problem of preserving the unique advantages of their class against challenge from all other classes in society. At the same time, however, they have to cope with the problem of protecting themselves against the competitive forays of other oligarchs.

An alliance of predators is bound to stir uneasiness among all who belong to it. But when such an alliance is composed of "super-predators," the tension of its members is likely to be very great indeed; and the respect of each oligarch for his collaborators may be inspired, in part, by an awareness of their common penchant for exploitation. In any event, the oligarchs run the most exclusive of all clubs[6] in our society. And while they may be understandably loath to publicize the predatory basis of their common interest, they can ill afford to admit to their club any incipient oligarch who is not wholeheartedly committed to upholding the privilege of their class to prey upon the rest of society.

Because such a privilege might be resented—if not repudiated—even in a society that is dedicated to aggrandizement and organized in terms of invidious distinction, the oligarchs are constrained to behave as if they were morally entitled to their hegemony and its material bounty. The very elegance of their possessions—their homes, automobiles, furnishings, and clothes—evokes a mystique of awe, as if such impressive personages ipso facto merited public indulgence; as if individuals so grandly bedecked could scarcely be motivated by any but the noblest of human concerns. Hence, quite apart from seeking the vicarious pleasures of conspicuous consumption, the oligarch may often feel compelled to adorn himself to reinforce an aura of his presumptive superiority as a person. Similarly, although they may despise such activities, oligarchs often strive to create the public image of an exceptional sense of social responsibility by devoting part of their time to highly visible philanthropic or educational activities.

Actually, in the deportment of their personal lives, oligarchs are greatly fettered by the very propaganda that their corporations would have the public believe. For they might imperil the machinations of their corporations by failing themselves to be publicly involved and identified with manifestly non-commercial causes. Not that their personal involvement on behalf of the "public weal" is without its mercenary dividends. On the contrary, the association of the trustee of a major corporation with an organization to aid crippled children cannot help but make a favorable impression on most people. And the effusion of warmth stirred by such an association is very likely to arise again in the heart of the housewife as she spies a carton of his corporation's product sitting on the shelf of the supermarket. Moreover, as an influential member of a community organization, the oligarch-cum-philanthropist is in a strategic position to funnel his ideology into the community and to determine the outcome of communal decisions that come within the sphere of that organization's jurisdiction.[7] Thus, he can directly help the interests of his class, not to speak of his personal fortunes, by seeing to it that the communal organization of which he is a trustee makes no decision that is inimical to the privileges of oligarchy.

The worrisome problem of assuring the superiority of his position in society does not permit the oligarch to extend his participation in public affairs only to activity in the philanthropic organizations of his community. On the contrary, it is at the governmental level that his prerogatives are most vulnerable—ultimately, if not immediately—to threat. For our governmental organizations are the only ones explicitly created to further the welfare of the whole society; and it is through their elected representatives that the people of our society have the fullest opportunity to express their will. But since most people in our society are not oligarchs, they may often find reason to be displeased with their lot and to raise their voices against any special privilege whose exercise obviously functions to their detriment. Under such circumstance, it would be foolish for the oligarch to remain aloof from politics, lest he find that his detachment permits the passage of legislation and the election of officials that prove antagonistic to his privileges. Hence, the corporate oligarchs feel it prudent to do whatever they can to insure that the government will never become unduly hostile to their proprietorship of the economy. But who is the government? The elected representatives of the people. Accordingly, it is the policy of oligarchy to bring its considerable resources to bear upon such matters as political nominations and elections, and the legislative decisions the elected officials eventually make.[8]

As has been often remarked in the past, the parliamentarian form of government permits a wide hiatus of time and space between the multitude of electors and the relative handful of persons that they elect to represent them.[9] Given our system of political parties, individuals who contribute heavily to the nominating and election campaigns of legislators tend to engage their political indebtedness more than individuals who make no such contributions. Thus, legislators are susceptible to the influence that special groups in the society can muster; and while oligarchs are by no means the only such politically active group in our society, the amount of money that they contribute to political campaigns far exceeds the amount expended for this purpose by the same number of representatives of other classes.

These modes of securing political influence, however reliable and effective, are still indirect. It would be much more effective, for any class zealous to promote its special privileges, to have members of its own socio-economic grouping *directly* represent its interests in the councils of state. And that is precisely what has begun to happen in this country—and quite systematically, it would seem. In regard to the Presidency, for example, it appears that none but members of the oligarchical class emerge as candidates of *either* of our two major parties. Not that we have previously risen up in wrath to prevent oligarchs from occupying the White House. George Washington, a double oligarch, both military and economic, set the precedent for a number of his class who were to follow in his place. But we now hear the proverbial man-in-the-street aver quite benignly that "it takes a lot of money" to run for President and that "only a millionaire" can reasonably be expected to contemplate the prospect. Evidently, one of the favorite of American myths—that any lad at all may one day become President—is being laid to rest without a whimper of protest.

But, even if the Johnsons, Rockefellers, Romneys, Scrantons, or Goldwaters do not take a temporary leave of absence from their corporate headquarters to promote oligarchy in governmental ones, the prerogatives of oligarchy will not be at a loss for legislative defenders. For as Mills took pains to spell out,[10] our legislators are not at all representative of all the classes in our society. In fact, they come predominantly from these favored classes: the managers, the self-employed professionals and entrepreneurs, and the oligarchs themselves. True, the oligarchs do not comprise the actual majority of our legislators. But the representatives of the managerial and self-employed classes are very apt to look up to the oligarchs as a class of people they would infinitely prefer to join than to fight. Hence, even without systematic prompting, legislators of the managerial and self-employed classes can generally be counted upon to protect the interests of the oligarchs. In fact, for legislators from the managerial class, this governmental superintendence of the oligarch's proprietorship is often a political counterpart of the job that he does for that elite group in the economy at large.

Let us reckon the human cost of these preoccupations to the oligarch. Here is the time of his life, a life no less, if no more, precious than that of anyone else in society, dribbling away in activity that produces for him, in the end, only an inflated image of himself; while this same activity is depriving untold others of elementary justice and causing them abject material privation. Even if the oligarch is never smitten by a bad conscience for the harm his very socio-economic existence necessarily inflicts upon others, he may well wonder whether or not there is anything else to life but the meanness of his rooting and snorting; but the aridity of his arrangements, deals, and conferences; but the monotony of penning herd after herd of underlings, erstwhile rivals, and potential enemies safely into his corral. What room is there in such a life for the sublimity of creation? For the tapping down into the deepest core of one's being to release the warmth and beauty that lies within?

And where is the freedom that the oligarch, at first glance, seems to possess in such enviable abundance? Can a person so concerned about his worldly possessions be so free? In this respect, can he be so much freer than the unemployed worker who has nothing left to lose? For while the unemployed worker is enslaved by the rusty chain of poverty, the enslavement of the oligarch results from the silken cords of intrigue that bind him to his proprietorship. Unquestionably, in terms of anything that money can buy, the oligarch is infinitely better off than his unemployed compatriot. But, it is the irony of his condition—the very bane of his existence—that the active guardianship and enhancement of his socio-economic prerogatives enchains rather than liberates him; that the more he concerns himself with the maintenance and furtherance of his special privileges, the less they function as forms of social license and the more they serve as social stocks, clamping him hand and foot to the very edifice of property that has been so widely assumed to be the basis of his freedom.

Through his manipulation and control of others, the subtle quality of the oligarch's debasement of his own human capacities reaches its greatest poignancy. The range of his manipulation of others is very broad, covering many persons within his own organization as well as those in communal and governmental organizations. But interpersonal manipulation is essentially, if not obviously, a reciprocal process. That is, he who manipulates others is, at the same time, manipulating himself. For the intent of his manipulation ties him as much to the persons whom he seeks to influence as the success of his efforts ties them to him. Moreover, successful manipulation is a difficult and uncertain process, which requires continual attention and reinforcement on the part of the manipulator, putting him under a greater strain, perhaps, than any single one of the many persons whose behavior he is attempting to shape.

The strain of manipulation does not arise simply from the output of energy it requires. More tellingly, it reflects the duplicity[11] that is inherent in the manipulation. And it is in regard to this duplicity that the oligarch most thoroughly debases his humanity. As long as he feels obliged to lie, cajole, dissimulate—to play one rival off against another, to make public utterances that contradict his covert motives, to pretend to be democratic in his political ideology while he runs his own organization along completely totalitarian lines, to seem to contribute to the welfare of society, the better to extract profit from it—the oligarch corrupts himself as surely as he does anyone else. And to the extent that this process of corruption warps his sensibilities—his spontaneity, his capacity for genuine feeling for others, his respect for tenderness and justice—the oligarch dissipates his one and only chance, his life, to realize himself as a human being.

Of all the manipulations carried out by the oligarchs, none are more immediately vital to their socio-economic interests than those concerned with the procurement of suitable recruits to their ranks. Accordingly, it is hardly surprising that the most likely recruits are those who have already clearly and consistently demonstrated a penchant for the debasement of their own humanity. Naturally, a goodly number of new entrants into their realm are bound to come from the families of the oligarchs themselves. This sort of nepotism is one of the prerogatives of oligarchy. Even so, the relative admitted to active control of the corporation must show that he is willing and able to manipulate others in the necessary manner. If he is too "soft" or insufficiently "hard-headed," his presence might pose too great a threat to the other oligarchs; and he might be considered inadequate, by his own relatives, to look after the fortunes of the family in competition with rivals. Typically, therefore, the relative of a reigning oligarch is "schooled" and "seasoned" in the realities of management and the problems of control before being admitted into the oligarchy itself; this preparation generally gives the young man a chance to practice the skills of manipulation at various levels of management.

But oligarchies cannot be perpetuated or extended merely through such a limited mode of recruitment. Intelligence and specialized knowledge are also required to rule the huge corporate enterprises—qualities that are not always sufficiently possessed by relatives. Intelligence and special knowledge are likely to abound in the upper echelons of management. But the matter of which manager is recruited—or, as the sociologist would say, co-opted—for membership in the oligarchy is decided, apparently, on the grounds of personality. Among the managers who possess the necessary intellectual attributes—at least the ones considered essential to oligarchical status—some also manifest traits of personality that inspire the particular regard and confidence of the oligarchs. What are those traits? None other, it appears, than the very ones possessed by the oligarchs themselves. Indeed, Presthus goes so far as to posit that, among managers, there is one type of person that is more likely to be co-opted by the oligarchy than all the rest. He calls this type the *upward-mobiles*;[12] and he portrays them as being uncannily attuned to the desires and whims of their superiors. In a word, the upward-mobiles are the most avidly manipulable of all men in management. Far from waiting to be persuaded to take a stance appealing to their superiors, the upward-mobiles virtually anticipate what their superiors wish of them and waste no time in getting it done. They are highly adaptable to changes in wishes emanating from above, and watch all the straws in the managerial wind whose drift has any bearing whatsoever on their chances for co-option to oligarchy. This adaptability and militant compliance evidently makes a most favorable impression, for the manager, in those ways, offers his behavioral pledge of allegiance to the policies of the oligarch, showing how fervidly he is willing to employ himself as an instrument of the organization's proprietors. And since he is eager to be so manipulated in the interest of the oligarch, why should he not be equally willing to manipulate those below him for the same purpose? We do not know with any certainty whether or not oligarchs base their selection of recruits to their class on exactly this reasoning. But it does appear, according to Presthus, that they have a great affinity for those managers who resemble them so closely as to guarantee the continuation of their policies and orientations. And Mills, too, has remarked upon the tendency of the corporate elite to search out living mimes of themselves.[13]

Since it is known, among the highest level of managers, that admission into the oligarchy is determined, in the last analysis, by the faithfulness with which they reproduce in their own behavior the prototype above them, the potential oligarch is obliged to suppress his personal idiosyncrasies to the utmost. Otherwise, the least expression of his own individuality might arouse doubt about his fitness to rise. Consequently, the manager who aspires to oligarchy is, if anything, caught in a more powerful psychological vise than the oligarchs. And, by the time he does join them, he may have so crippled his individuality as to be more a caricature than a person; he will most probably have become so enchained to the psychological confinement of oligarchy as to remain its captive for the rest of his days.

How Managers Are Molded and Mold Themselves to Their Class

Most managers never get within nodding distance of their oligarchical masters. Yet managers, no less than workers, require more than purely hypothetical incentives to keep them in their socio-economic harness. Essentially, these inducements consist of the promise of those things that are the criteria of attainment for the values of aggrandizement: promotion to higher rungs in the managerial ladder, more pay and material fringe benefits, a larger office, a private secretary, and a decanter on one's desk. Although both these symbols of advancement and their appeal to aspiring managers are well known,[14] it is instructive to examine the rites of initiation that usher persons into the managerial class and determine which of the initiates shall be admitted to higher and higher managerial positions; or, conversely, which of them shall be pegged at a specific level, unable to move upward in the administrative line.

The most obvious of these rites are the management training programs for neophyte executives. Typically, candidates for such programs are selected from graduating classes of colleges and *not* from the ranks of labor within the organization itself—a practice that does a great deal, of course, to keep workers "in their place."

Typically, too, each organization has its own system of market-ing, accounting, or production. These systems are often so special-ized that those who are trained in them cannot readily transfer to a different or competing organization whose equivalent system requires its own training program. Having fully absorbed his com-pany's way of doing things, a beginning manager may feel quite bound to that company. If he were to leave it for another, he might have to start anew as a trainee, losing the advance he has gained.

The training program, however arduous or demanding it might be, is usually oriented toward the learning of particular skills and methods. That is, its criteria of successful performance are often objective and clearly discernible, calling for a demonstration of competencies as well as attitudes. Having passed this hurdle, how-ever, the junior executive is faced with a much more ambiguous challenge. He must now play his role in administration without an entirely explicit set of guidelines to indicate which of his behaviors is most likely to ingratiate him to his superiors and, hence, lead to further advances upward in the hierarchy. He will be expected to practice the skills for which he has been trained by the organiza-tion; and many of his actions will be more or less predetermined by definite conceptions that the company has about how people in his position are supposed to do their job. However, apart from the exercise of his specific skills, the junior executive, like the senior executive who is a would-be oligarch, often finds that personality is crucial in determining who is earmarked for further advance-ment in the organization.

"Personality" refers to those traits that permit the individual successfully to manipulate others[15]—as well as himself—in order to advance his ambitions. Some of these are traits of ingratiation, which induce others to like and respond positively to the individ-ual; others are traits of guile, forcefulness, ruthlessness, and cun-ning, those that permit the individual to hurt others and to tolerate their hostility. The most successful executives need to be amply equipped with both kinds of traits and with a flexibility in their use—so that they will be able, *at the opportune moment,* to scuttle or betray someone whose favor they formerly curried. For while ingratiation may be a stepping-stone, it may also be a hindrance when the point is reached at which it serves the individual's ambitions to belittle the very persons whom he had formerly flattered, and, hence, by comparison, elevate his own prowess.

These "traits of personality" are not necessarily intrinsic to the individual, although they may well be for many persons. It is likely that these traits are developed, adopted, and cast off like so many costumes in order to fit the part required at any particular time by the actors in this drama of aggrandizement. It is of extreme functional importance for all of the aspiring executives to have a keen sense and awareness of what trait is called for in every interpersonal situation that has a bearing upon their advancement. But it is obvious that, within the organization of work, there is no situation that does not have such bearing. Even outside their organization *per se*—within the relationships they maintain in their neighborhoods, country clubs, and other social settings—executives often encounter situations that may have an indirect effect upon their organizational fortunes. Knowing "the right people" in the community and charming them may add to one's desirability as a representative of the firm. For the firm may be interested in creating a good public image. In addition, acceptance by influential persons in the community may open up new channels of mobility, allowing the individual to change organizations, if it appears that such a change would be advantageous to him.

Managerial employees are led to become polished actors, taking their cues from potential instruments of their advancement—a cast of characters that includes virtually everyone with whom they have occasion to interact—and playing their parts in such a way as to produce the maximal benefit for themselves. The eerie sense of artificiality that one often experiences in the company of a group of such people stems precisely from the fact that all of them are putting on a charade aimed at manipulating the rest. Each person in the group regards everyone else as someone of whom he should be wary and with whom he should attempt to ingratiate himself. The result, of course, is an unremitting atmosphere of vacuous tension—vacuous because nobody is expressing a spontaneous or genuine feeling or thought; and tense because nobody is quite certain of the impact of his dissimulation, especially since all are vaguely conscious—although it may be painful to be too conscious of it—of the fact that everyone else is being as cagey and falsely ingratiating as themselves.

Under such circumstances, the cultivation of interpersonal "skills" and techniques of dissimulation becomes a very serious endeavor. With everybody playing the same game, it behooves one to become as refined, resilient, and subtle an actor as possible; to build up an infinite repertoire of roles. Costuming and props are also brought very much into the act, since their contribution is no less vital in the managerial drama of self-aggrandizement than it is in the professional theatre.

As in the theatre, too, the leading character requires a supporting cast. The manager's wife must do her bit parts on behalf of aggrandizement—values which she has adopted as ardently as her husband—in scenes enacted at home, where she enters the stage as the gracious, charming, witty hostess, just exactly the right sort of helpmeet a rising executive needs to have on hand to keep the conversation and compliments flowing when he entertains his associates from the organization.

Nor are children exempt from the rigorous requirements of the unending drama. On the contrary, they are also quickly inculcated with the manners and attitudes likely to find favor among the adults who "count." They are sent to the "right" schools, the "right" camps, the "right" dancing instructors. They are given all these "advantages" not in the interest of realization—although that may not be entirely absent as a motive, even among parents clearly given over to aggrandizement—but in order to prepare them to play their parts in the drama of aggrandizement as capably as they can. By the time they reach college, many of these children have already been solidly "shaped up" for the roles their parents have trained them to perform. And they float blandly and unfeelingly through the academic side of college life as if it were merely a minor aspect of a foreordained sequence of attainments expected of children in their social class, a dallying point along the road to adult forms of aggrandizement. But, even the ones, among such students, who take their studies seriously are more inclined to see what they can "get out" of their courses rather than what they can fully realize and express of themselves. By "getting something out of a course" these students mean information that can be used subsequently to advance their occupational career or that can help them to maintain their presumably enviable class position. They are interested in what their instructor has to say about his subject; but they are not interested in the subject for its own sake. Yes, they can understand the passions that might move a faculty member to take ideas seriously, so seriously that he and other scholars might actually prefer a life of intellectual or artistic creativity to any other. But all of this understanding and appreciation is academic, so to speak. The important thing for these students is to learn all they have to learn about the implications of their various courses for the maintenance of their status in society, as well as for its enhancement. For such students, the college years are not periods of heightened self-realization, during which they seek to plumb and express the reservoirs of thought and feeling that lie within them. Liberation of their capacities for creativity or for contributing to the establishment of a more decent social order is not the objective of higher education for these students. Instead, having already become addicted to the values of aggrandizement, these students come to college to acquire even more polished methods of pursuing their enslaving ambitions than the ones they have previously developed in elementary and secondary schools.

Since managerial employees, as well as their wives and children, feel it necessary to cultivate the tactics of ingratiation in order to appease their aggrandizing motives, it is inevitable that their outward behavior should seem to slavishly conformist. The ingratiate oneself effectively, one has to assess the wishes and expectations of the other person and to act in accordance with them. But this is not conformity for its own sake. *This kind of conformity is a means to the end of furthering highly individualistic and extremely self-centered ambitions*; it is the common social mode by which a mass of unmitigated egoists have been forced, because of the historical changes in the conditions of their work, to pursue their values of aggrandizement.

Many of these "conformists" are "compulsive" in their conformity; that is, they do it automatically, unwittingly, and are not "acting" in a conscious and calculated fashion. Their numbers may increase as we increasingly rear[16] children with a stress on "interpersonal skills" rather than any other kinds of skills. However, "compulsive" as this conformity may be for such individuals, it seems highly unlikely that they are totally unaware of the impact of their behavior upon others and, especially, of the relationship between compliance with the wishes of others and the evocation of their approval and gratitude. Most of these "other-directed"[17] personalities are attuned to others largely as a strategy of conscious *manipulation* and not because of a helpless and unconscious drive to submit abjectly to their will.

In time, perhaps, the requirements of advancement through the managerial hierarchy may so broadly affect patterns of child-rearing in this country that we shall stamp in character traits that, from earliest childhood, lead a child to crave to "fit in" with the norms of whatever group he happens to belong to at that time. Such automatic conformity would be the surest "built-in" guarantee of doing what the leaders of the organization wanted members of one's working group to do; and hence of evoking their approval and gaining promotion. More likely still, the freezing of mobility—even *within* managerial ranks—may soon approach the same point that it has already reached within the class of workers. In that event, there may be a widespread movement to rear children with what might be called the conformity of apathy. For the acquiescence that workers already give to their organizations of work often has that apathetic quality. Nevertheless, whereas the conformity of workers may frequently reflect the numbness of stupefaction, the conformity of management, thus far, appears to be that generated by ambition.

This enslavement of the managers, like that of the oligarchs, is largely a voluntary and an avid one. It is only through conformity to the ground rules of their organizations that persons in the managerial class can hope to further their individual desires for self-aggrandizement. Their allegiance to the oligarchies above them is also buttressed by institutional forms of social control that have been established by those oligarchies. Among such controls are the standardization of salaries and fringe benefits for comparable positions in different organizations, a device that reduces the potential power of an executive to play one employer off against another in individualistic bargaining for his own advancement in salary. Another, and even more effective, coercion consists of the sort of pension plan that is contingent upon continuing employment in a given company. Under such a plan, a manager entirely forfeits his pension if he leaves his employer for another one before serving a specified number of years. Needless to say, the thought of jeopardizing one's future years of financial security is likely to quell many an incipient impulse to bolt to another organization or, indeed, to take up any other kind of employment.

The Tethers That Keep Workers in Their Stalls

The common cultural heritage of American society leads all of its members—of all classes and castes—to cherish the values of aggrandizement. As a result, individual members of the working class develop motives that are just as oriented toward self-aggrandizement as those of the managerial class. In fact, the development of such motives among workers is virtually inescapable. For they find themselves on the bottom of a hierarchy of invidious distinction, from which lowly vantage point they are urged on all sides—by educators, the mass media of communication, and the very humiliation of their daily lives—to covet that which is possessed in such tantalizing profusion by those at the top of the hierarchy.

What are they to do with these gnawing motives? How are they to grasp more and more of what their society holds it most desirable for all to pursue? The general answer to these questions is that workers have a very difficult time in attaining the criteria of aggrandizement that our dominant values require. Many workers have succumbed in a variety of ways[18] to the frustrations attendant upon the gap that separates their aspirations from their attainments. And, it has taken the concerted efforts of the leaders of their own unions to devise the arrangements under which workers have been disarmed into an acceptance of both the oligarchical control of the organizations in which they labor and the chronic disadvantage of their position within those organizations.

In fact, the "conflict" between organized capital and organized labor has settled down into a rather cozy "understanding" that is based on an acceptance of the socio-economic status quo by both sides. Essentially, this meeting of minds assumes that it is the business of unions to look out for the vested economic interests of labor, while it is the job of the corporate business to look out for their own economic interests. Further, it recognizes the legitimacy of oligarchical control and the hierarchy of invidious distinction within the organizations of work. This means, specifically, that labor unions in this country do not question the right of the corporate oligarchy to pursue greater and greater profits from the efforts of its employees, nor to determine the basic purposes and policies of the organization without the participation of its employees, nor to maintain every other kind of distinction of status that emphasizes the superiority of the oligarchy over the other socio-economic groupings under its control.

In return for this acceptance of their prerogatives, the corporate

oligarchies have acknowledged the legitimacy of unions as representatives of the workers, as well as the inherent obligation of the
unions to demand higher and higher wages and more and more
fringe benefits for their membership. Naturally, the corporate
oligarchies strive to retain as much profit for themselves and to
drive as hard a bargain as they can. However, they do not question the right of the oligarchs of labor to bargain similarly for a
greater share of the profits to be dispensed in terms of wages and
fringe benefits to the workers they represent.

In practice, the corporations have often lost nothing in giving
the unionized workers a little more each year or so, since they
have merely passed on the cost of such raises to the consumer in
the form of higher prices. It is also becoming increasingly feasible
to absorb such raises in the cost of labor through the simultaneous
introduction of automation and the reduction of the number of
workers employed. Labor-industry relations have, in fact, evolved
into a quite predictable game, whose ground rules are well known
and accepted by the principals concerned. As a consequence, the individual worker has been enslaved not *only* by his own values of
aggrandizement but also by the restricted boundaries within which
his own unions have agreed that they shall be pursued.

Therefore, American workers are kept in their socio-economic
"place" by their desire to pursue the values of aggrandizement in
any way they can. But since the chief ways set down for them is
the one defined by the relationship between the oligarchies of
industry and the oligarchies of labor, unionized workers are
largely dependent upon the outcome of negotiations conducted
under that relationship for indications of their own aggrandizement. These indications consist of steadily increasing wages,
shorter hours, pension plans, and other fringe benefits. True, the
worker's increases in salary may seem like pathetically feeble
criteria of "advancement," but they are all he has and they are
concrete. True, he may drive a Ford rather than a Cadillac, but he
can trade in his old car periodically, and, with an assist from a
credit company, obtain a newer, flashier model with which to

titillate his ego. True, his home or apartment is modest and in-
commodious, but he can embellish it with knickknacks that flatter
himself. True, his entertainment may consist largely of a bottle of
beer and a TV program; but he can afford to drink enough to
experience a mellow glow and to identify himself temporarily with
the heroes that parade across the screen.

Yes, the unionized American worker has been given and is
being given enough of the national wealth to induce him to go
along with the socio-economic status quo and to feel that he is
making some progress on the plush road to aggrandizement. With
the ever-increasing threat of technological unemployment hanging
precariously over his head, he may well be inclined to see in the
security of a permanent job even more allure than he has seen in
the past, and to swallow some of his resentment in gratitude for
the safety of his position.

The "contentment" of workers with their place in society is
probably only sufficient to undermine their will to do anything
about altering the conditions that produce the distress that they, in
fact, feel. As a number of sensitive observers[19] have agreed, it is
not easy for grown men, even ones of only average talent and
intelligence, to abide the boredom and humiliation of the monotonous jobs that millions of American workers are obliged to perform. And it is harder still to tolerate such monotony when one is
assigned to it as a mere robot, carrying out a mechanical and
repetitive function in a plan formulated entirely by others. Yet,
this is precisely the situation that the American worker faces and
bears, salved only by the few more dollars and few more trinkets
that he can annually acquire to enhance his image of himself.

As he punches his clock and performs the stereotyped, machine-
tooled motion of his specialized task, the worker is grinding himself into a mush of addled sensibility. Even a grazing sheep, roam-
ing freely over a hillside, encounters more novelty and beauty than
the worker does on the assembly line. And while the shepherd's
dog may occasionally bark at his straying hoofs, the sheep is at
least permitted considerable leeway in his meandering. But the

clerical or blue collar worker is typically lashed to the demands and limitations of his machine. It is the machine that dictates his movements. It is the machine that makes him its robot.

So, the worker contributes further to his own bondage by dulling his senses and feelings in performing tasks that are inherently debilitating and inherently opposed to the fulfillment of the distinctive capacities of our species. Those who "merely" become emotionally blunted may be counted as "fortunate" in comparison with those driven to insanity and agitated despair. Yet it is singularly difficult to regard a bland automaton—seriously deprived of empathy even for his own woeful plight, much less that of others —as a paragon of either happiness or mental health.

In classifying the types of accommodation made by employees to bureaucratic organizations in which they work, Presthus lists the *indifferents*[20] as the most numerous of the three types—far outnumbering the *upward-mobiles* and the *ambivalents*,[21] who are caught in a conflict between the values of aggrandizement and those of realization. Presumably, the indifferents are emotionally alienated from their organizations, having either abandoned or never seriously entertained hope of rising in the hierarchy. Presthus also assumes, as would appear to follow most logically from the realities of their position, that workers are much more susceptible to the indifferent mode of accommodation than are managers and oligarchs. But what Presthus has failed to note is that, if borne long enough, that indifference and alienation may be applied to oneself as well as to one's organization; and that a worker may come to disregard his own needs as a human being, just as he may learn to discount the possibility of either aggrandizing or realizing himself through his work.

Actually, the majority of workers—inasmuch as they continue to voice demands for a greater material return for their work and for better working conditions—can scarcely be considered indifferent in the sense just described. For they have not yet resigned themselves completely to whatever uses the corporate oligarchs may wish to make of them. Nor have they rejected, at long last, the values of aggrandizement for which they receive such a pittance of attainment. Instead, most workers still seem to be clinging to the formula that the oligarchs of industry and labor have contrived for their pursuit of those values: a few more pennies an hour, a little more money in the pension fund. And it is for rewards such as these that they continue to turn themselves into living machines.

Enticed at every turn to aggrandize themselves through consumption, if not through earnings, American workers have shown no hesitation to draw upon credit to buy what they cannot properly afford. The result is a fantastic rate of national indebtedness.[22] And, with the steady stream of unpaid bills[23] flowing into their mail boxes, workers are caught up in a current that presses them still more tightly into the maw of the system. A vicious whirlpool is set up: the worker, his ambitions frustrated by the receipt of insufficient criteria of aggrandizement from his organization of work, seeks to aggrandize himself outside that organization—through the purchase of commodities that are perceived as possessing ego-enhancing qualities. He is exhorted by every means of advertising to make such purchases—and explicitly told, moreover, that the commodities he acquires do, in fact, contain the very properties of self-aggrandizement for which he longs. At the same time, credit is quickly and easily made available to him. Thus, everything conspires to impel him to purchase many more things than he would buy on the strength of essential need alone. Naturally, this "psychic" spending soon plunges the worker into a state of habitual debt, and he is squeezed even more tightly into his emotionally deadening routine.

The Pressures That Bind
Those Outside Organizations of Work
to Their Places in Society

The great majority of Americans are bound to their socioeconomic strata primarily by pressures that concern their position in bureaucratic organizations of work. However, the minority of Americans who continue to function economically outside such organizations are by no means free of constraints that hold them fast to their particular place in society. And, if those constraints are, in some cases, less obvious than the organizational ones, they are no less oppressive in their effects, no less injurious to the humanity of those who suffer from them.

The Demoralizing Freedom of the Idle Rich

Since money is what everyone in our society is taught to desire above all else, one might conclude that the possession of great wealth would be the handmaiden of ecstasy. Indeed, if we were to judge by the magical powers that Marx, of all people, attributed to money, we could scarcely imagine a person of wealth to be anything but a living Aladdin, delighting in the materialization of his slightest wish, transcending personal shortcomings that might chronically oppress those of lesser means. "I *am* ugly, but I can buy the *most beautiful* woman. So, I am not ugly, for the effect of *ugliness*, its repulsive power, is eliminated by money. . . . I am an evil, dishonest, unscrupulous, dull-witted man, but money is held in honor—hence so is its possessor."[24]

In a society that upholds money as its most revered vehicle of aggrandizement, money can no doubt effect many of the transformations to which Marx alludes. And one can readily appreciate the facilitation that money gives to the pursuit of megalomania. But, are all the psychological implications of wealth really that simple? Are they all so unequivocally productive of joy?

Admittedly, the rich can buy the most valuable commodity of all—life itself. And, without a doubt, money can release one from many limitations, both small and large, that poverty imposes. However, the *sheer possession* of wealth can be its own source of distressful bondage, impelling its possessor, as in the case of the corporate oligarch, to manipulate himself no less ruthlessly in his efforts to preserve and augment it than he manipulates others. Certainly, in such instances, the possessor of money is propelled by it into states of tension and harassment that are as acute as any experiences of happiness it may also make available to him.

Quite apart from the strains involved in caring for and multiplying it, wealth contains a hidden snare that becomes agonizingly evident only to those who possess it in great quantities—and especially to those who are seriously engaged in no other activity save its consumption. It is only the idle rich who fully savor the burdens of large incomes that are not contingent upon their own active participation in the economy. Difficult as it may be for us to entertain the proposition that money and happiness are not equated—all the more so since their equation is one of the most, if not *the* most, sacred beliefs of our society—we should try, for the sake of our common humanity, to look at the unhappiness that may be found among the idle rich.

Having been reared in this society, the idle rich have been exposed to our minor values of realization as well as our major values of aggrandizement. Indeed, because of their educational advantages and their unfettered time to do as they wish, members of this class have the implicit encouragement and the explicit opportunity to cultivate the values of realization to a greater extent than members of any other class—including the oligarchs, who devote themselves so assiduously to the active maintenance of their corporate proprietorship. Unquestionably, the idle rich have contributed a good deal of their time, money, and influence to the support of intellectual, esthetic, and humanitarian activities. Nor is there any doubt that many of their charitable efforts have mitigated the sufferings of many persons at the bottom of the socio-economic heap. It may be quite true, as in the case of the oligarchs, that much of this involvement in philanthropic, esthetic, and intellectual affairs is motivated by enlightened economic self-interest or by an egoistic intent to pursue aggrandizement through the evocation of public acclaim. On the other hand, a goodly amount of that involvement may well reflect a sincere effort to fulfill the values of realization; in still other cases, guilt over the acute awareness of their special privileges must impel the wealthy persons to harken to the needs of their infinitely less affluent fellows.

Apart from experiencing twinges of conscience and uneasiness about the possibility, however remote, of depleting their fortunes, the idle rich might be supposed to live in a rosy state of untarnished bliss. And, if one were rash, one might attempt to support such a contention with empirical evidence. For example, a recent study of the sociology of mental illness suggests that the relative incidence of psychosis is inversely correlated with socio-economic class; that is, the higher the class, the lower the incidence of psychosis.[25] Yet, the idle rich are unlikely to be included among the statistics of such studies for the very simple reason that they do not participate in them. But while they may not permit sociologists to count or interview them, they surely comprise a large proportion of the clientele of such genteel insane asylums as the Menninger Clinic, the Austin Riggs Foundation, and Chestnut Lodge. No one knows how many psychotics among the idle rich are kept at home, under the watchful eye of a personal nurse or attendant; or how many psychotics, alcoholics, and drug addicts of this class are being treated as outpatients by expensive specialists.

Setting aside the matter of comparative statistics, however, let us ponder the nature of the psychological stresses that afflict the idle rich, and that may even cause them, in unknown numbers, to break down as completely as the poorest of unemployed workers. The peculiar stresses of the idle rich should stem from the very infinity of possibilities by means of which they can pursue self-aggrandizement. Despite their great opportunity to fulfill the values of realization, the idle rich, as a class, are undoubtedly no less smitten by the values of aggrandizement than are any other classes in society. But, if everything is possible for them—if no limits of either time or money curb the extent to which they can aggrandize themselves—they are more vulnerable than all the other classes to the empty but frenetic egoism that is inherent in the limitless quest for aggrandizement. Thus, many an independently wealthy person may eventually find himself driven by the insatiability that his money, in concert with his aggrandizing motives, has unleashed—driven by it, victimized by it, dissipated by it. As quickly as he acquires one object, it is possible for him to obtain another and another and another, until the very act of acquisition may become a joyless mania. Grand as his home may be, he can, at his merest whim, make it grander; and if his first home soon pales in its aggrandizing effect upon his image of himself, he can quickly obtain a second and a third—all of different styles and in different locations; and if his present wife no longer sufficiently flatters him, he can easily divorce her and find a woman who seems like an even higher compliment to his taste; and so it goes with cars and planes, furniture and friends.

Yes, insatiability consumes the consumer at no less a rate than he himself consumes. Sooner or later, he finds himself listless and jaded. Whereas he may at first have been thrilled beyond measure at the opportunity to exercise his choice in the avenues of aggrandizement, the individual gradually begins to feel indifferent to such choices, indifferent to yet another trinket, another adornment. By that time, his energies have been too exhausted and his will too undermined to find more meaningful and fulfilling purposes for his life. So, he repeats his formula for aggrandizement in a rather perfunctory and listless manner—not really expecting an increment in "kicks" from his next bit of grasping, but grasping, nonetheless, for want of anything else to do. And, if he finds himself spent altogether, he may deaden his aimlessness through drink or drugs; or put an end to it altogether in suicide.

It was Durkheim[26] who first called the attention of social scientists to the psychological consequences of the complete freedom from constraints against egoistic self-indulgence, the complete lack of commitment to any goal other than grasping self-centeredness. And it must be said that, in this respect, Durkheim's insights into the psychology of money were deeper than those of

Marx. For Durkheim saw what Marx did not see: that the liberating power of unlimited money contains the seeds of abject slavery when it is spent for exclusively egoistic purposes. From this standpoint, Durkheim could ascribe some psychological comfort to poverty, since the very lack of money precludes the demoralization that comes from the insatiability of egoistic indulgence. He held that the idle rich may begin to suffer from an apathy as profound as that often present among unemployed workers, who are so disaffected from their society that they can take no pleasure in living and can anticipate no future attainment with enthusiasm. Thus, Durkheim underscores one of the paradoxes of freedom that is all too easy to overlook—that a surfeit of choice can, in time, become psychologically equivalent to an absence of choice; that freedom to choose one's destiny, in small matters as well as in large, derives its exhilaration from the quality of the alternatives that relate to the choice. If the range of choice, while theoretically unlimited, refers only to alternative criteria of aggrandizement, the individual's choices will inevitably lead him into a limitless desert, where all possible pathways only stretch further into the arid wastes.

Since this condition is prevalent among the idle rich, they have just as great a stake as any of the other classes in the transformation of our present social order into a more humane and meaningful one. And, even if such a transformation were to involve the loss of their fortunes, their human condition might be so improved that they would not regret it. For the loss would be one of unrestrained egoism, from whose demoralization their money condemns them to suffer.

The Agonizing Dilemmas of Self-Employed Persons

Of all socio-economic classes in our society, the self-employed professionals and entrepreneurs are the ones who still seem to approximate the virtues of hard-working financial independence that we associate with the idealized image of the Colonial farmer and the rugged individualist of the Westward movement. Yet, the very fact that the number of self-employed persons has been rapidly diminishing in our society is a strong indication of their beleaguered independence. The ones who continue to stay in business for themselves are finding that the freedom of their mode is more illusory than real, that the price they pay for their presumably self-sufficient way of earning a living and pursuing aggrandizement is in excess of the rewards they get.

Although they may function as individual entrepreneurs, virtually all private practitioners must previously have received the stamp of approval and acceptance from their professional organization. Typically, these organizations not only lay down educational specifications that must be met for admission to the "profession" but they also determine, as legal surrogates for the State, the examinations and other criteria of competence governing the award of certificates or licenses.

Hence, entrée into a profession means submission to many rules, regulations, and stipulations that have been established by a bureaucratic organization composed of those already practicing in a given field. After a person is given permission to practice, his professional organization may still continue to exert considerable influence over the conditions of his practice through committees of review that are empowered to withdraw his certificate or license if he fails to practice in accordance with the standards drawn up by that organization; or even, in some cases, if his personal behavior —quite apart from those aspects directly involved in the provision of his services to clients—deviates from certain stated norms. Through such devices as committees of "public information," professional organizations—a choice example of which would be the American Medical Association—may unloose propaganda in favor of or in opposition to legislation that it perceives to bear upon its vested economic interests. Yet, any number of practitioners, who contribute dues to support their professional organization, may be in personal disagreement with the stand taken by the officers of their organization.

The establishment and maintenance of a private professional practice requires considerable capital—a fact that plunges many neophyte practitioners into a morass of debt for many years. Even in the uncrowded field of medicine, in which acute shortages of physicians of every specialty characterize many sections of the country, the new practitioner may find himself unwelcomed by colleagues in places, such as large cities, where a concentration of doctors exists—albeit that the physicians already on the scene are doing a thriving business and that the "concentration" is still pathetically inadequate to meet the crying social need for medical care. The young physician may find himself unable to practice in the community of his choice, lest he incur the enmity of potential competitors who resent the slightest inroads into their source of income. Certainly, without cooperation and referrals from his colleagues, a physician's life in a community can be quite miserable; and if he is, further, denied an affiliation with the local hospital, he is severely hampered in the discharge of his medical responsibilities to patients who require hospitalization.

In more crowded professions, such as law, the prospects for beginning one's own practice are much more unfavorable. It is not uncommon to find many young lawyers entering bureaucratic organizations directly upon their graduation—never to emerge as independent practitioners. On the other hand, the competitive conditions in that field tend to stimulate "group" practice as a compromise between independent and bureaucratic functioning. But group practice brings with it the paradoxical requirement of cooperation among persons who, by the slant of their training (not to speak of the pressure of their egoistic ambitions), are oriented toward the individualistic pursuit of aggrandizement. Surely, it is not difficult to imagine the tensions that arise within and among individuals whose partnership, while expedient to each, in no way reflects a genuinely altruistic orientation of mutual aid.

The most disturbing aspect of the private practice of a profession concerns the conflict between the values of realization, which the professional service explicitly aims to fulfill, and the values of aggrandizement, which the practitioner often seeks to pursue through his professional services. Manifestly, the rendering of service to one's fellow men is an expression of humanitarian values; and, depending upon the nature of the service rendered, it may also greatly involve the expression of esthetic values as well. The architect, for example, has the opportunity to fulfill his gift for artistic creativity at the same time as he helps to produce something useful and delightful to others. Self-employed professionals, more than members of any other socio-economic grouping, are in a position to fulfill the values of realization in their day-to-day work. It is this very possibility of doing work that is its own reward that attracts many persons into the professions. For, depending upon one's talents, the professions permit one to exercise them and, at the same time, to contribute, as a result of that exercise, to the welfare of others in their society.

However, this linkage of the professions to the values of realization is severely strained, if not entirely broken, by the professional's desire to use his work as an instrument of the values of aggrandizement. While some professionals struggle valiantly— with themselves as well as with their professional colleagues— against the intrusion of those values upon their work, the *very principle* of private practice is destructive to their cause. When *any* professional practices privately (*or* in the employ of a profit-making organization), he involves himself in a gross contradiction between the values of realization, which his profession *per se* represents, and the values of aggrandizement, which the practice of his profession for economic gain promotes. When any recipient of professional service becomes a source of the professional's financial fortunes rather than exclusively an object of the professional's selfless concern, his relationship to the professional is inevitably damaged. For he then is perceived by the professional not merely as someone in need of service but also as someone who possesses more or less of the resources—ultimately, money—that the professional has to have in order to pursue his aggrandizing motives. Instead of simply being someone to whom the profes-

sional has an opportunity to give of himself, the recipient of service also becomes someone from whom the professional must
extract his coveted criteria of aggrandizement. The egoism thus
introduced into such relationships demeans the humanity of both
parties.

The professional demeans his own humanity the moment he
makes the giving of his services contingent upon a fee. From that
moment, he is no longer free to extend his helping hand to others
as spontaneously and warmly as the promptings of his heart might
otherwise lead him to do. On the contrary, he begins to restrain
his spontaneity and to discriminate among all potential recipients
of his services—all his brethren in society—in terms of their relative affluence. In this way, he begins to manipulate himself, however unwittingly, into a restricted purveyor of money-making
skills.

Thus, the private practitioner numbs his sensibilities and re-
stricts not only the field of his professional vision but also the
variety of fulfilling experiences that he could realize from work
with the kinds of persons and problems that fall outside the limits
of his financial stipulations. Knowing full well that his monetary
demands exclude many needy persons from his services, he further
constricts his own humanity by accommodating to the implicit
callousness of his entrepreneurial orientation. By directing the
bulk of his energies toward the money-making aspects of the practice of his profession, he contributes very little to the prevention or
amelioration of conditions that give rise to the problems that come
to his attention in the form of requests for his remedial services.

By and large, in fact, private practitioners in the professions
related to health take very little time out from their practices in
order to participate in research aimed at the prevention of many
of the ailments that they are currently asked by their patients to
treat. Nor are many lawyers in private practice avidly involved in
the implementation of social and legal reforms that might reduce
the incidence of the infractions or disputations for which clients
solicit their services. Yet, the long-range humanitarian and equali-

tarian aims of these professions—health and justice—would be best expressed by eliminating the very factors that necessitated their emergence as separate fields in the first place. Indeed, the highest ideal for the professions would be one that impelled their members to work toward the dissolution of the very profession in which they practice.

It would scarcely be humane, of course, to abandon all ministrations on behalf of living sufferers in favor of work toward the prevention of problems among generations of men yet to be born. Even so, it is conceivable to imagine living professionals spending at least part of their time on the work of prevention. So long as they withhold such expenditure of their time, they show as great a disregard for the future of humanity as they do for the existing segments of mankind whose poverty puts them outside the ken of the private practitioner.

In the case of the potential client or patient, the demeaning consequences of private practice exactly reflect those that debase the humanity of the practitioner. Standing as commodities in relation to the aggrandizing motives of the private practitioner, those in need of the practitioner's services cannot obtain them unless they possess sufficient funds. Accordingly, their very lives may be forfeit—as in the case of someone whose survival depends upon the outcome of a delicate surgical operation—for want of the price that a private practitioner may set upon his services. And, even if a client or patient has enough money to initiate a relationship, he may not be able to continue it if his funds run out. To be sure, many professionals have made some provision for the granting of their essential services to the indigent. Still, these charitable or semi-charitable organizations of professional service are not likely to enjoy more than the token participation of experienced private practitioners, some of whom may devote a half-day or whole day per week to such philanthropies.

The non-professional entrepreneur faces none of the grating conflicts in value of the professional in private practice. For the lone entrepreneur who operates his own commercial establishment does not pretend to be in business for anything else but his own profit. True, he may prefer selling shoes to beef; but he is selling a tangible commodity whose exchange value is the characteristic that interests him most about it. And, if he sells a service, such as brokerage in stocks and bonds, he can hardly convince himself that he is performing humanitarian activities that are essential to the welfare of his fellows.

However, because he is free of the conflict between the values of aggrandizement and those of realization, the individual entrepreneur is not necessarily likely to be any less distraught than the self-employed professional. On the contrary, whereas the professional may sometimes be able to derive a modicum of gratification from his daily expression—even if only for a price and to a restricted clientele—of the values of realization, the pathos of the lone non-professional entrepreneur lies in his difficulties in pursuing his single-minded dedication to the values of aggrandizement. For he is as a dwarf among giants, a David among Goliaths, an embattled trading post in a rapidly consolidating economy of commercial empires. It is his peculiar, if ironic, fate to be steadily engulfed by the growth of those empires, although he may still be widely regarded as an exemplar of the American system of free enterprise.

But the individual entrepreneur continues to cling to his economic self-sufficiency as tenaciously as he can—seeking to compensate in effort and personal attention to his customers for what he lacks in financial resources to compete with the chain stores, discount houses, and national organizations that have begun to market goods and services in every corner of the country. These large organizations, because of the volume of their purchasing, can obtain goods more cheaply than the individual entrepreneur; and they can benefit from other economies, such as those obtained by having manufacturers produce goods exclusively for sale in their stores.

Like a barnacle weathering high seas, the individual retailer clings to the recesses of local neighborhoods. There, he seeks to retain enough trade to resist bankruptcy; and he drives himself mercilessly to keep his business going. For example, he may remain open long after the chain stores have closed for the day; and his vigil for the stray customer may extend through the weekend. He may extend credit to his customers, retaining their patronage while stretching his indebtedness to a perilous point with his own creditors. Similarly, whereas the large discount house may operate on a self-service, self-delivery basis, the independent merchant may feel compelled to provide his customers not only with delivery service but also with all manner of personal compliments and attentiveness. Because of the enticing and glamorous settings that large chains use to display their merchandise, the solitary entrepreneur is under pressure to "dress up" his own store, a procedure that requires further expenditures for operating overhead, which he cannot easily pass on to his customers via higher prices, since his prices may already be higher than those of the chain. Whereas the chain store has large reserves of capital to invest in advertising as well as in surveys on the preferences and motivations of consumers, the individual entrepreneur must husband his profits to meet financial crises that are often occasioned by the very success of the chain in its advertising and research activities. Certainly, for example, the individual merchant cannot devote himself on a full-time basis to such specialized tasks as determining the correct height at which to stack his goods to catch the housewife's searching glance. Nor can he afford to re-arrange his store periodically, as is the practice of some chains, deliberately to force the shopper to look afresh at goods she had gotten into the habit of passing by without notice.

Nevertheless, the individual entrepreneur, living by his agility and willingness to cater unsparingly to his customers, may succeed in remaining in business for his lifetime. Yet, long before he dies, he may well begin to wonder whether he is a hero or a martyr to his culture; whether his self-imposed years of exhaustion, harassment, and obsequiousness brought him either aggrandizement or independence. He may spend his life in an eerie state of pseudo-independence or quasi-slavery, in which his apparent freedom of run his business as he sees fit is countered by the host of things he *must* do if he is to withstand the relentless economic pressures imposed upon him by the bureaucratic organizations with which he is obliged to compete. While he is buckling under the weight of such pressures, he can hardly feel too sanguine about his progress in aggrandizement. Even if his profits continue to increase from year to year, he can obtain them only by being constantly alert to the moves of his towering competitors and by picking upon the bones of trade, as it were, that the big organizations still condescend to drop in their ravenous pursuit of the mass market and the quick sale. The role of scavenger among sharks can scarcely be inflating to the egoism of the individual entrepreneur, although he may experience a sense of vindictive triumph over his deadly competitors merely by virtue of continuing to remain in business.

On the other hand, having remained in his business for a number of years, the self-employed entrepreneur has backed himself, however inadvertently, into an occupational cul-de-sac. For while he may have become rather accomplished at running his own modest enterprise, he has not acquired any of the technical skills that might permit him to seek employment in one of the specialized arms of management—such as the production or accounting division of a corporation. Nor has he even developed the "interpersonal" skills appropriate to the supervision and manipulation of the work of others—since the personnel of his own enterprise has been very limited. Because he is not used to "fitting in" with a hierarchy of superiors and a legion of organizational peers, he may find the thought of entering a bureaucratic structure too abhorrent for serious consideration. Similarly, the idea of joining the ranks of the workers is hardly likely to appeal to him, for such a descent to that class would represent a most damaging blow to whatever measure of aggrandizement his individual entrepreneurship has produced for him. In the light of these adverse factors, he may well choose to stay where he is, gnashing his teeth in wearisome anger as he braces himself for the next blow from his great and proliferating competitors.

The Blighted Freedom
of the Creative Artist

Whereas the private practice of a profession or the individual conduct of a business is a manifestation of our particular economic system rather than an intrinsic necessity for the rendering of humanitarian services or the distribution of goods, the solitary and independent functioning of the creative artist is both a universal and an inherent requirement of artistic creativity. Only in full-time devotion to their art can artists hope to develop their capacities to the fullest; and only by creating entirely on their own can they unlock their unique visions and voices.

If all our artists could be relieved of economic concerns, therefore, they would be able to apply that freedom to the end of nurturing the qualities of their artistic idiosyncrasy; and the art that they created would reveal the heterogeneity of their individual differences. But our artists are, on the contrary, cruelly oppressed by our economy. Unlike the widespread public demand for professional services, the market for original works of imagination is so minute that only a very few can ever acquire a steady and appreciable income by selling creations that express no other perception, no other taste, no other heart or hand except their own. Thus, unless a creative artist is willing to subvert his uniqueness by adapting it to some mercenary objective, he is likely to face a lifetime of grinding poverty, subsisting either on the charity of others or on occasional periods of paid employment in some other field. Alternatively, if he wishes to earn a decent living and still retain his artistic integrity, he must spend a good deal of his time in non-artistic activity, devoting the remainder of his hours and energies to his art.

Because our artists of all media are implicitly under severe pressure to produce works that conform to the demands of the artistic marketplace, however restricted and competitive it may be, many of them are quick to join transient fads that seem to have caught the public's fancy. In the field of painting, for example, the recent trends in abstract expressionism and pop art followed each other with startling alacrity, the latter style literally clearing the former off the gallery walls once it had become *de rigueur*. And, when these fads were at their height, it was often very difficult to distinguish the paintings of one artist from another of the same "school."

While not submerging their individuality in these passing genres, some artists manage, nevertheless, to subvert the development of their own uniqueness by cultivating special "gimmicks." One artist may begin to depict nothing but rifle targets; a second, nothing but saccharin and doe-eyed children; a third, nothing but vacuous self-portraits. Presumably, this specialization in content, which seems to be a dreary esthetic counterpart to that found in industrial production, gives the artist a definite, if pathetically shallow, identity.[27] And although such an artist may condemn himself to a life of painting essentially the same picture over and over again, he may realistically hope to corner any market that may arise for his specialty.

But the fads and grotesqueries of this sort can be found in all the creative arts. If anything, the pressures to submit to the esthetic dictates of others are more crushing in the field of playwriting than in any of the other creative arts—verbal, visual, or musical. True, a painter or sculptor cannot ordinarily expect to be exhibited unless the owner of a gallery covers the expense of his show; or unless, as is now possible in some "vanity" galleries, the artist himself raises the money to defray the costs of his own exhibition. But the costs of a showing, depending upon the gallery, need not involve a tremendous investment on the part of the dealer. Besides, if the artist is sufficiently determined to have others view his work, he can find an outlet in non-commercial exhibits run by local community centers and municipal organizations, an outstanding example of which is the outdoor art festival that is held each year in New York's Greenwich Village. And, if all else fails, the artist can simply invite people to his studio to see his work.

But the playwright cannot consummate a communication with

anyone else unless his work is actually performed. Yet, the cost of staging a professional production of a play is greatly beyond the means of most playwrights, no matter how intensely their vanity might desire it. In fact, the production of plays is rapidly becoming a joint corporate venture in which many persons invest part of the necessary capital, sharing the production's profits or losses. Under such conditions, the potential sponsors of a play are likely to be quite cautious about backing any script that represents a departure from theatrical formulae already proven to be financially successful. It is little wonder, therefore, that the theatre in America has, in general, become so stereotyped and lackluster. And it is a miracle, in view of this state of affairs, that any young American playwrights still have the courage knowingly to write plays that deviate from the commercial canons of popular acceptance.

The channels of communication for the novelist may be a little more open, but they are also closing very quickly. Even our largest and most prosperous publishing houses are deserting[28] serious fiction in preference for more reliably lucrative areas: nonfiction, textbooks, and trifles, such as murder mysteries, which are intended only as the lightest of entertainment. Thus, notwithstanding the publicity received by the rare best-selling novel, publishers are taking fewer and fewer financial risks in bringing unconventional and previously unknown authors to the attention of the American public. On the other hand, in the last few years, we have witnessed the emergence of the contrived and co-authored pseudo-novel,[29] which does not even presume to be a work of inspiration but which is, instead, a calculated effort to put a highly topical political or social issue into fictional dress.

The Humiliating Imprisonment
of the Unemployed Workers

All the other socio-economic classes have, in terms of the values of aggrandizement, some positive incentives for accommodating themselves to their places in society. Even the workers may obtain a sop to their ambitions by getting periodic increases in salary and fringe benefits. But, lacking even these slight incentives, how is the unemployed worker kept from vigorous protest against a social order from which he is so manifestly dispossessed?

Thus far, the answer to this question has been in the form of a dole—direct governmental payments to the unemployed. And when that "unemployment insurance" is exhausted, the still unemployed worker is obliged to "go on relief"—to obtain permanent subsidies from the State. But such payments are minimal, based upon estimates of the cost of bare subsistence. Owing to the differences in the amounts granted by various states, the "relief" checks may be so small that they provide their unemployed recipients with very little relief indeed—even from the goadings of hunger. Still, the device of subsidized unemployment seems to have been successful in giving the unemployed worker just enough money to dull the cutting edge of his resentment and to keep him in a state of passive despondency.

Naturally, no unemployed worker can feel that he is aggrandizing himself through his meager allowance. And, if his aspirations continue to be predicated by the values of aggrandizement, his quickest avenue of attainment lies in the realm of fantasy. Hence, he is drawn increasingly toward insanity, whose delusions and counterfeit euphoria mock the grandeur that the individual failed to experience as a participant in his confined segment of social reality. Fundamentalist religion, with its offer of the immediate and passionate appropriation of godhood, is another possible channel for the pursuit of the megalomaniacal aspirations that the unemployed are incapable of pursuing through active participation in the economy. For those who can neither endure the pain of chronic humiliation nor resort to such extreme modes of vicarious aggrandizement as they may find in psychotic delusions or religious ecstasies, there remain the anodynes of alcohol and narcotics.

But some of the unemployed workers are unable to reconcile

themselves to self-manipulative containment within the confines of their misery. Some, quite simply, attempt to run away from their daily wretchedness, leaving behind them thousands upon thousands of fatherless children and husbandless wives. To make matters worse, the degradation of unemployment is so great for many potential husbands that they are discouraged from assuming the responsibilities of marriage, although they may not hesitate to father children. The women and children involved in such relationships simply inherit the pain and humiliation from which their unemployed lovers and fathers have sought to flee.

Other members of our most downtrodden socio-economic class may try to aggrandize themselves through direct action on their own behalf. Although they are blocked, by reason of their unemployment, from the legal means of such actions, they may undertake illegal ones. For such persons, crime may be seen as the only realistic means of improving their circumstances in life and, thereby, of advancing the aggrandizing motives that they have learned; they may regard their crimes as acts of retribution, in much the same way as the legendary Robin Hood justified his poaching upon the rich.

But crime often leads to arrest and punishment, in the course of which the individual is further alienated from the rest of society. And the social ostracism that the unemployed ex-convict meets is likely to make it harder for him to obtain work than it was before his incarceration. Thus, a vicious cycle is begun, the frustration of the unemployed worker provoking criminal behavior whose treatment by our legal institutions insures that it will be harder still for him to find a job. Indeed, these added barriers to employment augment the individual's desperation and, perhaps, increase the likelihood of his committing more crimes in an effort to get that which he feels he cannot attain by any other means.

Frequently, this kind of vicious cycle has its counterparts in those set into motion when unemployed workers choose some of the other methods of dealing with their blocked aspirations and the resentments engendered by that blockage. Thus, alcoholism and drug addiction are not habits that generally make a favorable impression upon prospective employers. Nor is raving insanity usually considered an excellent qualification for a job.

The most insidious aspects of these cycles of degradation are those that impinge upon the children of unemployed workers. For these children are born into entrapping poverty and demoralization; born to parents who cannot help but pass on to them the effects of their own sufferings. The unemployed workers are the pariahs of our society, and their children inherit not only their lowly status but also the ruthlessness of society's disregard.

6

Injustice, Crime, and Delinquency

INEXORABLY, THE SOCIAL and economic realities of our historical development have severely confined the ambitions of most Americans, requiring them to modulate the initial extravagance of their Dream and to harness their pursuit of aggrandizement to the constraints inherent in our bureaucracies of work. Indeed, some Americans appear almost ready to trade aggrandizement for security and stop dreaming altogether, stop hoping for anything more grandiose than a weekly paycheck.

But the Dream dies hard, especially when it is continually reinforced by all the major organizations of education and communication in our society. And most Americans have been reluctant to give it up quietly and passively. However, since they do not have, as yet, strong commitments to the values of realization, they are disinclined to channel their resentments toward the creation of social changes that might produce a more fulfilling society for themselves and their children. Instead, still motivated by the hunger for individual aggrandizement, they are simply tempted to take from others what they feel themselves to be lacking; or to strike out destructively against those whom they perceive as more favorably placed in the hierarchy of invidious distinction. The result, of course, is crime.

Whereas the criminal or juvenile delinquent has often been portrayed as an enemy of society, he is likely, in fact, to be an avid exponent of its most prized values. Far from being ideological rebels, the majority of our criminals are probably the staunchest adherents of our dominant social values. While they may use more drastic means[1] of obtaining what they want from others, their intent is no different, for example, from that of the advertiser who dupes people into buying his product by appealing to their unconscious motivational vulnerabilities.

Actually, we have two varieties of crime in our society: legal and illegal. Nor is this classification merely a facetious play on words. On the contrary, the existential reality of these two types of crime is one of the most demoralizing aspects of our way of life.

Illegal crime consists of those actions that are specifically proscribed by our legal statutes and that are covered by our penal codes. In general, the acts prohibited and punishable by law are those that inflict injury upon the person of a victim or that deprive him of his property by cunning or force. However, while defining illegal behavior, our law has simultaneously thrown its full moral and punative power into the support of economic practices whose effects are as injurious and exploitative as any that it has condemned as criminal. These legally approved and socially idealized criminal practices involve nothing other than the ordinary conduct of capitalism. For the very cornerstone of our economy rests upon the concept of private property and the right of proprietors to derive income from property.

But as Proudhon has articulated with impeccable logic for all posterity to know, there exists no ethical justification for the institution of property—if we hold ethics to be an expression of justice. On the contrary, since the property contained in a society is finite, he who permanently appropriates any part of it unto himself implicitly deprives his fellows of an equal chance to share the blessings of their common earth, upon which the very fact of birth entitles every man to an equal claim to whatever life has to offer to all. It can readily be seen that he who profits from the labor of others is taking from them something that they do not bestow upon him as a voluntary gift. When any man is denied the possibility of enjoying anything that property or profit can buy, including nourishment and medical care, that man is being injured. The extent of that injury may even be fatal, as exemplified by the differences in longevity between our highest and lowest classes. Thus, in the words of Proudhon,[2] property is both robbery and murder; and he who asserts his right to property declares his intention to rob and murder his fellow men.

It follows, therefore, that our economic system is based upon legalized crime. And all who put the system into practice are criminals; those who own property and profit from it; those who draw interest on capital and savings; those who receive dividends from stock; those, indeed, who receive more pay for their work than that granted to persons doing other categories of work. Virtually all of us are parties to these legalized crimes, although some of us commit more and larger ones than are committed by many of our fellows.

Viewed from this standpoint, the function of law in our society is, first of all, to condone the plunder and injury that are inevitably wrought by the *normal* operation of our economy. Secondly, by directing its reproach to an arbitrarily and illogically restricted range of unjust acts, the law obscures the intrinsic criminality of our economic system. Finally, the law protects the loot obtained by legal criminals from the encroachments of illegal ones.

At a time when the land of our continent was fair game for all who desired property, the contradictions of our legal system were not so painfully apparent as they are today—although at no time in our history were all Americans owners of property. But as property became translated from arable land to industrial plants, and as profit from property came to depend not upon the labor of its proprietor alone but, instead, upon those in his employ, the function of law as an instrument of special privilege became increasingly evident. And it is far from inspiring to listen, now, to the hypocritical indignation[3] of those who, while bewailing the steady and seemingly unstoppable rise of illegal crime, would not for an instant consider renouncing their privilege to commit the legal crimes that are necessarily involved in their extraction of profit from the labor of others, in their ownership of property, or in their relatively high wages.

Yes, we are a nation of criminals; and we can hardly expect each other to exercise a restraint that is implicitly denigrated by the fundamental principles of our economy. For the very attainment of financial success involves, by definition, robbing and inflicting injury upon others. And since financial success is the most honored of all our modes of aggrandizement, its pursuit inflames the criminal tendencies that are latent in property and profit.

To make matters worse, the other values of aggrandizement—prestige and power—also require the evocation of responses from others that they may not be disposed to give freely; that, in fact, they may be competing with others to obtain. Hence, ambitions for prestige and power also impel Americans to exploit and harm each other in the interest of their attainment.

Since the inability to attain continuous increments of aggrandizement through the commission of legal crimes is likely to be frustrating, such failure paves the way for illegal criminality. The frustrations of thwarted aspiration may stir hatred[4] that is vented in acts of violence against others: at those perceived to be in higher social class or caste; at competitors within one's own socioeconomic and caste grouping; or at those who, because they are "below" one's own class or caste, serve as conveniently helpless scapegoats for anger that they themselves did nothing to provoke. On the other hand, blockage in the pursuit of aggrandizement through the application of legal criminality—that is, through the approved means of exploiting and manipulating others—may quickly induce experimentation in the use of illegal forms of crime. For if success is too long in coming by recourse to one form of crime, why should the aspiring person not avail himself of means that seem to promise its more rapid attainment? True, the potential penalties that attend detection and conviction for illegal crimes may act as a powerful deterrent. But the pain of social failure and the racking tensions of unappeased ambition may be even more powerful goads to the commission of such crimes. The fact that our population is becoming increasingly willing[5] to risk punishment for illegal crimes bespeaks the pressure they feel to commit them.

With commendable lucidity, Proudhon describes fifteen major ways in which robbery may be committed—ranging from "murder on the highway" to "making profit on a product." In discussing these methods in detail, he points out that they "have been very cleverly distinguished and classified by legislators according to their heinousness or merit, to the end that some robbers may be honored, while others are punished."[6] Exposing the spurious character of such distinctions, Proudhon reveals, in his comments about usury, the essential injustice—that is, the essential criminal-ity—of any transaction that permits one person to profit econom-ically from his relationship with another. "This species of robbery, so odious and so severely punished by the Gospel, is the connect-ing link between forbidden and authorized robbery. Owing to its ambiguous nature, it has given rise to a multitude of contradic-tions in the laws and in morals, contradictions which have been very cleverly turned to account by lawyers, financiers, and mer-chants. Thus the usurer, who lends on mortgage at ten, twelve, and fifteen per cent, is heavily fined when detected; while the banker, who receives the same interest (not, it is true, upon a loan, but in the way of exchange or discount—that is, of sale), is protected by royal privilege. But the distinction between the banker and the usurer is a purely nominal one. Like the usurer, who lends on property, real or personal, the banker lends on business paper; like the usurer, he takes his interest in advance; like the usurer, he can recover from the borrower if the property is destroyed (that is, if the note is not redeemed)—a circumstance which makes him a money-lender, not a money-seller. But the banker lends for a short time only, while the usurer's loan may be for one, two, three, or more years. Now, a difference in the duration of a loan, or the form of the act, does not alter the nature of the transaction. As for the capitalists who invest their money, either with the State or in commercial operations at three, four, and five per cent,—that is, who lend on usury at a little lower rate than the bankers and usurers,—they are the flower of society, the cream of honesty! Moderation in robbery is the height of virtue!"[7]

If our laws were really just, therefore, almost every American would qualify as an active criminal. But since the laws are unjust, they unfairly place the onus of criminality upon an artificially delineated segment of our population. Even so, this segment has been widening with great speed in recent years. The volume of legally prohibited offenses has already achieved the notoriety of a national disgrace and the prevalence of a national anxiety; and the dimensions of the problem are so unpleasantly familiar and menacing that they conjure the terror of an irrepressible cancer. Moreover, since our rates of statutory crimes have been running very much ahead of our rise in population, they cannot be reasonably attributed to increases in the sheer number of people in the country. In the years 1958-62, our population rose by 7 per cent, whereas our criminal offenses rose by 27 per cent. Some categories of offenses have skyrocketed; for example, from 1956 to 1962 the number of bank robberies increased almost threefold, while embezzlements, over the same period of time, were committed nearly twice as frequently. Nor have the overall rates of illegal offenses risen most precipitously in our largest cities. On the contrary, the greatest rise in these rates has been in cities of 500,000 to 1,000,000 persons; and cities of both 25,000 to 50,000 and 50,000 to 100,000 people have shown steeper increases than cities of more than 1,000,000 people.[8]

While the rates of these offenses are understandably greater among those in the lowest class and caste groups than those of higher class and caste—understandable not only in terms of greater provocation but also greater defenselessness against arrest —the incidence of statutory crimes is by no means insignificant among our more advantaged socio-economic groupings. "Edwin H.

Sutherland, the well-known criminologist, observed many years ago that 'if two persons on different economic levels are equally guilty of the same offense, the one on the lower level is more likely to be arrested, convicted and sent to an institution.' Several recent studies have confirmed this discrepant treatment of offenders who are members of different socio-economic groups.

"In a study entitled 'Our Law-Abiding Law Breakers,' Wallerstein and Wyle summarize the admissions of some seventeen hundred law-abiding men and women, overweighted with professional businessmen of substantial standing, regarding their 'delinquent' and 'criminal' acts. Almost all of these individuals confessed to having committed offenses under existing laws. Two-thirds of them admitted engaging in behavior which, under the laws of their state, were felonious. In another study by Austin L. Porterfield, a randomly selected group of college students all acknowledged committing a considerable number of offenses similar to those found among those brought into court. However, the offenses of these college students rarely appeared in any court statistics. The fact that delinquency cuts across social stratification lines has been statistically supported by a recent study made by James F. Short, Jr., F. Ivan Nye and Virgil J. Olsen. These researchers found that of two thousand three hundred and fifty high school boys and girls, examined in six Western and Midwestern communities, there was 'no significant difference in delinquent behavior in the different socio-economic strata.' "[9]

Juvenile Delinquency and the Limitless Quest of Aggrandizement[10]

What forces are driving more and more of our children into flagrantly criminal behavior long before they participate, as adults, in the more commonplace and legally authorized crimes required by the regular functioning of our economy? Why is it that more and more of our children commit such acts before they reach the age of eighteen? Why, for example, did these children account for

62 per cent of *all* automobile thefts, 51 per cent of *all* larcenies, 49 per cent of *all* burglaries and 29 per cent of *all* robberies that were committed in this country during 1962? Why did the arrest of youths under eighteen years of age increase by 9 per cent in 1962 as compared to 1961?[11]

Like their parents, American children are still being urged to adopt, as the highest of all ideals, limitless progress in the personal pursuit of aggrandizement. Nobody who commits himself to such a pursuit can ever hope to experience an enduring state of contentment. On the contrary, the best he can expect to find in the course of his strivings is transient relief in specific instances of attainment. But any such success merely becomes a new base from which the aspiring individual faces the future. Accomplishments in the future, new levels of aggrandizement to be attained, now engage his attention and energies. What he has already acquired for himself is, as it were, dead and gone; his former acquisitions cannot relieve the tensions that his grasping aspirations continue to generate. Instead, these tensions push the individual toward fresh successes, denying him the comfort of resting on his laurels.

Under these circumstances, a person's social class position *per se* is no absolute guarantee of his continual progress toward greater and greater self-aggrandizement. Of course, a child born into a managerial family begins life with considerably better chances of making such progress than a child of the working class, since he can draw upon the resources of his economically advantaged parents to appease his aspirations. For instance, as an adolescent, he can get a car from them, acquiring one of the important symbols of prestige of our culture. However, depending upon the intensity of his aspirations and the available resources of his parents, even the managerial child may begin to feel acutely deprived; even he may begin to feel frustrated when he gauges his family's current socio-economic position against the aspirations he has developed; or when he finds that he lacks the intellectual ability to prepare himself for occupations that are commensurate with, if not superior to, the socio-economic stratum into which he was born. A good deal of the recent unrest among adolescents of the managerial class has been attributed to the fact that many such children realize, well before the age of 18, that they simply do not possess the capacities and talents required for successful competition in the occupations they were taught to admire and in which, in fact, their own parents may have already built successful careers.[12] Accordingly, the managerial child may come to feel quite as blocked as his working class counterpart who, in purely objective terms, has fewer economic resources.

Keeping the social psychology of aggrandizement in mind, we may be able to account for a seeming paradox: the sharp rise of delinquency in a period of proliferating national wealth.[13] According to the premises of that psychology, the more wealth people have acquired, the more they will need to acquire in the future in order to enhance their image of themselves. The recent acquisition of a small house in the suburbs begins to pale, if its owner regards it primarily as a criterion of aggrandizement. Eventually, he will wish to purchase a newer house, a bigger house, a house in a more expensive neighborhood—a house that represents an advance over the last one in terms of the yardstick of wealth. The inciting forces of advertising continue, all the while, to stimulate the individual's cravings, lest their insatiability begin to wane in the slightest degree. Lust for aggrandizement is kept at a white heat by the relentless appeals of oligarchs whose own limitless aspirations can be pursued only by fostering patterns of public consumption that are congenial to the concept of "planned obsolescence."

In a period of booming prosperity, however, members of most of the socio-economic classes improve their material conditions more quickly than they are ordinarily able to do. But prosperity, as welcomed as it may be by the aspiring individuals, tends to shorten the span of time between their increments in aggrandizement and the strivings that they subsequently feel obliged to undertake. Consequently, under these circumstances, individuals come to expect ever quicker and ever greater results for their efforts. Psychologically speaking, these circumstances give rise to a reduced threshold of tolerance for frustration; and barriers that were once tolerated with considerable patience may seem insufferable. And, if one sees others as having prospered much more rapidly than oneself, one may grow extremely dissatisfied—even if one's economic condition is manifestly better than it had been in the past.

Several years ago, Bohlke[14] attempted to delineate two contexts of delinquency that relate to this psychological state. One condition for delinquency, Bohlke holds, may arise when families of the working class have acquired sufficient income to permit them to move into residential areas that were formerly the exclusive preserves of members of the managerial and self-employed classes; or when, having made the rare jump from the status of worker to that of manager or self-employed entrepreneur, a former worker moves his family into a neighborhood occupied by the class grouping into which he is newly arrived. However, as Bohlke postulates, children of families who have made such moves come into their new location without having first acquired the manners and attitudes of those among whom they now reside. As a result, they may be socially rejected by age peers, who have been reared in families of a higher socio-economic class. Angered by this social rejection, children of the nouveaux arrivées may commit acts of violence against those who have rejected them, who have impeded their aspirations to attain the prestige that is commensurate with their freshly elevated economic fortunes.

Bohlke argues that another type of delinquent may be discerned among children who have grown angry because of the failure of their parents to keep on moving upward in the economy. Presumably, unlike the children just described, these adolescents come from families who have long ago become solidly ensconced in positions and neighborhoods occupied by members of the managerial and self-employed classes. Having grown restive because the stationary economic condition of their parents is not consonant with the very aspirations their parents preached to them, these children may be inclined to resort to quick but illegal means of appeasing their aspirations. They may engage in automobile theft and other forms of stealing, which represent means of accumulating goods that their parents might not approve or use to advance the family's economic position. The crimes of the children, however, *may* reflect the accumulated frustrations of their parents' aspirations.

The values of wealth and prestige contribute to the definition of the hierarchy of invidious distinction on the basis of which our society is structured. These two values tend to be highly interrelated variables among our socio-economic classes. As Mills[15] has remarked, many of the listings in the *Social Register* can be traced back to the "merchant princes" who founded the fortunes that give their progeny a firm place among the elite. Accordingly, people who strive to move upward in the socio-economic hierarchy may be motivated by limitless aspirations for prestige as well as economic gain; and if they achieve some success in the economic dimension but not in the dimension of prestige, they may well feel, as Bohlke hypothesizes, a great deal of resentment toward those who thwart their desires for prestige.

Still, from the standpoint of its insatiability, the limitless pursuit of aggrandizement renders any success, however impressive, exceedingly *relative* in its meaning to the striving individual. And, to understand an individual's reaction to success, it is necessary to view it in the light of that which the individual feels he must do in order to reduce the discrepancy between his present attainment and the next accomplishment or acquisition; between what he has, at the moment, and what he must have, in the future, in order to feel that he is continuing to make progress in aggrandizing himself.

Because this element of psychological relativity is so crucial to our understanding of the behavioral implications of the limitless pursuit of aggrandizement, it is equally important to assess both the individual's aspirational history, as it were, and the current obstacles in the path of his striving in order to make predictions about the extent to which he may be inclined to behave in an illegal manner. Some of these obstacles may be objectively more difficult to surmount than others. The physically handicapped individual, for example, may be said to be confronted by greater barriers than the healthy person—holding constant all other variables relevant to their chances for success: e.g., social class, motivation, education. On the other hand, given the same objective chances, the same potential obstacles will be perceived as barriers more readily by those who have developed intense aspirations than by those who have only mild ones.

It is impossible to spell out all of the various combinations of aspirations and barriers that may be found to coalesce in the general population of children. However, it is possible to postulate several patterns that may prove to be very commonplace in our culture at the present time. A good example of the more objective barrier might be seen in the child of a working class family who has developed strong limitless aspirations for material gain, but whose lowly socio-economic position creates an enormous gap between his goals and the realities of his daily life. Such a child is restricted, first of all, by very limited familial resources. He cannot buy the things he has to buy in order to adorn himself with the manifestations of wealth. His daily cultural experiences do not provide him with the niceties of manner or social skill that he could use for his material advancement. Certainly, the knowledge and orientation of his formal schooling are difficult to apply in an environment in which sheer survival is a genuine attainment. Literally, he may be unable to afford a leisurely, long-range educational program. And he may be pressed into working for his own economic support long before his vocational attitudes and skills can crystallize.

Looking upward in the socio-economic order of our society, such a child may see himself implicitly humiliated by those who can succeed more easily at what he wishes to do—simply because they were born into a family with material resources. Looking ahead to his future, such a child may realize that he may never rise in the socio-economic hierarchy no matter how diligently he works. Admittedly, children of the working class may not have a sophisticated knowledge of these implications of the social grouping into which they are born; but they surely must obtain a fair glimmer of those realities in the course of their own daily experience. For such children, therefore, the legal means of economic striving may not be too alluring. These means may be seen as an equivalent to their attempting to bag a tiger with a pea-shooter. Accordingly, they may resort to illegal means—such as thievery— as a direct and rapid way of acquiring that which they feel they may otherwise never be able to acquire. And the fact that the highest rates of delinquency are still to be found in the urban slums[16] lends support to the foregoing notions of the frustrating effects of environmental obstacles that severely restrict the pursuit of limitless aspirations for wealth, prestige, or power.

Other kinds of delinquent acts may also arise from similarly real frustrations. Interpersonal violence that has no other object but to inflict injury, for example, may be spurred by the displaced aggression aroused by balked aspirations. Sometimes, as in attacks by children of low classes against peers in higher ones, this aggression may be mingled with jealousy and directed against those who symbolize a socially enviable position.

Apart from the obstacles presented by membership in a deprived social class, other objective barriers may create intolerable states of tension in the intensely aspiring child—states that lead him to illegal activities. Such previously mentioned factors as physical handicap and intellectual insufficiency may be numbered among these obstacles. Additional barriers might include social unpopularity for reasons of appearance or personality, or membership in ethnic minorities against which members of the majority group have developed prejudiced attitudes and discriminatory social and economic practices. Certainly, in regard to the latter points, the frustrating effects of prejudice and discrimination upon the aspirations of a social minority are dramatically illustrated by the fact that rates of delinquency are much higher among Negroes than whites. "Thus, although Negroes represent about 10 percent of the total population of the Nation, they contribute nearly twice that much to the delinquency rate."[17]

In all such cases, the child, even if he belongs to the managerial or self-employed class, is likely to be at a disadvantage in the competitive struggle to attain relief from the pressure of his limitless aspirations. We must keep in mind that, as children grow, they begin more and more to anticipate their place in adult society, to test out their capacity for success in later life. Admittedly, while they are still in school, children do not compete for the identical criteria of success sought by their parents. But the school environment provides no shortage of dimensions of striving and indications of success that ape and symbolize the areas of aspiration, in pursuit of which the children will subsequently be devoting their adult energies. For example, grades in courses, class offices, memberships in fraternities or sororities, and participation in various extracurricular activities of the school are among the media through which the child can directly strive to pursue his aspirations for prestige and power. But academic and social successes in school also portend similar successes in college. And, since a college education has become so mandatory to the pursuit of most vocational objectives that children are encouraged to develop, successful graduation from college becomes a most important instrument for the pursuit of economic aspirations. In high school, and often years before, children begin to realize that their grades are omens of future success; and that present academic records may pay off, literally, in terms of future entrance into famous colleges whose graduates are likely to earn incomes higher than those received by graduates of less noted institutions.

Possessing an awareness of the relationship between his success in school and that which awaits him later in life, the aspiring child may be expected to put forth a great deal of effort to attain such criteria of ongoing success as are available to him in the school environment. Hence, the school becomes transformed into an arena for the child's version of the adult "rat race"; and the child who is not "making it" in this "rat race"—or not "making it" as much and as fast as his aspirations require—is likely to resort to whatever means he can use to "get ahead." The child whose intellectual limitations do not permit him to get the grades he wants, for example, may well be motivated to cheat during examinations. As the competition for college placement becomes keener, we may expect the rates of cheating to increase among children in high school and elementary school.

A child's sense of being blocked in the pursuit of his aspirations may often stem more from his subjective assessment of his performance than from any objective factor that may stand between him and that which he covets. For example, a child may have shown steady progress in his academic work through his years in elementary school and in junior high; in high school, however, he finds the intellectual competition to be greater than anything he has previously encountered. In addition to grades, he finds that a number of special prizes and awards are offered to children whose academic record surpasses all of the others in the school. As a result of this encounter with new competition and new criteria of attainment, the child may feel that his past efforts must be redoubled if he is to continue among the elite and if he is going to attain the levels of achievement that he must now reach in order to feel he is making satisfactory progress in the pursuit of his limitless aspirations for self-aggrandizement. However, despite his redoubled efforts, the child may fear that he will fall short of his mark. Under such conditions, even a brilliant child may be driven to cheat in order to insure his success.

But not all forms of delinquency stem from children who, frustrated in their aspirations, either resort to devious means of pursuing those aspirations or strike out in resentment against successful competitors. Some children may be led to illegal acts as a means of expressing their resentment against the very institution that serves as the social context of their failure. Some acts of vandalism against schools, for example, may be committed by children who have failed to attain those criteria of success that are promoted by the school.

Other illegal acts may be committed by children who are attempting to express contempt for the blatant hypocrisy of their parents who preach one set of values but practice another. Those children may have church-going parents whose Sunday piety is entirely contradicted by their avid pursuit of materialistic, self-seeking values during the rest of the week. Recognizing this discrepancy, the children may be unable to contain their resentment for parents whose daily lives debase the humanitarian values to which they may give ritualistic adherence once a week. And they may engage in acts of vandalism against the very building their parents have erected as a token gesture to values in which they do not sincerely believe.

Similarly, such children may wind up in juvenile court as "incorrigible," because they refuse to obey the authority of parents whose moral turpitude has lost them all genuine right to command respect. In the same vein, given the "double standard" of sexual morality that still prevails in the culture at large, some cases of "sexual delinquency" among girls may stem from their refusal to submit to codes of behavior whose ethical bases are inherently hypocritical and discriminatory.

In regard to sex differences in the rates of delinquency, court records show more than four times as many referrals for boys as for girls.[18] Assuming that males are still expected to be the chief pursuers of the conventional aspirations of our society—the chief strugglers for success—we may interpret the existing ratio as reflecting the results of the greater stress and greater frustrations to which boys are exposed in the course of pursuing the more intense aspirations that they are taught to possess.

Paradoxically, some children may appear in the statistics of juvenile delinquency because they take the values of *realization* seriously. If a teenager works too sincerely on behalf of racial equality in some states in this country, he may well be arrested and charged with the violation of a local ordinance. Surely, in such cases, the delinquency is in the law rather than in the behavior of the adolescent.

A final type of delinquency that may be mentioned concerns those children who have never committed themselves to any goals whose pursuit or expression might engage their energies over a lifetime of purposive activity. Such children may seek, through fleeting and sporadic emotional experiences, to fill the void created by a lack of adherence to any set of values that could imbue their lives with meaning. Children of this kind may engage in illegal acts for "kicks," for the momentary thrill that they derive from them. These children may have been reared in families whose parents never taught them to develop firm attachments to values of any sort. Consequently, their very aimlessness becomes an emotional burden to them; and they may seek to lighten this burden through the diversion of daring or criminal exploits.

The non-delinquent teenage "beatnik" may be similar to the foregoing type. He may have become repelled by the major conventional values of society—material gain, prestige, and power—without having found a strong substitute in the values of realization. Yet he may be sufficiently attracted to the latter values to express them passively, as an appreciator of the efforts of those who put them into practice. Lacking sufficient motivation to make their own contributions to the furtherance of the values of realization, these juvenile "beatniks" may at least refrain from illegal acts as a way of infusing their lives with meaning.

The Prevention of Juvenile Delinquency and the Values of Realization

Given *both* the conventional aspirations of our society and the obstacles that block their limitless pursuit, juvenile delinquency, like adult crime, is an inevitable outcome of the ordinary functioning of our social order. Under this formulation, the juvenile delinquent, again like his adult counterpart, may be regarded either as a model of the very values to which his society devotes the bulk of its energies and resources or as a victim of those values.

Certainly, the measures likely to reduce the rates of delinquency do not lie in the direction of increasing opportunities for more and more children to pursue the values that give rise to delinquency in the first place. Yet this is precisely the kind of recommendation contained in one of the most influential approaches to juvenile delinquency that has been published in recent years, *Delinquency and Opportunity*.[19]

It may be quite true, as the authors of that book suggest, that the opening up of job opportunities may reduce the anger harbored by many children in the classes of workers and unemployed workers, who are severely hampered in the pursuit of the conventional materialistic values that they, no less than children of more favored classes, have made their own. But we already know how relative is the experience of success, how quickly people adapt to their attainments when they are motivated by the limitless quality of the aspirations nurtured by our culture, how rates of delinquency rise more rapidly in eras of prosperity than in those of economic stability. If one could somehow magically guarantee that—having created the initial opportunity for him to rise above the material conditions of his birth—the aspiring juvenile will continue to move upward as quickly and as extensively as his unleashed aspirations demand, one might find the logic of the thesis advanced by Cloward and Ohlin somewhat more compelling. However, such guarantees are patently impossible to offer; and the aspiring individual, however sanguine his initial opportunities, must soon face the constraints inherent in our contemporary bureaucratic structures of work and the stress of competition that bears in upon him from his aspiring fellows. No matter what his initial opportunities may have been, the aspiring individual rapidly runs into obstacles in the path of his constant advancement. And when he hits those snags, his reactions to them may be all the more resentful because his aspirations had been elevated by his earlier opportunities; and he may be all the more vulnerable to the employment of illegal or devious means of surmounting the obstacles that he encounters after his initial success.

But its sheer impracticality and *its likelihood of exacerbating the problem of delinquency* are not the only arguments that may be raised against the views of Cloward and Ohlin. From the standpoint of our long-range functioning as a decent social order, their formulation may also be criticized because *it takes for granted and presumes to promote the very values that sow strife and antagonism in our population.* Yet the remedies for our problems of crime and delinquency are to be found, if we are serious about finding them, in quite the opposite set of values from those implicitly advocated by proponents of increased "opportunity." But this opposing set of values, the values of realization, cannot be properly implemented within the hierarchy of invidious distinction that exists both within and outside of our bureaucracies of work. What is needed is a transformation not only in our basic system of values but also in our socio-economic system; not only in the goals we teach our children but also in the means by which they may, as adults, realize those goals.

7

Sanity and Love Besieged

EQUATING CRIME with injustice, we have seen that ours is a criminal society. For the very conduct of our economy requires acts of injustice; and our socio-economic hierarchy of invidious distinction provides injustice with structural support. And if we define madness as alienation from the realities of one's being, we also have reason to conclude that our society is basically mad. All who pursue the values of aggrandizement are bound to be more or less estranged from their humanity, since such a pursuit sets them upon the megalomaniacal quest of becoming more than men can be. Because the values of aggrandizement are the ones most strongly held by the majority of our people, madness is as characteristic of our social order as is crime.

Madness, like crime, takes two forms: legal and illegal. As in the case of crime, the differentiation between legal and illegal insanity reflects the hypocritical imposition of a double standard of moral evaluation upon essentially similar behaviors. We commit to mental institutions some persons who, without benefit of ministerial training, fancy themselves to be spokesmen of God. Yet we give great deference to thousands of clergymen of all faiths who hold themselves forth as missionaries of the Lord. Similarly, anyone who proclaims himself to be the True Messiah is likely to be a candidate for a psychiatric ward. But our dominant religion was founded by a self-styled Messiah; and the psychiatrist who is put in charge of the "new" Messiah may well be a devout follower of the old one.

Nor are the contradictions in our criteria of insanity confined to the spheres of religion or mysticism. On the contrary, they extend to the most trivial as well as the most vital areas of public concern —even to matters that pertain to our survival. On the mundane side, we are curiously loath to tolerate the demented conceits of persons who, for example, are inclined to use parks or streets as stages for the enactment of maudlin dramas of themselves; persons who, with the aid of bizarre clothes—including, perhaps, military ribbons and decorations purchased at a pawn shop—strut about in vainglorious splendor; and as they harangue us about their fictitious accomplishments, we may wonder how long it will be before someone complains to the police about them, at which time they are likely to be escorted to the nearest madhouse. However, the millionaire who displays an identical proclivity may be regarded as a quaint eccentric; and if it is his caprice to glorify himself by having a Venetian Ball at his estate—during which he is transported to his guests as a Doge of antiquity, an authentically attired gondolier propelling him across his private lake under the light of a specially constructed electric moon—his antics are gushingly described in the society pages of the newspapers. Far from being reported as a lunatic, he is presented to his fellow citizens as the most charming and praiseworthy of men.

Lastly, consider the pathetic case of an individual who, as part of an attempt to regard himself as a personage of inestimable importance, harbors the unwarranted belief that foreign agents are conspiring to trap and kill him. If he begins to act upon his delusion by threatening to harm innocent persons, he is properly perceived to be not only out of touch with reality but also a danger to the community. But how do we regard the military strategists who concentrate all their intelligence and knowledge upon the single objective of devising offenses and defenses against every nation that could conceivably be our enemy at some time in the future? Or the scientists who devote their talents to the contrivance of increasingly dreadful means of destroying such potential enemies? Or the experts in psychological warfare who systematically imagine the most effective ways of sowing panic among other nations under a variety of hypothetical conditions?

Instead of censuring such persons as incipient menaces to mankind, we shower them with awards. We may even go so far as to avow that these conjurers of death are the best guardians of peace in the world, the bulwarks behind which we can take shelter from all who would presume to plot our destruction. In this way, we inflate their egoism and exacerbate whatever megalomaniacal tendencies they originally brought to their work.

But certainly, even if we restrict ourselves entirely to the legally recognized forms of insanity, we cannot deny the endemic madness of our society. More than half of the beds in all our hospitals are occupied by mental patients,[1] most of whom are diagnosed as psychotic or, to use a more generic term, insane. In a recently conducted and nationally representative survey, approximately one out of every five American adults reported that he had, at some point in his life, felt himself on the brink of a "nervous breakdown."[2]

Crime and madness are not mutually exclusive modes of behavior. The paranoiac who is alienated from the reality of his limits as a human being may eventually be led, by the extremity of that alienation, to behave unjustly toward his fellow men—to hurt and, hence, to commit crimes against them. And we have special legal categories and penal codes for statutory crimes committed by persons who are also judged to be officially insane. At the same time, some conditions that psychiatry considers its province involve behaviors that are proscribed by law. Sexual perversion is one such condition; and the homosexual, voyeur, or exhibitionist who is caught in the act of accommodating his symptom is liable to criminal prosecution. Psychiatry, on the other hand, is inclined to regard such persons as emotionally disturbed, although psychiatrists may differ with respect to their theories about the nature of this disturbance. Psychiatrists of the orthodox Freudian persuasion[3] tend to regard perversions as manifestations of unresolved psychological conflicts that first arose very early in the pervert's life, assuming that adult patterns of sexual behavior continue to reflect the interpersonal difficulties and upsets an individual suffered in his relationship with his parents. Other psychiatrists, of a more sociological predilection, have postulated that the pressures involved in playing adult roles in our competitive society may account for some cases of male homosexuality, if not other varieties of perversion. Clara Thompson has hypothesized[4] that some men may retreat into homosexuality as a refuge against the responsibilities that married men and fathers must necessarily assume if they are to live up to our culturally defined standards of masculine maturity.

The so-called psychopathic personality[5] is another example of the individual who may be regarded as criminal by the law but as disordered by psychiatry. Psychopathic personalities are those individuals who seem capable of hurting or manipulating others without the slightest moral hesitation, without the slightest qualm of conscience. Such persons are often quite intelligent and charming, although they may also be dull and surly. When their misdemeanors and felonies bring them to the notice of the courts, they are treated as criminals; and since full foreknowledge of the destructive implications of their actions is a legal criterion of sanity and, hence, culpability, these psychopaths generally cannot qualify as being legally insane. Still, Cleckley, one of the leading authorities on psychopathic personalities, regards them as possessing a very subtle form of insanity, which "consists of an unawareness, and a persistent lack of ability to become aware, of what the most important experiences of life mean to others."[6] But this blunting of feelings for others is universally and implicitly encouraged by the institutionalized injustices of our society, as well as by the priority that it gives to the values of aggrandizement. Since these social forces discourage both the development of genuine empathy for others and the commitment to humanitarian values, they may be expected to increase the numbers of psychopathic personalities —or, at the very least, the numbers of individuals with strong tendencies toward that syndrome. Alienation from others is but the interpersonal manifestation of alienation from oneself. And if an individual has lost touch with his own humanity—if he manipulates himself for his own greater glory—why should he hesitate to use others for the same purpose?

But, after all, as widespread as it may be in our culture, insanity is distributed in varying amounts throughout our population. Americans thus vary in the extent to which they are alienated from themselves. And insanity *per se* is only *one* of the psychological conditions that bespeak the poor state of our nation's mental condition. Indeed, when asked, virtually one out of every seven American adults has admitted that he at least once felt sufficiently distressed about his emotional problems to seek out the help of someone he thought competent to bring him relief—a clergyman, physician, or some other professional specialist in the field of mental health.[7]

Naturally, the variety of conditions that may be listed under the broad category of mental disorder could include ailments that are quite independent of social forces. Organic deterioration of the brain, for example, may be the immediately precipitating factor in the abrupt downfall of an individual's usual pattern of behavior. Even among such cases, of course, societal forces may have played an important etiological role. Thus, damage to the brain that results from warfare or acute deficiencies in the diet of an impoverished group of people can scarcely be considered independent of social circumstances. And, when millions of people become alcoholics,[8] the statistics of organic psychosis stemming from the excessive use of alcohol are properly comprehended only in the light of the social determinants that stimulated the increasing use of alcohol in the first place. Nevertheless, we can at least theoretically conceive of organic—perhaps even genetic—predispositions to behavioral aberration, factors that might cut across cultural and sub-cultural influences.

It must also be admitted that the very process of socialization—of inducing the child to become a member of society, taking on its values, attitudes, manners, and skills—may be terribly upsetting for those whose native temperaments do not quite mesh with the schedule and the map of behavioral development that their culture lays down for them to follow. From this point of view, we might expect a certain number—however small—of persons to become disturbed in the most wholesome of societies.

In Eden itself, fortuitous but distressing events may jar an otherwise happy life: accidents, illnesses, and the death of loved ones, events whose impact may so unnerve individuals of frail constitutions that their emotional equilibrium is very difficult to restore. And even in a society deeply committed to the values of realization, many people would suffer personal upsets from failure to express those values as fully as they might wish—because of a lack of talent or because their commitments exceed their capacities. But, assuming that instances of emotional distress would occur in the best of all possible worlds, we cannot thereby feel justified in concluding that our present society is a harbinger of the millennium. On the contrary, the volume of our most severe mental casualties alone—those who are so incapacitated that they must be cared for entirely by others—constitutes as fearsome a national blight as do our rates of statutory crime.

Actually, alienation from oneself is likely to be experienced as considerably less painful than the anxiety, guilt, despair, loneliness, and emotional conflict that are so commonplace among contemporary Americans. In fact, alienation may not even be noticed by the alienated individual for the very reason that he tends to assume it to be a natural state of affairs. For, if he has learned to crave aggrandizement, why should he regard his own megalomania—of whatever intensity—as anything but a "normal," indeed, a most desirable condition? Hence, we can witness the paradoxical result that the most megalomaniacal of the socially acceptable insane are likely to be as self-congratulatory as the most successful of the authorized criminals. We can now see that success in legalized crime—in entrepreneurship or management, for example—tends to heighten the individual's degree of legalized insanity, alienating him further and further from his human limits and propelling him further and further in the direction of super-human grandiosity.

In statutory crime, the destructive strains of our society erupt in behaviors that merely caricature the interpersonal manipulation and injury that people are obliged to inflict upon each other if they wish to pursue aggrandizement as participants in the ordinary functioning of our economy. But many Americans, however self-seeking they may be, still have too much respect for our laws—despite their gross injustice—to violate them knowingly. Other Americans may simply be too frightened of arrest to break our laws, although they do not really respect them. There are other citizens who, while possessing no such respect or fear, are too deeply committed to humanitarianism to do injury to others will-fully and consistently—that is, above and beyond, as it were, the harm they are implicitly called upon to do in the course of their regular economic duties.

For whatever reasons they forego statutory crime as a tool of their ambitions, those who fail—or who perceive themselves to be failing—in their pursuit of aggrandizement must find some outlet for their tensions. For some such persons, unrestrained delusions of grandeur and flights of pseudo-euphoria may be appealing ways of seeking to overcome impediments of reality; and, if such com-pensatory devices fail them, these people may lapse into troughs of stuporous and vegetative withdrawal, their processes of percep-tion and powers of reasoning vulnerable to rapid deterioration. On the other hand, many Americans who are chagrined about the crimes of everyday life that they commit on behalf of their un-relenting ambitions—their lying, cheating, and duplicity—pay for their derelictions in anxiety and guilt, in nervous agitation and dulling depression, and in a veritable catalogue of psychosomatic complaints, such as ulcers, asthma, and colitis.

Loneliness is another result of our extremely individualistic and grasping aspirations. In our smiling combat with our competitors, we are constrained from being completely open and forthright. Instead, we water our secret ambitions with private tears, and we strive to be cool and composed and light-hearted as we interact with those who covet what we covet. At the same time, our preoccupation with our own aspirations renders us quite oblivious to the sufferings and needs of those with whom we come into daily contact. Consequently, we may begin to feel isolated and cut off from others, victimized by the lack of genuine trust and warmth that the prudent cultivation of our personal aggrandizement has necessitated.

Yes, the worst casualty of our social order is love; perhaps because it is the most fragile, if most precious, of human emotions. And it is crushingly sad, in this abundant land, to realize that our desperate cries of lovelessness are drowned by the hysterical songs of love that blare forth from our radios, television sets, movie screens, and juke boxes. And the more we insist in song and saga that love is everywhere, that we are a nation of perennial romance, that the ardor of our affections is boundless, the more difficult it is for us to face the reality of our emotional aridity.

Our need to give and accept love is very great; yet so is our fear of lasting intimacy, of binding attachments to others. For such relationships conflict with the unencumbered and limitless pursuit of our self-centered motives. Nor, assuming that others are similarly egoistic, are we disposed to entrust them with our innermost vulnerabilities, much less our seething ambitions. It is probable, therefore, that the loneliness of their genial detachment from each other is largely responsible for the willingness of many Americans to spend a great deal of money on individual psychotherapy.[9] For the psychotherapist is paid not only to listen wholeheartedly but also to accept and hold in the strictest confidence everything that his patient feels he must share with at least one person in the world in order to relieve his oppressive feeling of isolation. The psychotherapist may often perform the same role for an American that a friend performs for a European.

Inevitably, therefore, the social graces of Americans have frequently mystified foreign observers, who may be more inclined, at least in regard to the communication of affection, to say what they mean, to mean what they say, and to accept responsibility for both their actions and their words. As compared to their European[10] counterparts, Americans of all socio-economic groupings seem much less reserved, but are emotionally more inaccessible. It is not uncommon for an American tourist—outwardly buoyant but inwardly starved for intimacy—to regale a stranger, a fellow passenger on a journey in a European country, with stories of his family, capping his catharsis with a display of photographs of his wife and children. The same American may also invite his traveling companion to address him by his given name—and use an equally familiar mode of address in return. By the time the trip is over, the American may seem exceedingly jovial, as if he had been conversing with an old friend. Yet, he may bid his companion farewell and stride off on his business without any thought whatever of continuing their relationship, even if considerations of time and space fully permitted it. If he does assert such an interest, the American may simply be making an empty comment that he has no intention of remembering.

Similarly, Americans are very liberal in their use of the word "friend." They may, in fact, invoke it when referring to almost anyone they happen to know, effectively obliterating any distinction between the connotations of friendship and mere acquaintanceship. Thus, it may take a long time for a European to learn that his American "friend" regards as *genuine* friends only those whom he describes as "close, intimate, personal friends." And, if the European is a member of the opposite sex, it may take him even longer to realize that the fact that his friend kisses, hugs, and fondles him is no necessary indication of either the depth of her feelings for him or the extent to which she is prepared to go any further by way of physical demonstrations of affectionate feeling.

But the fact that Americans are familiar with their own contraditions and make allowances for them in their interactions with each other is little solace to them. It is all very well for a boy to know that the girl who kisses him goodnight may merely be performing a ritual she is expected to perform with all the boys who take her out. Still, that boy might wish to know whether or not there was any affection in her kiss—any "close, intimate, personal feeling" that expressed her reaction to him as a unique human being. Similarly, a girl may realize that a boy's effusive compliments may simply represent a "line" he feels it necessary to spin in order to draw her into a seductive glorification of his own prowess. But she may hope, all the while, that he or someone else will one day speak to her in words that contain more love than flattery.

Similar instances could be given of the myriad of essentially ritualistic parties and social gatherings at which Americans "entertain" each other, repay their "social obligations," "make contacts," or cultivate "good impressions." At these joyless affairs, everyone concerned may be perfectly aware of their forced cordiality or feigned show of interest in each other, and of the vanity that compels them all to participate in such hypocritical antics. And yet, even as their smiles stick to their lips, the "celebrants" at these occasions might be hoping for a moment of real attention from others, for a flash of genuine concern about themselves in the eyes of others, for the courage to reveal openly that they are dying of emotional suffocation.

Undoubtedly, our enormous concern with our ambitions, with the profoundly demanding task of continually aggrandizing ourselves, cripples our ability to love. And, among the victims of that crippling are the very persons who are closest to us: our spouses and children. Indeed, it is just because our closest relationships are presumed to be based upon love that our "loved ones" expect the most love of us, just as we expect it of them. Yes, it is within the hearth of the family—if nowhere else in the society—that Americans look for the give and take of love whose warmth need not be lessened or restrained by any consideration of ambition or

self-defense; where the tactics of successful competition have neither place nor function. In fact, speaking of function, the principal
function now accorded the modern American family by some
sociologists[11] is the psychological one of providing its members
with emotionally fulfilling relationships.

And yet, what is the fate of marital love in contemporary America? The statistics of divorce give us a clue: The latest census,
taken in 1960, revealed that, while 1,523,000 marriages were
performed, 393,000 divorces were granted;[12] and countless others who refrain from divorce for religious or economic reasons
remain tied together in unremitting lovelessness. The upsetting
implications of divorce and loveless marriage for children affected
by them are obvious, as are the implications for the rejected or
semi-rejected children of parents who, while they may remain
together in somewhat compatible marriages, become too involved
in their own ambitions to give their children more than a fleeting
gift of love. Since love breeds love, the absence of love in a child's
experience is very likely to undermine his own confidence in himself; and it also tends to make it difficult for such a child to love
others. Hence, a vicious cycle is established, unloved children
becoming loveless parents.

Love, Marriage, and Aggrandizement: An Impossible Mixture

Society—every society—stipulates an ironical sacrifice for marriage: that the spouses sufficiently attenuate their original love for
each other to permit them to perform the roles that accompany
the attainment of marital status. Cultures differ in the extent of
this sacrifice; the one implicitly required of married couples in our
society is so great that it often consumes the marriage itself.

Typically, in our society, the married man is expected to expend
a considerable portion of his daily life in the process of "making a
living." By and large, this process still occupies most American
husbands for at least eight hours a day, five days each week. For

her part, the American wife is typically expected to devote no less a share of her life to the chores of homemaking and child-rearing. Many millions of American wives also work part-time or full-time at jobs outside their homes in order to supplement their husbands' incomes or in order to pursue vocational aspirations of their own; and millions of other American women voluntarily participate in community organizations in addition to their wifely duties.

Expectations of this kind are not foisted on the couple at their wedding ceremony. On the contrary, most children in all cultures are reared in such a manner as to convey the soundness and moral excellence of the social roles that men and women are supposed to play when they are married. Owing to this early and protracted learning, the potential husband and wife arrive at marriage with commonly held conceptions of their marital roles. Of course, members of our different socio-economic classes and castes may hold somewhat differing ideas about the proper roles of husband and wife. Nevertheless, certain expectations—for example, that the husband should engage in some form of remunerative employ-ment and that the wife should have the principal responsibility for child-rearing and housekeeping—seem to run throughout virtually all of our socio-economic groupings.

Since most couples enter marriage with the clear anticipation— indeed, the desired prospect—of diverting large amounts of time, energy, and affection from their relationship to other activities, objectives, and persons, they are unlikely, at the outset, to be concerned about the possible consequences of such diversions for their marriage. Instead, they may throw themselves busily, even gleefully, into the challenge of performing their roles with the utmost success. And they may become so enamored with the pur-suit of this success that they fail to notice, for some years, that the fervor and scintillation of their pre-marital love is seeping from their relationship. They do not yet miss the savor of their initial love for each other, for they are relishing the taste of their growing competence in the worldly affairs of adulthood. Indeed, they may remain quite unaware of the steady decline of their exchange of affection for each other as long as they are inflated by public acclaim; by the diluted and often false expressions of affection that are contained in or read into the handshake, the pat on the back from an employer or supervisor, the promotion or the award. Nor is it easier for many husbands and wives to realize that their mates can only share vicariously in these social figments of affection; and that no amount of vicariousness can fill a mate's need for the soft and tender touch of his or her beloved.

In time, however, the symptoms of affectional deprivation crop out in a chronic laugh, a shade too shrill and highly pitched; in the involuntary furrowing of a tense brow; in the pulsating movement of facial muscles in the clenched jaws of a restive dreamer; in fingers clawed red from scratching nameless itching; in the furtive weeping of a man whose eyes fill up—unexpectedly, frighteningly —during a mawkishly sentimental movie; in periods of gray emptiness that descend upon a woman while she is shopping for a new dress.

The occurrence of these symptoms is not always followed by insight into their cause. On the contrary, whole legions of loveless husbands and wives troop daily to their ministers, psychotherapists, and fellow sufferers for comfort that only the giving and receiving of heterosexual love can really provide. And although their potential cure resides at home with them, they search futilely in every relationship but their own marriage for the balm they need.

For some spouses, however, the source of their distress becomes increasingly apparent as their years of marriage pass. Still, in correctly identifying the general problem, one is not necessarily led to an entirely adequate differential diagnosis. For example, each partner may suppose that the other is not giving him enough attention, nor being as kind, considerate, and physically demonstrative as he used to be. And, of course, both partners are correct in their mutual recriminations, which are seldom explicitly stated because of a desire to avoid the humiliation of begging for love; to avoid the risk of being openly rebuffed or the possibility of inflicting pain upon the presumably unsuspecting partner. Sometimes, in addition, the secretly aggrieved partners may feel too grateful for the love already received from each other, too guilty for their own growing indifference, or too proud of the image of their happy marriage of former days to bring their dissatisfactions to light and reveal the nakedness of their need for love.

Such people are apt to sink into the limp posture of unuttered desperation, going through the motions of marriage but feeling condemned to a life without love. In some cases, their resignation may be accompanied by the dubious gratifications of imagined martyrdom. In other cases, however, even the illusion of martyrdom cannot be created or sustained; and the loveless spouses come to feel increasingly apathetic, lonely, and dead. Under such conditions, the marriage is shorn of its original verve and meaning; and the partners may maintain it only out of a sense of moral obligation (to each other or to their children), out of fear of social ostracism or out of a cold terror of being alone in a world of indifference, cruelty, and ambiguity. Finally, in still other cases, a marriage grown loveless remains cemented, nevertheless, by the passion of mutual hatred, into which the initial love of the mates for each other has been transformed by the black chemistry of unassuaged disappointment.

For many persons, resignation to the soured relationship seems more horrendous than any consequence of its dissolution. These persons have too much sensitivity, too much respect for their own humanity, too great a desire to live—to endure the waking death of a marriage without love. Consequently, they prefer to break their moral scruples and jeopardize their emotional security—to inflict pain on themselves, their spouses, and their children—rather than remain accomplices to an impossible lie. Separation and divorce become, for these people, constructive alternatives to the destructiveness of their marital status quo. Or they may begin, while still married to their original spouse, to establish adulterous liaisons in search of a more loving and a more lovable partner.

In some cases, divorce may be the healthiest course of action—not only for the estranged husband and wife but also for their children. Some marriages may have been a mistake from the outset, since the spouses did not really love each other before they married. But for those who entered marriage with love, divorce may reflect a premature surrender to fatigue and bitterness, a failure to mobilize and direct their energies toward the renewal of the love that they had given each other for years, the love with which they had sustained each other in facing the demands of their marital roles.

Most of all, the aggrieved spouse in search of a new love is likely to forget, if he had ever been aware of the fact in the first place, that it is one thing to carry on an extra-marital romance that is uncluttered and untaxed by the baggage and burdens of familial responsibilities and social roles—an affair that can be kept pure and pristine, entirely reserved for love—but quite another thing to manage to preserve and nurture the flame of love while, at the same time, coping with the responsibilities and roles of marriage and family. The adulterous lover might often be chasing merely an illusion of contrast that, surely, could not remain impervious, after remarriage, to the same social stresses, the same pressures of insatiable ambitions, the same constancy of routine as dispelled the magic of love between his first spouse and himself.

No marriage—however sanguine the emotional auspices of its beginning, however well-intentioned its participants—can continue to be host to love unless both partners have the will and the consciousness to make it so. Not only in our society but in all societies does the social order conspire against love in marriage. True and mature love is the most heroic enemy of the established order of things, since its proper cultivation and maintenance requires a large measure of disengagement from the values of aggrandizement toward whose pursuit most societies are ideologically dedicated and socially organized.

Love, quite naturally, shrinks from megalomania, which is its antithesis. For love is the giving of ourselves fully to other human beings, and the giving and receiving of love is so inherently gratifying, so patently the be-all and end-all of human experience, so reassuring of the meaning and value of life, that those who know it cannot be easily persuaded to turn from it to other purposes.

But the requirements of sheer subsistence, of course, demand some participation in the economic activities of society; and the rearing of the children of love draws away additional energies and feelings that married lovers might otherwise have available for each other. Yet, if one's work is intrinsically creative or undertaken for humanitarian or equalitarian objectives, it is not antagonistic to love. It extends love to others, albeit in less intense forms than it is expressed between the pair of lovers; and much the same is true of the love that parents give their children.

Neither work nor child-rearing have to be destructive of marital love. What is so destructive is the intrusion upon those activities of the values of aggrandizement. When work becomes not a celebration of love but a channel of self-aggrandizement, and when the rearing of children becomes not an expression of love but a vicarious pursuit of egoism, the relationship between husband and wife is placed in jeopardy. Under these conditions, each of the spouses is bound to look outside the relationship—and far, far into the limitless future—for indications that their individual conceptions of self are constantly growing in importance; for more wealth, more power, more prestige—from their work, from their children, from the adornment of their homes and persons. At last, the insatiability of aggrandizement insidiously drives husband and wife to expect egoistic worship from each other; having long since taken their initial love for granted, they proceed to bury it alive under the tombstones built by their vanity.

Megalomania demolishes their marriage, just as love had created it. Yet, because even the most megalomaniacal of persons finds it difficult to live without love, the couple may begin, subsequent to the process of disaffection, to scan their interpersonal horizons for new partners. And, if and when they find them, they may well repeat the same heartbreaking cycle, their newly evoked love giving way imperceptibly to the inroads of their aggrandizing motives. Thus, the problems of divorce, like those of crime and mental disorder, can be understood not merely as a personal tragedy to those who contribute to the statistics but also as a predictable consequence of our society's system of values.

8

Palliatives in Purgatory

DESPITE THE BRUTALITY and madness that engulfs them, contemporary Americans find it very difficult to comprehend the social sources of their personal malaise. The more they surround themselves with material symbols of their aggrandizement, the harder it is for them to see why so many of their children should be delinquent and disturbed, why they themselves should be so often distraught, edgy, and joyless.

Actually, we have always been so convinced that the material road to limitless aggrandizement also leads straight to salvation that our puzzlement is quite understandable. After all, the majority of Americans still accept the premise that personal progress in the accumulation of wealth will yield increasing contentment as its by-product; that there is scarcely any problem that cannot be happily resolved by money.[1] And yet, somehow, the two sleek cars in our garages, our sparkling homes in the tidy suburb, the acquisition of gadgets that we bring into our dens, and the size of our wardrobes seem unable, for long, to fill the emptiness of our days or calm our fretful discontents, which growl within us like beasts at bay.

We tell ourselves that we are a nation to be admired. And so, indeed, we are: let there be no doubt about that. Our economy, unjust as it is, has yielded an abundance whose extent is unparalleled among countries as large as ours. And our high standard of living can be matched by some of our less tangible benefits. We enjoy as much freedom of political and personal expression as can be found in any society as massive as our own; and there still exists here a great concern for the welfare of the individual and a social atmosphere that is definitely democratic, although the values of realization are not as influential as those of aggrandizement.

Still, even as we congratulate ourselves, our voices grow hoarse from cumulative muscular tension; our eyes blink wearily from chronic insomnia; we clutch at aches in our heads, hearts, and backs. And when we finish the inventory of our good fortune, we cast a furtive glance at our wives, dozing before our television sets, and wonder what has happened to our relationships with them. Wherein have we—or they—failed? Or, we reach, with somewhat tremulous hands, for a Martini to help us relax from the strain of the discourse upon our blessings. And as we take our first, long sip of the drink, our relief may be sullied by the awareness that we have tended, these days, to become rather heavily dependent upon the crutch of alcohol. Is this a sign of incipient alcoholism? Or, perhaps, we suddenly spring to our feet in a recoil of anxiety as the telephone rings later in the evening. Has our teenage son or daughter, who had not kept a promise to call earlier in the day, gotten into some sort of trouble with the gang of rowdies who seem so reckless and irresponsible of late?

Yes, questions of this kind hound us in all the comfort and material progress of our days. And it is just *because* we have so much, just *because* we can find no material basis for our crippling tensions and the inner void of our lives, that we are at such a loss to identify and diagnose the causes of our pathology. How much easier it would be to pin the blame for our problems on blatant material deficiencies! Such an explanation would jibe nicely with our existing misconceptions; and while it might not suggest a specific personal solution for us, at least it would point toward the general direction in which such a solution could be found. If we could assume that lack of money is at the root of our misery, we could try to overcome that lack; and, if we were not able to do it on our own, within the ground rules of our present economy, we might feel it wise to band together with those in similar straits in order to bring about the necessary improvement in our common economic circumstances.

The continued existence of widespread poverty and unemployment in our society does suggest that the general welfare of many millions of Americans could, in fact, be bettered with a marked improvement in their material conditions. But the prototypical quandary of our society is seen among the majority of Americans whose economic circumstances cannot be described as dire, although they may feel relatively deprived in comparison with more affluent socio-economic groups. Since most Americans cannot put the blame for their discontent upon material hardship, in an absolute sense, they face a dilemma that intensifies their anguish. They are led to conclude that—in spite of every evidence of their own demoralization and that of their fellows—they are living in the best of all conceivable societies. Hence, they may be smitten by guilt and humiliation, because they have failed to feel as happy as their system of values leads them to conclude they should be; and they may throw themselves all the more strenuously into the task of persuading themselves how lucky they are to be Americans.

Nor do our political leaders really help us when they insist[2] that our society is superior to Soviet society. Surely, comparison with the Soviet Union is not the only frame of reference within which the value of our own society can be assessed. Yet, by thus unduly limiting the context of our evaluation of ourselves, comparisons of this sort not only reflect a poverty of imagination but also set up an alternative whose rejection leaves our problems unsolved. Even if we agree, as it is by no means difficult to do, that we prefer our present social order, with all its defects, to the Soviet way of life, we have no reason to cease our search for basic social, political, and economic changes that might vastly improve not only the plight of our people but that of the Russian people as well.

Americans who find it impossible to criticize the fundamental institutions of their own society may place the onus of their dissatisfaction upon the idiosyncratic vicissitudes of their personal upbringing; or they may search vigilantly for scapegoats to whom they can attribute the fact that Americans are rapidly falling apart and producing spiralling rates of crime and insanity. It is possible to locate a host of such scapegoats within our society itself; and to proceed to condemn them without ever realizing that they are not only symptoms of our social order but inter-related ones at that. For example, reduction of parental discipline[3] may be marked as the culprit behind our dramatic rates of juvenile delinquency; yet, whoever puts forth such a "theory" fails to recognize that such discipline is less likely to be administered when the father's ambitions take him out of the home in pursuit of his own aggrandizement, giving him little time even to converse with his children, much less to show them love or disapprove their violations of justice. As long as the father, in the course of his own strivings— in his personal example—shows that he is ready to commit acts of injustice to further his ambitions, his efforts at moral education at home are likely to be vitiated by his own manifest hypocrisy. Unfortunately, parents are also increasingly constrained against implanting the values of realization—which alone contain the seeds of decency in human relations—for fear of reducing the child's chances of successfully pursuing the values of aggrandizement. For the more the child is constrained by his ethical scruples and his commitment to the values of realization, the less free is he to do whatever may later be opportune for him to do in acquiring money, prestige, or power. Finally, by looking to their own children for vicarious success in the pursuit of aggrandizement, parents often convey the fact that they consider the values of realization to be infinitely less important than the values of aggrandizement.

The upsetting ramifications of our own way of life may also lead those unable to acknowledge them to look for the source of their problems in the arena of international affairs. Competing forms of government—especially communistic ones—can be singled out as instigators of disturbance within our own. And any movement toward change within our own society—such as the demand of Negroes for greater social, political, and economic justice—may be branded as a threat, inspired by alien philosophies, to the presumably hallowed state of our status quo. Thus, a number of ideological rationalizations are available for Americans who cannot bear to admit that the wellsprings of their personal sufferings and anxieties inhere in the very nature of their society; that the torments besetting them are not foreign to that society, but, for all its admitted virtues, intrinsic to its dominant values and its fundamental socio-economic structure.

Palliative Platitudes

One of the principal palliatives to which Americans can turn in their unabating distress consists of shibboleths, however worn or meaningless. Neither our political parties nor our media of communication show any reluctance to repeat them. On the contrary, our politicians, journalists, advertising men, and script writers pour forth enough syrup to dull the senses of any one who has the slightest wish to sweeten the bitterness of his life with inane platitudes. Indeed, a person would have to be extremely ingenious to avoid exposure to the sticky flow of homey reassurance injected—free of charge—into so much of what is to be found in our newspapers and magazines, over our radios and television sets. Over and over again, the distraught and troubled citizen is told that we are the envy of all people; that no people anywhere have as good a life as we have here; that ours is a land especially endowed by God with abundance, peace, and harmony; that we are a united and indomitable people; that the future contains nothing but inestimable vistas of happiness for each and every one of us; that our past is glorious beyond measure; that our might is invincible and our right unquestionable; and that we are the friendliest and coziest group in all the wide world.

Yes, both those who form our opinions and those who seek to benefit from the opinions thus formed are eager to have us believe that our life in this land and at this time is nothing short of an incredible piece of good luck; that we have no cause whatsoever to complain, no legitimate recriminations against our social order; that nobody except a crackpot or a subversive agent of a hostile and jealous foreign power would ever suggest that our society is in urgent need of alteration.

In offering the public this pap, our publicists and politicians do not hesitate to draw upon all the enticements to superhumanity that have found favor in our society. Nationalistic and religious feelings are freely evoked, the individual being implicitly invited to identify himself with the grandiosity of God and the State. Often, the two concepts are welded into a joint invitation, the listener being given to understand that his endorsement of the status quo would advance his megalomania on both fronts.

It is noteworthy that even the monstrousness of President Kennedy's assassination failed to shock our most responsible and respected political leaders and analysts into uttering full truths about the dilemmas of our society. Instead, while sounding high alarms and pointing the accusing finger of guilt at all of us, those who best eulogized the late President, who sought to put his murder in an honest social perspective, stopped short of complete candor.[4] They rightly declared that an atmosphere of lawlessness encourages crime; that the American people seem, somehow, to have lost some of their traditional respect for justice and order; that the selfishness and egoism that are rampant in the country implicitly sanction willful acts of injustice. However, having properly indicted the whole population as implicit accomplices to the crime, our preceptors fell strangely silent, as if that were all that could be said about the matter; as if their moral flagellation would spur the American people to resolve, henceforth, to be more just and less self-seeking than they had been before Mr. Kennedy was shot.

But criminality is woven into the very tapestry of our society, since no one can participate in our economic system without committing gross acts of injustice. And our values of aggrandizement just as inevitably stimulate egoistic megalomania. So, when Americans are exhorted to be more just and more sane, more humanitarian and less selfish, they may well be puzzled about how to put those exhortations into practice. For justice and sanity require the buttressing of values and institutions that are clearly and unequivocally consonant with them. And, since our leading values and institutions are diametrically opposed to those humane ends, their effects and implications must be openly articulated in any sincere and realistic attempt at moral reform. Unfortunately, however, such a candid articulation was not voiced by those who would raise the question of the ethical stature of our people, who would hold out Mr. Kennedy's assassination as the basis for the beginning of a genuine change in the ways in which Americans treat each other.

Despite their minority status, the values of realization are not dead in this country. And we should be thankful for that. By invoking those values in a time of crisis, one may succeed somewhat, if only for a short while, in inducing people to give them greater priority in their daily behavior. And, it must be admitted that eulogies are not the most appropriate media for a thorough analysis of our social difficulties. Nevertheless, no enduring alteration in our prevailing moral atmosphere will be possible short of an alteration of the systems of value and invidious distinction that make flagrant immorality an integral part of our way of life. Those who—learned or not, informed or not, powerful or not—disregard that fact, are bound to be disappointed in the long-range impact of condemnatory speeches that chastise our symptoms without illuminating their social origins. If anything, such speeches function primarily as passing palliatives: we may temporarily expiate the guilt we feel for our complicity in the inherent injustice of our social order, while neglecting to propose the ways in which we might act to create a social order in which justice may be less beleaguered than it is now.

The Stupefaction of Canned Entertainment

Many commentators have lamented the crassness, vulgarity, and mediocrity of the bulk of our television shows, movies, and radio programs; both the commercialism and the pandering to less than the highest standards of esthetic taste have been amply and properly criticized. What has been rather less frequently brought to light is the fact that these media may function not so much as vehicles of entertainment or instruction—high or low in quality— but as soporifics. Television, now by far our chief[5] medium of "entertainment," probably has the most stupefying effects.

Inspecting the schedule of programs presented by our major networks, which have local channels that blanket the nation, one finds that they fall into the formula of a rather uniform pastiche: situation comedies, Westerns, variety shows, sporting events, mysteries, and re-issued movies. True, new series of Westerns or situation comedies are introduced from time to time and old ones are withdrawn. New casts may be added to these series as they are changed and fresh personalities may appear on the variety shows. But the basic formula seems to have settled down into a quite predictable monotony; and a regular viewer must be dim-witted indeed if he fails, after a full year before his set, to anticipate when the next laugh is supposed to come or the next Indian will bite the dust.

Given this monotony, one would have expected the average viewer, who is not dim-witted but of average intelligence, to give up the practice of watching television altogether, or to so badger the networks that they would be coerced into offering more imaginative and varied programs. Yet, nothing of the sort has happened. In fact, it appears that the planned monotony of programming in television is the very thing that the regular viewer wants from it: a monotony so bland, so expectable—yes, so deadening —that it can dull his mental anguish. As the familiar figures, scenes, and themes lull him away from the reality of his personal distress, he may experience a growing torpor—neither pleasant nor unpleasant, neither acute nor ambiguous; as he gives himself over to this innocuous mesmerism, he may begin to feel drowsy and, perhaps, fall asleep. Indeed, many persons seem to rely upon television as a nightly treatment for the insomnia to which they are prey, owing to their accumulated tensions; and the placement of television sets in bedrooms[6] is one indication of this reliance. But, even if they are not lulled into the complete unconsciousness of sleep, viewers often lose sufficient consciousness to feel "re-laxed." This feeling of relaxation, however transient, however much it may have to be attained anew each night, is an exceed-ingly powerful psychological reward for the regular viewer. As a result, his viewing habits are reinforced and he becomes more and more addicted to his set—precisely because he can look into its hypnotic eye and find, in the sameness of its gaze, an antidote to his pain.

Consequently, the regular viewer does not turn to the mass media of entertainment—as exemplified by television—for fresh and novel dimensions of experience. Undoubtedly, he might find confrontation with the problems of his existence irritating salt on wounds whose hurt he wishes desperately to deny. He is inclined, therefore, to hew to, nay, to insist upon the soporific concoctions that the commercial entertainers have brewed for him.

It is also quite true that the commercial implications of public opinion inhibit experimentation in television programming. A sponsor may balk at underwriting a program that may be viewed by only 2 million people—if he knows that his alternative is to present a program that will surely reach 20 million people. So, a vicious circle of monotony is established, the networks simply presenting more or less what they have presented in the past, since that is what most regular viewers want to see.

It would be interesting to learn what the reactions of the people might be to programs that sought to probe beneath the surface of their problems and to examine alternatives for social change that are directed toward the prevention of those problems on a societal basis. Perhaps such programs, offering not merely the dramatization of the viewer's problems but also an analysis of their relationship to his social order and an exposition of the ways in which they might be dealt with via social change, would arouse many a viewer from this torpor. These presentations would confront him with problems in a context of possible ways in which he could cope with them. If such programming were once begun, many regular viewers might eventually be moved to demand its continuance in preference to what they now desire; they might be moved to drop addiction in favor of comprehension and action.

Yet the prospects for the initiation of such mature programs are not bright. Neither the sponsors nor the networks themselves greatly desire basic changes in the socio-economic status quo; both are corporate oligarchies that, as yet, have shown little disposition for encouraging any enlightenment that might jeopardize their economic prerogatives and power. So, the regular viewers—many of whom might conceivably prefer an engagement with reality, if they saw themselves as having a genuine chance to shape their destinies—are implicitly offered no alternative approach to their misery than electronic anesthesia.

Our Chemical Anodynes

The palliative effects of political obscurantism, ideological platitudes, and canned entertainment are very subtle in comparison with those that are produced by alcohol, tranquilizers, or narcotics. These chemical means of deadening pain have a very direct impact on the brain, eliminating troubles, worries and anxieties and, most of all, unsettling consciousness itself, in a swift and efficient manner.

Alcohol is without a doubt the most accessible and socially approved of our chemical palliatives. It is both cheap and plentiful; and it is almost universally regarded as an appropriate beverage to serve at social gatherings for adults. It is also customary for restaurants to have on hand some form of alcoholic drink.

The corrosive effects of alcoholism—upon the interpersonal relations of the alcoholic as well as his own body—are by now so familiar to the population at large that one might have expected a brake to be provided against the excessive use of this palliative. However, the general need[7] for alcohol still seems greater than concern about its destructive consequences; and millions of people prepare themselves daily for chronic addiction to alcohol by basking in its rosy glow. Indeed, for many Americans, the hours of work represent a nagging, if necessary, prelude to the "happy time" of the cocktail hour, during which they can begin, with a long-suppressed sigh, to dissolve their problems in alcohol. The next day, of course, they awaken to the apprehensive darkness of their lives—which they seem able to bear only because they can look forward, at evening, to the warm and confident light with which alcohol will suffuse them.

Tranquilizers are certainly pressing alcohol for popularity as a palliative. In 1962, 85,113,000 prescriptions for tranquilizers were filled.[8] Many varieties of these pills can now be purchased without a doctor's prescription. In any event, millions of Americans feel sufficiently agitated to take the same medication as is now being given to inmates of our mental hospitals. The exact effects of these drugs differ from person to person, as well as differing in the variations of their chemical composition. Some may have only a mild and virtually unnoticed impact in reducing the agitation of some people; while the same tranquilizers may induce almost unruffled calm among persons who would otherwise be extremely jumpy.

Lest the effects of their products be too unpredictable and heterogeneous, the pharmaceutical concerns that manufacture these tranquilizers have been conducting and supporting many research projects that aim to assess and pinpoint the physiological and psychological reactions triggered off by the various tranquilizers. Among these investigations, there are none more interesting and fraught with potential social significance than those seeking to locate the specific areas of the brain that mediate our experience of fear and anxiety.[9] Presumably, to the extent that such regions can be surely isolated and subjected to the numbing effects of specific tranquilizers, to that extent can individuals be relieved of the psychological experience of anguish. Ultimately, therefore, it may be possible for persons, under the proper dosages of anguish-removing drugs, to function with consummate calm under the same frustrating and noxious socio-economic conditions that now render them chronically upset and discontent. Eventually, it may even be possible, with such drugs, to induce placidity in a population that is subjected to much more acutely trying social conditions than those with which our harassed people must presently contend.

Another dramatic and potentially ominous development in the field of chemical palliatives concerns the quite recent discovery that mammalian brains contain discrete areas which, when stimulated via electrodes implanted in the interior of the brain itself, apparently produce the experience of pleasure rather than of pain. Experiments[10] with rats, cats, and monkeys have repeatedly demonstrated that these creatures avidly learn all kinds of tasks in order to gain the rewards of this specific kind of internalized stimulation to their brains. The values of such stimulation as an incentive to learning may be quite as great as food is for a hungry animal or water for a thirsty one.

Thus far, scientists have refrained from the widespread use of human beings as subjects for experimentation on the pleasurable effects of such stimulation. However, some work[11] along these lines has been conducted with mental patients considered sufficiently hopeless to justify the requisite surgical assault upon their brains. But while the judgment of "hopelessness" may be handed down by anyone determined to place his own curiosity before the humanity of others, there scarcely seems to be any hiatus of knowledge that would merit the deliberate and permanent damage of the brain of a single human being.

Quite apart from this ethical consideration, however, the work already done with humans suggests that they, like members of infra-human species, tend to react with pleasure when equivalent areas of their brains are stimulated by implanted electrodes. Theoretically, it is also possible to develop chemical rather than electrical means of stimulating the relevant areas. It is, therefore, conceivable that we shall one day see the production of "happiness" pills on a mass basis—pills that do not merely lessen an individual's agitation but actually generate feelings of pleasure, regardless of how abysmally unhappy his life in society might be if he were deprived of his "fix."

Anticipating the day of the "happiness" pills, we already possess chemical "stimulants" that appear to lighten the depressive state of some individuals, giving them a "lift," a chemical nudge into mild euphoria. Conversely, for those whose distress is manifested by a false state of euphoria, we have "depressant" drugs that reduce their mania. All in all, we have now, or will soon have,[12] chemical palliatives designed for every type of person, every nuance of mood. As these drugs become readily available, they will represent a quick and easy way of diminishing the painfulness of our lives; we shall only have to reach for our favorite bottle of pills to feel inured to all and anything that troubles us.

Interestingly, while the palliatives of alcohol and tranquilizers are abundantly available in almost every region of the country, the use of narcotics is everywhere forbidden by law. A physician can prescribe or administer narcotics for individuals whose physical condition generates such intractable pain that the relief provided by an opiate seems necessitated on humanitarian grounds. But the habit-forming properties of narcotics quite properly lead medical men to recommend them most sparingly.

Nevertheless, illicit narcotics continue to reach those bent upon addiction, the ranks of whom include an appalling proportion of young persons.[13] Actually, in comparison with alcoholism, narcotic addiction is a "small" problem, encompassing "only" 46,798 active addicts as of 1961.[14] Yet it is psychologically, if not statistically, impressive that there are even this many Americans so intensely motivated to flee the realities of their daily lives that they are willing to enslave themselves to opium. Although the population of known addicts is kept small[15] by the laws regulating the sale and use of opium—laws, incidentally, whose far from perfect enforcement costs millions of dollars yearly—it might swell strikingly if opium were as accessible and as socially acceptable as alcohol.

It might be argued that one of the incentives for the current usage of narcotics is their very illicitness; that many addicts are attracted to narcotics as a means of expressing their contempt for social conventions or, perhaps, as a substitute for the adventure or purpose of which their lives are ordinarily bereft. In spite of such possibilities, however, the eagerness with which the Americans now swallow tranquilizers and cocktails suggests that many of them might well be willing to try yet more efficient means of killing pain if such means were readily available to them.

Consumption as a Palliative

Using consumption as a vehicle of aggrandizement, members of the various socio-economic classes may be motivated to spend as much money as they can—indeed, much more than they actually earn—upon the acquisition of material goods, which are so widely regarded in our society as the criterion of progress in self-aggrandizement. But the spending of money can also serve another major function: it can be an escapist activity in its own right—a semblance of a meaningful goal for those who are basically aimless and a drug for those who wish to flee from their existential problems.

For many Americans, shopping is a substitute for living; or, to say the same thing a little differently, many Americans appear to live for the sake of shopping. The most extreme instances of such persons are, perhaps, housewives in the higher socio-economic classes, women who have both time and money on their hands, and who do not know what to do with themselves—who have no strong commitments to either the personal pursuit of the values of aggrandizement or the personal expression of the values of realization. Such women are often—and quite understandably—restless, quite unable to resign themselves to the shiny boredom of their household routines. In such cases, shopping may assume the role of a quasi-purposeful activity, although it is instigated neither by a felt need for the use of a particular object nor by the desire to display a particular object as a symbol of aggrandizement.

Typically, for shoppers of this kind, "shopping" is not a sporadic act, undertaken to purchase specific objects, whose nature, if not precise brand, is determined in advance. On the contrary, these "shoppers" generally have no idea of what they intend to buy before they leave their homes for the stores "downtown" or the "shopping plaza." They may quite frequently return empty-handed, having spent all or part of a day browsing about, peering into windows and shelves, fingering and trying on articles of clothing, chatting with sales clerks about the merits and demerits of this item or that. When they do buy something that momentarily strikes their fancy, they may bring the article home with them and quickly return it, having decided, upon second thought, that they do not really need or want it or that it is not quite "right" for them. If they retain their purchase, they may put it away without any further notice, or, if it is an article of clothing, they may wear it once or twice and then relegate it to the limbo of their closets.

Consumers of this variety return regularly to their stores—almost as regularly as if they were employees reporting for work. Sometimes, they may be joined on their rounds by similar "shoppers"; or they may spice their day with luncheon at the restaurant of their favorite department store. But their principal mission is to wander among the counters and racks: searching, comparing, weighing, measuring, buying—and searching again.

The most curious aspect of the orientation of such women is the note of briskness that often pervades their "shopping" days, from beginning to end. They may descend upon the stores with a certain bounce, as if they firmly believed that they were embarking upon an activity whose inherent value is self-evident to all right-thinking persons; as if saying that one is going shopping conveys a sense of laudable purpose to all who may be concerned—husband, children, neighbors, and friends. And, when she arrives at the store, the shopper may look and act as if she had definite objects in mind, masking from herself, as well as others, her essential aimlessness.

These compulsive but aimless shoppers are given plenty of pretexts by the commercial advertisements that reach them from every medium of communication. And they may, in fact, begin their day of shopping with a half-hearted yen for something that their eyes happened to light upon while browsing aimlessly through the pages of the morning newspaper. However, upon entering the first store, they may quickly forget what it was they thought they came for, their attention captured by placards in the lobby or signs announcing sales not listed in their newspapers.

The profusion of goods available in our stores is vast and changeable enough always to give such shoppers something new to buy. And if these women are abashed at the thought of buying things only for themselves, they can always "pick up" something for their husbands or children, friends or relatives. The special holidays that our commercial enterprises have been ingenious to invent—Mother's Day and Father's Day, for example—supplement the gala occasions, such as Christmas, in connection with which unrestrained shopping is encouraged by those enterprises as a virtually religious, if not civic, duty. Such celebrations as birthdays and anniversaries can also give the compulsive shopper a temporary focus for her addiction—much as they may give an alcoholic a socially approved justification for getting drunk.

With or without external justification, it can hardly be doubted that shopping of this sort is extensively practiced in America; and while certain categories of housewives—because of their relative idleness and affluence—may be most numerous among such shoppers, single women as well as single and married men may also be similarly addicted. Indeed, "shopping" trips may often be events that include an entire family—husband, wife, and children all setting off to browse through stores in a familial failure of purpose; each goes searching for something to purchase—not because it is avidly desired in advance of the spree, but because it engages his fancy within the store and because its purchase lends a rationale to the irrational proceedings.

For those to whom shopping is too tame an escape, gambling may hold forth the exciting possibility of consuming a great quantity of money in a short time and under conditions in which the painful sense of one's existence can be much more fully obliterated. The gambler may seek to defend his particular addiction by invoking the most conventional values of our society. Thus, he may say that he is interested in making money as quickly and easily as he can. And, if it is pointed out to him that, over a period of time, the odds of chance implacably undermine the attainment of his avowed goal, he may reply that he has been or will be an exception to the laws of mathematical probability; that he is sufficiently confident in his uniquely lucky fate to pit himself against the impersonal tendencies of the wheel to produce more winnings for the owners of the casino than for those who place their bets on red or black, on their magical number 19 or their clairvoyant number 57. But even if he forgoes conventional rationalizations, the gambler may be unable to acknowledge or to express the psychological basis of his passion. He may ascribe his love of gambling to the thrill it affords him; to the moments when he feels the outcome of his own life to be riding on the back of a racing horse; to the instants when he lets a tumbling roll of the dice determine a part of his destiny; to the hanging pause before he defies the unknown with the last draw of a card.

Gambling, like the other palliatives, may appeal to different people for different reasons; more than a single motive may be engaged by the total situation within which a given palliative is indulged in. Yet those who have observed rapt gamblers in action, who have seen them sit for hours upon hours at the gambling table, cannot help being struck by the fact that they seem lost to all space, all time; that whatever consciousness they possess is diverted away from all things—including themselves—and fixed intently and exclusively upon the limits of space and time that enclose the present spin of the wheel, and the next and the next and the next.

Yes, the gambler often succeeds in losing himself quite as effectively as he loses his money. And while he may subsequently regret his loss of money, the fact that he returns to the gambling table at the earliest possible moment indicates that he scarcely regrets the transient loss of self-awareness. It is precisely this escape from the reality of his being that he seeks again to experience. If his money lasts, he may be able to blot out that reality for days at a time. If sheer exhaustion impels him to get some sleep, although he still has money to lose, he may well install himself again in his "lucky" seat at the gambling table as soon as he awakens.

As with so many of our legal codes, our laws concerning gambling are replete with inconsistency and hypocrisy. On a national level, we have no laws forbidding gambling, since that sphere of behavior falls within the jurisdiction of the states. For their part, the states have no consensus on this matter. Gambling casinos are disallowed in New York State. However, the same state allows Bingo to be conducted by churches and other organizations as a form of fund-raising. But it forbids a lottery, popularly known as the "policy" or "numbers" racket, in which individuals place bets on a given combination of numbers that will be yielded by some arbitrary tally—for example, the last three digits in the day's "pay-off" to horses that come in first, second, and third at one of the many race tracks whose betting operations are officially sanctioned and supervised by the state.

The State of Nevada, by contrast, licenses gambling casinos, which flourish like glittering cacti in its desert wastes. Nor does Nevada prohibit the ubiquitous installation of slot machines, which are probably more numerous than postal boxes in Reno and Las Vegas. It is quite apparent that millions of Americans avail themselves of whatever palliative effects they can derive from our diverse forms of gambling. And it is equally clear that, wherever gambling is "wide open," it is a tremendous lure to Americans from other localities. The gambling centers of Nevada attract a steady influx of Americans from every part of the country.

Dice, roulette, poker, racing, and other similar games and "sports" are not the only avenues open to those who want to gamble. The Federal government itself licenses our national "casinos," the various exchanges through which any American in any of the states can attempt to gamble on the purchase and sale of stocks, bonds, and commodities. Indeed, on the bond market, one is free to gamble on the government's own issues, buying or selling them with the hope of obtaining a quick profit, if the course of events—over which the individual gambler in securities has no more control than the gambler in roulette has over the fall of the little white ball—proves that luck was with him.

To be sure, the exchanges that transact sales in securities and commodities might hotly disclaim the notion that they function as gambling houses. No doubt they would wish to be seen as institutions that provide an indispensable service to investors. It is true that an investor may not regard himself as a gambler. He may simply wish to obtain safe and, hopefully, maximal dividends for his invested capital. Following Proudhon's definition of property, he is but a petty thief. But many—certainly a great, if highly fluctuating, number of people who "play the market" are not mere investors. They are, to use a term that is a shade less honorific, "speculators"; that is, their avowed objective is to gamble on fluctuations in the prices of the securities they buy, fluctuations that, they hope, will go in the direction—either up or down—that is in accord with the gamble that they have made. They may, conceivably, win by betting either on a rise in price—"buying long"—or a decline in price—"selling short." Still, they regard their activity in the same way that gamblers regard their "investments" in the outcome of a race; before placing his bet, the gambler may arm himself with no less thorough an encyclopedia of data concerning the performance of the relevant horses and jockeys than the speculator does before gambling on a particular stock.

For Americans who find the usual forms of gambling offensive to their dignity or sense of propriety, the exchanges of the nation stand ready to provide as fast a flow of "action" as a gambler could find in any medium for his addiction. In brokerage houses throughout the country, such gamblers can track the course of their bets almost as closely as they could follow a speeding horse with binoculars; the moment-to-moment fluctuations in the price of securities are recorded on ticker tapes and flashed on screens before their very eyes. And, the avid gambler in securities may often spend as much time during the day as he possibly can in such offices, his stare never leaving the moving quotations that report the fate of his bets. For the majority of those "traders" that cannot leave their work to follow the momentary changes in the "market," the mass media of communication offer periodic summaries; and many newspapers contain quite complete and detailed reports of the trading after the markets close for the day.

Thus, whoever seeks a palliative in gambling need not look far, nor surreptitiously, for accommodations. The most respectable of commercial exchanges stand as ready to welcome his patronage as the most nefarious of illicit gambling dens. And, the person who takes his addiction to a national exchange is spared whatever implication of immorality may still adhere in the minds of others concerning illegal or esoteric means of gambling; as he gazes transfixedly at the clicking ribbon that runs into his hands from the ticker, he may temporarily forget, like his counterpart at a dice table in Las Vegas, the oppression of himself.

Keepers and Asylums

While the human wreckage of America continues to mount, we persist in treating crime and mental disorder as if they were exceptional blemishes upon a spotless society; as if they represented idiosyncratic departures from universally upheld standards of emotional well-being. For our general approach to the disposition of these problems still puts the onus of blame or the focus of correction upon the particular individual in question. If he is ruled a serious offender or diagnosed as gravely disturbed, we are inclined to remove him bodily from the mainstream of society, letting it run its habitual, if reckless, course without his interfering or troublesome presence. However, if his case is judged to be less severe—in either its criminal or emotional aspects—we tend to keep him in the community, offering him a variety of professional services aimed at siphoning off his tension to a degree that may allow him to go on absorbing the stresses of our inhumane social order. In both instances, the effects, however they may be explained by penologists and mental hygienists, are such as to immobilize the individual and, at the same time, to protect the dominant values and institutions of our society.

Pacification by Physical Containment

Our classical reaction to formally adjudicated criminals and the insane has been to sequester them from daily life for varying periods of time. We put them into containers constructed specifically for the purpose of housing these differing groups of outcasts: prisons for criminals, hospitals for the insane, and hospital-prisons for the criminally insane.

Although prisons and mental hospitals are supposed to serve mutually exclusive functions, they often resemble each other quite remarkably. The prison is explicitly required by law to be an instrument of retributive punishment. But the mental hospital, while ostensibly devoted to the restoration of the sanity of its patients, also imprisons them. Consequently, it often happens that the prisoner and the mental patient spend the same amount of time under lock and key, although very different reasons may be given for their incarceration.

True, many patients in mental hospitals are accorded the privilege of walking freely about the grounds; but so are many trustees within the walls of a prison. On the other hand, many patients are confined to "locked wards," where they are under the constant surveillance of attendants. And such wards often contain cells for the solitary confinement of particularly disturbed patients, just as penitentiaries have similar cells for especially obstreperous prisoners. Finally, the patient discharged from the asylum may encounter as much ostracism as the prisoner who has completed his sentence or is released on parole. Indeed, the word "parole" is also frequently used in reference to the status of mental patients who are granted trial visits to their communities before being officially discharged.

Naturally, the analogy between the prison and the mental hospital could be pushed to the point of absurdity. Undoubtedly, there are many patients who voluntarily commit themselves to mental hospitals, a course of action that is impossible for a would-be prisoner, who must first be apprehended and convicted for violating a legal statute before he can be sentenced to jail. And surely, within the plush atmosphere of a private "lodge" or "sanitarium," where he is called "guest" rather than "patient" and where he lives in his own cottage with his own aide, the insane person of wealth is spared many of the jarring reminders of his confinement. But even in state institutions for the indigent, the medication and psychotherapy given to the mental patient are meant to diminish his distress, whereas the prisoner is often put to work on tasks that increase his pain and humiliation.

Still, private or public, the mental hospital separates the individual patient from the outer world; and while that separation may be voluntarily initiated and carried forward with the highest of therapeutic goals on the part of patients and staff alike, it is no less real than the separation of the prisoner from society. Not too long ago, in fact, even in the least oppressive of private institutions, mental patients were often subjected to modes of "treatment" whose painfulness might well have led them to wish to change places with most prisoners. A favorite form of "therapy" then consisted of the administration of massive electric shocks[16] to the brain; and patients selected for this procedure were violently catapulted into an electrically induced epileptic seizure, as a result of which they sometimes fractured limbs or spines—or even died. And it was not uncommon to administer a series of these shocks to the same patient over a span of months, at the end of which the unfortunate wretch might be so terrified at the prospect of further electrical assaults that he showed sufficient "improvement" in his behavior to cause his "therapists" to desist.

Similarly, and yet more ghoulishly, our mental hospitals, during the same era that electric shock was in vogue, demonstrated a weakness for surgical operations[17] upon the brains of patients regarded as unusually recalcitrant in their quirks of lunacy—often patients whose frightful obsessions or compulsions created difficult problems of management to the administration of the hospital. By systematically and gratuitously inflicting irreparable damage to the brains of these patients, the hospital authorities succeeded, in many cases, in rendering them more tractable. However, this gain for the staff was more than balanced by the loss for the patients, who could, henceforth, never hope to have an intact brain with which to deal with their environment. Thus, the hopelessness perceived in the patient's pre-operative condition by his physicians was objectified by virtue of their operations. Here, indeed, we have a grisly instance of a "self-fulfilling prophecy."[18]

Obviously, in comparison with individuals who are tortured with convulsive electric shocks or reduced to chronic vegetative states with surgery, persons who are quite well cared for behind the bars of a prison may be considered fortunate. Admittedly, some persons who submitted to electric shock and surgical damage of the brain may have shown behavioral changes that pleased them no less than their physicians. It is also true that medicine may have learned something as a by-product of these procedures. Moreover, given the shortage of beds to accommodate the insane who need special care, the administrators of our public hospitals are under constant pressure to admit new patients. Thus, they may be receptive to experimentation with any device that produces sufficient change to warrant the discharge of a patient. But the fact remains that the ordinary prisoner is not exposed to the terrors and the neurological insult that many, many patients of our mental hospitals have endured in the name of medical treatment.

Yet, the popularity of these drastic measures has been eclipsed not so much by humanitarian considerations as by the development of tranquilizers. These new drugs induce tractability among patients for whom electric shock and brain surgery formerly seemed to be the only recourse open to those charged with their care. However, it is paradoxical that these tranquilizers can also produce toxic "side effects,"[19] such as impairment of the liver. Thus, in some cases, the physical "side effects" may exceed the psychological "gains" of the tranquilizers, raising the question of how great an "advance" they represent over the more gruesome forms of "treatment" they have replaced.

Our rates of mental disorder are so great that it has begun to seem impractical, even to laymen, to attempt to build and staff enough new asylums for the confinement of all the people who have previously been thought to require hospitalization. Thus, Congress has recently authorized funds[20] for the development and expansion of outpatient psychiatric clinics as well as for the treatment of even grossly insane persons within the community itself. But this dawning recognition of the societal scope of the problem does not necessarily presage a growing readiness to grapple with its societal origins. For the use of tranquilizers and similar drugs may simply permit mental hygienists to mollify patients at home, thereby obviating the necessity of their custodial care elsewhere.[21]

Since our prisons may be expected to become as crowded as our mental hospitals, it is possible that penologists may follow the lead of their opposite numbers in the field of mental disorder. And Congress may one day be asked to pass legislation for keeping criminals at home, where they may be given sufficient dosages of drugs to keep them subdued.

Pacification by Psychological Containment

The violently criminal and the incapacitated insane are merely the avant-garde of those millions of Americans whose discontent constantly impels them in similar directions, Americans whose level of disturbance is at least great enough to qualify them as "delinquents" and "neurotics," if not "criminals" and "psychotics."

Those who are considered "only" delinquent or neurotic may well become more blatantly disturbed if no provision is made to calm them; but they may not be sufficiently dangerous or unmanageable to warrant imprisonment or hospitalization. Hence, we have been training more and more specialists whose particular function is the pacification of individuals who, despite their agitation, are attempting to remain active and conventional participants in our society.

Among these specialists, only psychiatrists are legally authorized to employ pharmaceutical palliatives, such as tranquilizers. All the other professionals involved in this work—and a great many of the psychiatrists as well—rely exclusively upon psychological means of placating their charges (variously called "patients" or "clients"), and keeping them out of prisons and mental hospitals; keeping them from killing themselves or others; keeping them from suffering as much as they might if they had no social caseworker or clinical psychologist or marital counselor or psychologically sophisticated minister in whom to confide.

The specialists engaged in these psychological endeavors (variously called "psychotherapy," "counseling," "guidance," or "casework") do not necessarily see themselves as performing a holding action on behalf of the existing social order. On the contrary, many choose to perceive themselves as emissaries of change —surely of individual if not social change. For example, Freud, whose writings inspired much of the activity of these diverse professional groups, regarded his invention, psychoanalysis, as a powerful technique for the production of lasting and fundamental changes in the personalities of those who undergo it. Certainly, he felt that a successful psychoanalysis would decrease the individual's incapacitating symptoms and liberate his capacity for sexual gratification.[22] Similarly, since Freud's time, other innovators of psychotherapeutic "schools" have asserted that the proper application of their methods[23] can lead to profoundly positive alterations in the individual's interpersonal relations, as well as in his feelings toward himself and others.

As things now stand, we lack the objective and systematically gathered data required to assess the scientific validity of these claims.[24] However, it seems plausible to assume that these various modes of psychological intervention may have significantly altered or repaired the lives of some of the individuals exposed to them, eliminating old and trying symptoms or creating more optimistic and buoyant frames of mind. Undeniably, too, the theories of personality upon which these psychotherapies are based[25] have contributed enormously to man's efforts to conceptualize the inner determinants of his behavior, and to imagine how his relations with others may have resulted in the enduring configuration of behavior from which we infer his psychological uniqueness.

But in spite of the avowed remedial goals of the practitioner and the conceptual illuminations offered by the theory of behavior that guides his psychological practice, the net *social* impact of the "mental health professions" in America can hardly be more than a palliative one. For our society is so replete with stress that it counteracts[26] whatever impetus toward beneficent change individuals may acquire through regular consultations of a psychological nature. In fact, because most of those who have sought such assistance are, like their fellow Americans, deeply committed to the values of aggrandizement and just as deeply enmeshed in bureaucracies of work, they continuously generate a high, chronic, and destructive state of tension. And since most members of the mental health professions are similarly affected by their culture, they are not likely to address their ministrations to the liberation of the ailing individual from the toxicity of either his dominant values or the institutions within which he strives to pursue them. On the contrary, our most influential theories[27] of psychological treatment tend to by-pass these crucial issues, largely focusing their concern, instead, upon the vicissitudes of the individual's affectional experiences with those who molded his childhood years.

Doubtlessly, parental rejection, neglect, and constraints against the expression of sexual and aggressive feelings may exert noxious effects upon the growing child. Nor can these effects fail to abound in a society that implants egoism and lovelessness among adults. Thus, detailed discussions of the misfortunes of one's childhood with sympathetic persons who are expertly trained to explore their most subtle and devious nuances—in the language of dreams no less than that of conscious thought—may be truly remedial for distressed adults, permanently freeing them from the grip of harrowing memories. And it is pleasant to divulge one's nagging worries to a kindly, intelligent, unshakably accepting, and entirely attentive listener. But despite the relief that he may obtain from insight into the formative aspects of his relations with his parents or from a cathartic airing of his present anxieties, the individual remains tied to a rack fashioned by his very adoption of the leading values of our society and by his very membership in our leading institutions. Indeed, his emotional undoing lies not in his *deviation* from those values and institutions but in his *adherence*[28] to them.

9

Musings on Utopia

EQUIPPED WITH INSIGHT into the specific qualities of our pain, despair, and inner emptiness—realizing also how those symptoms necessarily emerge from the basic assumptions and institutions that define and direct our way of life—how can we help ourselves?

Certainly, we might try to avoid a drift toward a worse society than the one we have at the present time. In this regard, a realistic assessment of our future prospects would be helpful, an assessment that seeks to take into account the worst as well as the best of our chances in the light of ongoing trends. But before we can properly discuss the possible,[1] we should voice the desirable; and before we consider how we may change social reality, we should envision the goals that the alteration of existing realities would help us to fulfill. We must conceive a view of life that would evoke and merit our best efforts on behalf of its fruition.

The Values of a Humane Society

To create a humane society, it would be necessary to effect a harmony between its dominant values and its major institutions. Such a society would be deeply, clearly, and unequivocally committed to the values of realization. Conversely, the values of aggrandizement would not only be minimized in every possible way but would also be regarded as a direct threat to humanity.

The vision of man would not be man the producer or man the consumer, but man the creator and man the source of his own solace; not man the egoist or man the shark, but man the helper and man the giver; not man covetous of superhuman glory, but man joyous in the expression of his humanity. Precedence would be given to humanitarian and equalitarian values—which nourish life itself and justice among men; to esthetic and intellectual values—which stimulate men to realize their unique capacities. Taken together, these four values would provide boundless scope and incentive for the exercise of ingenuity—not only in the ways people could care for each other but also in regard to the ways they could express themselves and develop their talents.

Beginning with this view,[2] men would be offered all the challenge, excitement, and fulfillment they might wish for. No one need feel bored or stifled; creative activity as an end in itself would be universally encouraged, making available to all the sublimity of experience that only acts of creation stir into being. Because humanitarian and equalitarian values would be translated into practices that relieve men of both the dissipation of competition with each other and the debilitation of monotonous work, the time and energies of men would be freed for intellectual and esthetic creativity. The exercise of this creativity would, in turn, have a beneficent effect upon the implementation of a worthy life. For men would be oriented toward applying their capabilities as completely and selflessly as possible in devising technological and social solutions for their existential problems and in making innovations that would give fuller and fuller expression to humanitarianism and equalitarianism.

Since the values of realization are capable of infinite expression and fulfillment, they would continuously motivate men to find new and better ways of putting them into practice. Efforts to fulfill those values would be just as limitless as are the strivings for aggrandizement in our existing society. But the endless attempt on the part of men to *realize* themselves would lead to further and further articulation of and intimacy with their humanity rather than to the growing alienation from themselves that follows from the limitless pursuit of aggrandizement. Men would become ever closer to themselves and each other as their attempts to express the values of realization increased. Instead of inducing greater and greater thirst for megalomania, this ceaseless effort would reconcile man to himself, imbuing him with more confidence in his powers to cope with his existence and with more reliance upon himself as a fount of his happiness.

A humane society would be rid of the three concepts that have stimulated man's pursuit of limitless aggrandizement: property, God, and the State. These concepts have been the traditional instruments of man's own inhumanity to and alienation from himself. They have not only been the principal pathways for pursuing the values of aggrandizement, but they have also served as the principal bases upon which men have sought to justify the injustice and insanity that have attended that pursuit. A decent society would not wish to perpetuate either these conceptual incitements to superhuman megalomania or their institutional supports; nor would there be any place for the concepts and practices of class and caste, also major purveyors of the crime and madness of aggrandizement.

The Economy of a Humane Society

The economy of a humane society would be entirely cooperative and devoid of any motive to profit from, exploit, degrade, manipulate, or humiliate others. Rejecting the concept of private property altogether, there would be exclusive devotion to the production and distribution of the goods and services that would help people to express the values of realization.

The *organization* of the economy, like its *objectives*, would be along non-hierarchical lines. Wherever possible, the division of labor would be ended, since it might induce the establishment of psychological, if not socio-economic, hierarchies of invidious distinction based upon differences in the intrinsic satisfactions or frustrations contained in the performance of various jobs. Automation could eliminate many of the divisions in work that are still required by our current technology. And such division could be further broken down by agreements to rotate participation among a range of the various specialized tasks that may still be required in the production of particular goods or provision of particular services. Such division of labor as might still be needed would *not* be differentially rewarded in terms of differences in money, prestige, or power. On the contrary, *everyone* would be *explicitly* recognized as being equally valued by the society, as an equal contributor to its totality and diversity.[3] Since technological efficiency would be so great, people could take for granted the production of goods in whatever abundance they were desired; everyone would be permitted to spend most of his time on other than economically productive activities. In fact, work would be defined not in regard to its economic functions or consequences but, instead, in regard to its relationship to self-realization and to the realization of others.

No man's economic activity would be regarded as more essential than the like activity of any other person. Similarly, all work performed outside the spheres of production and distribution would be regarded as equally crucial, important, or worth while. Work would be taken out of the arena of aggrandizement. For if one man's vocation brings him no more or less money, fame, and might than that of another, he cannot use it as a way of aggrandizing himself. Under these conditions, the rewards would lie in the fulfillment of one's humanitarian and equalitarian values as well as in the realization of one's potentials for esthetic and intellectual expression. Work would be both its own reward and a contribution to the well-being of others. With the incentive for egoistic glorification eliminated, people would be motivated to make work as enjoyable and as intrinsically interesting as possible for all concerned; and to make the conditions of work as democratic as possible.

Eliminating grandiosity and exploitation, and bringing intellectual resources unstintingly to bear upon the technological problems of production and distribution, would so reduce the amount of tension in the economy that no one would have to do anything boring for more than a very brief period of time each day. People would not feel humiliated or set upon during these intervals, for they would know that they were making a contribution that was crucial to and appreciated by their society. Everyone would be able to look forward to spending most of his time on activities of his own choosing, determined by his unique talents and interests.

Every organization of work would be a cooperative association of peers, in which each person would have an equal voice in the determination of its fate and administrative affairs. No oligarchies, no authoritarian tables of organization, no separation among proprietors, managers, and workers would exist. The association of peers would elect some members to assist in the coordination of activities within their organization as well as between themselves and others. This delegation of responsibility would be decided by democratic vote among those involved; and the delegates elected for service within and between organizations would be subject to recall by their electors. To insure the rotation of such special responsibilities, the tenure of these delegates would be limited to a single term.

A humane society would have no employees or employers, no pecking order of prestige or authority. Everyone who worked would be working of his own free will—not for fear of starvation, not for competitive advantage, not for material gain, but out of a sense of responsibility for his fellows. No one would have any incentive to hoard goods, to waste them, or to exhibit them for self-aggrandizement. On the contrary, because the leading values would be those of realization, it would be completely feasible to institute the old socialistic slogan, never yet put into practice:

"From each according to his ability, to each according to his needs!"[4] Yes, material produce and services would be available without question to all who felt the need of them—and in whatever measure. For in a society oriented toward creating and giving, people would feel no desire to take anything that they did not regard as essential to their health, safety, and security; and anything they took for vanity's sake would do little for whatever egoistic motives they might still have, since neither adornments nor possessions of any kind would elevate their stature in the eyes of others. Egoistic acquisition would be universally regarded as an aberration potentially destructive to the individual as well as to others.

Since the entire society would benefit equally from the highest quality of workmanship and the soundest possible economic policies, the members of each organization of work would arrive at their decisions within the context of the deepest and broadest humanitarian concerns. There would be freedom from the obnoxious pressures of advertising, together with all its manipulative intent to induce people to fritter away resources on products that neither delight nor edify; and to want what they do not need in order to fulfill themselves.

Such an economy would, therefore, be characterized by justice. With the end of profits, interest, dividends, and wage differentials, people would be free of the motivations for robbery that abound in existing societies, including socialistic ones, all of which presently give institutional support to various forms and degrees of economic injustice. The inherent justness of the economy would be mirrored by the interpersonal relationships functioning within it.

All these activities, requiring cooperation among many persons, would be organized on a democratic basis, every precaution being taken against the growth of apathy and the reliance upon authoritarian control. In every conceivable instance, the basic unit of economic organization would be a face-to-face group, small enough to permit its members to know each other and to relate directly to one another. It is only in such groups, scaled to human proportions, that men can feel that they know the people on whom they confer responsibility. It is only through groups of such size that individuals can have a full and complete exchange of views and experience the most complete sense of participation in the affairs of their daily lives.

We are so conditioned by the authoritarian structure of our present bureaucracies of work that it is difficult for us to imagine a complex economy thriving under democratic conditions. And yet, in a society both humanitarian *and* equalitarian, it seems quite reasonable to suppose that its economy could be both planful *and* democratic. Being dedicated to such values, people would scarcely have to be persuaded of the desirability of long-range and society-wide planning—if the alternative to such planning meant privation or hunger, death or disease to any of their fellows. Persons in every locality would be motivated to contribute ideas to such planning for the welfare of the community as a whole; what each contributed would be of benefit to all. With the elimination of all vested economic interest, it would be pointless to take anything but the broadest possible view of the economic needs and capabilities of the entire society. Individuals would have every reason to play their full part at the local level in fulfilling the overall plans for their sphere of economic activity—plans in whose formulation their voices would be heard through representatives they elected. There would be no "bosses" and no commissars. Educated, enlightened, and imbued with the values of realization, people could trust themselves with their own destinies.

Since the population of the world is very much on the increase, a humane society of the future would also doubtless be an exceedingly populous one. To develop an economy capable of meeting even the minimum physical needs of its population, it would be necessary to provide for international economic organizations whose membership would be vast—conditions that certainly might militate against the ideal of close human relationships. Still, functional equivalents of a small community could be created by structuring economic organizations so that their local units would consist of face-to-face groups characterized, as would be the total organization to which the local groups elected representatives, by a complete absence of invidious distinction and a complete sharing of the powers of decision-making among its members. Everyone would then welcome and contribute to international planning and cooperation.

It follows that the private practice of professions would be inimical to the humanitarian concerns of this society. Persons who were inclined by their interests and abilities to learn a profession in order to fulfill their own human potentials and to help others in fulfilling theirs would practice in an organization with their fellow professionals. Nor would people who chose to do these modes of work be accorded any special social or economic distinctions, the lack of which would preclude the possibility of attracting persons to professional service merely or largely because of such extrinsic considerations as money or prestige. In fact, the whole concept of professionalization would have little meaning when everyone could have a chance to develop his particular talents to the finest level of competence and expression of which he was capable; where it would be both possible and feasible for a person to become very proficient in more than one field of human endeavor, since he would be free of economic pressures to become a narrow specialist.

Far from feeling in any way deprived because he gains no egoistic distinctions for his work, the person who works in what are now considered professional areas of activity would be grateful for the opportunity to practice his freely chosen vocation, developing his skills and deriving an increasing sense of competency and fulfillment as the years go by. The same would apply to scholars, scientists, artists, and others who choose a particular mode of creative activity for the lifelong expression of their talents. By removing economic considerations from man's most sublime activities, people would enjoy a brilliant outpouring of creativity.

The artist and the intellectual would not be men set apart from their fellows—to be adored or despised, gilded or impoverished, lionized or cast into ignominious obscurity. Every man would be encouraged and permitted to develop his capacities for artistic and intellectual activity as completely as possible. With a technologically efficient economy draining off little of their time and energy, men could give themselves over to the fulfillment of all the activities—all the arts and sciences, all the creative expressions and humanitarian services—that are now considered the special prerogatives of an exceptionally gifted or affluent minority of the population. Men would be allowed to grow as creators without the threat of poverty or the megalomaniacal inducements of grandiosity. They would be able to develop their intellectual and artistic talents without becoming grotesque; without asking anything more of their work than the transports of experience they find in it; without being asked by others to be anything but true to themselves.

In an atmosphere of this kind, many whose creative tendencies now languish or lie fallow would find expression. This is particularly true of those who are now so oppressed by the constraints of class or caste that they cannot even begin to know what grace of movement, what fineness of feeling, what sweetness of voice, what eloquence of thought they carry stillborn through their barren days.

Education in a Humane Society

Education would have, as its major task, the implantation of the values of realization and the means by which those values may be expressed. It would focus upon the teaching of humanitarian, equalitarian, esthetic, and intellectual values—a focus that would be not only explicit in all the contents of its curricula but also implicit in the way in which those contents are taught.

It is evident that one cannot anticipate the specific technological skills that would be needed to further the economy and welfare of a society of some future epoch. But education would surely utilize the scientific method to the fullest, relying upon its objectivity to settle factual questions and to uncover even more valid conceptions of natural phenomena, including the behavior of man himself, and ever more effective ways of liberating man from the drudgery of boring work and the ravages of disease.

Because they would not have to spend much time in attending to the actual processes of industrial and agricultural production, people would be able to devote themselves to the provision of humanitarian services to each other as well as to the development of their creative potentials as ends in themselves. Included among the humanitarian services would be those inventive activities that make the work of the economy *per se* increasingly less arduous for all members of society. But preventive medicine, urban planning, and architecture would also be examples of the kinds of services that would flourish. Hence, education in skills in a humane society would give great emphasis to the general knowledge and specific techniques necessary to advance such services.

However, the other major areas of skill fostered by the educational practices would concern esthetic and intellectual activities —all the arts, crafts, studies, and modes of self-expression that make the use and continual development of their creative potentials a source of self-evident enjoyment for all. Even in a humane society, specific and exceptional talents would not be the natural gift of every person. Intellectual and artistic capacities, inasmuch as they are inherited, would continue to be inequitably distributed throughout the population. But these accidents of biology need not lead to either the glorification of the gifted or the degradation of those of lesser native talent. With all spheres of life removed from the invidious distinctions of the marketplace, with no person's work—productive or otherwise—receiving greater extrinsic reward than that of his fellows, the entire population would be equally motivated to realize whatever creative capacities they possess. They would be free to develop themselves in any medium of intellectual or esthetic activity that they found congenial to their aptitudes and personalities; and they could follow their chosen activities without feeling deprived of any external reward that could be granted to those who engage in other modes of self-expression.

Nor would such a freedom from deprivation invite mediocrity in any field of art and intellect. In fact, just the opposite would occur. For if anyone who wished could paint or write or act or dance, genuine freedom of choice would result in a self-selection based only upon the recognition of one's deepest interests and one's dearest talents rather than upon any other consideration. Whereas untold numbers of talented persons cannot now, because of economic constraints, select for themselves their truest vocation, a humane society would not only permit everyone to opt for that which he does and loves the most but it would also give him both the education consonant with his option and the chance to exercise the fruits of that education in the realm of social reality.

Education would, therefore, be an avenue of fulfillment, one which the individual could traverse as many times as he wished in the course of his life. Certainly, since knowledge in all fields would grow at an exceedingly fast rate—all the faster for all the people who would be free, able, and motivated to contribute to it—its adequate transmission would make it sensible for citizens to regard education as a lifelong process. They would wish to be as well-informed as possible of the advances in knowledge that might help them to improve the humanitarian impact of their work, as well as to increase the depth of their artistic and intellectual fulfillment. And since the gratification of curiosity is a prime object of intellectual activity, many individuals might wish to remain in studious contact with a variety of subjects. It would then be possible to maintain a broad and ongoing set of intellectual interests while, at the same time, concentrating upon the development of special aptitudes. Released from the economic necessity to specialize in work that they might find too confining for the range of their interests and aptitudes, people could decide for themselves how much they wished to concentrate upon one sphere of activity or another. In addition, they would be able, at any time they chose, to shift the focus of their energies from one field to another, accommodating the changes in their personality that might take place during the periods of adulthood and old age.

How refreshingly—yes, how humanely—different such an educational prospect would be in comparison to the one that confronts our youth today. Education in our society is attuned primarily to the needs of an economy whose inherent principles and organizational structure are unjust and degrading. Although the values of realization still play some part in contemporary education, they have quite obviously been shunted aside in favor of education in skills that are calculated to prepare the individual to assume a given position in a particular bureaucratic hierarchy of invidious distinction, as well as in the general socio-economic hierarchy. Contemporary education takes as its mission the dissemination of those skills and values that lead its charges not only to accommodate to but also to perpetuate the destructive premises and institutions of our society.

Inevitably, our present system of education is organized along the same lines of invidious distinction that run through the entire society. Our schools are bureaucratic organizations of work, structured by orders of rank and power and monetary reward—exactly like the economic oligarchies they serve with a stream of specialized manpower, exactly like the class and caste groupings from which they draw their clientele of students. Invidious socio-economic distinctions are maintained not only within schools but also between schools. These distinctions are spelled out in terms of various "streams" of pupils—"bright" versus "dull"; various levels of instruction—elementary, secondary, college, graduate; various titles of instructors and degrees; and various degrees of esteem accorded to the schools themselves—"Ivy League," "Private Prep," "State College," "Public High," "Local Elementary." The relationship between students and instructors tends to be an authoritarian one, reflecting, in the daily conduct of education, the inequity of the social relationships that prevails in society.

Such an educational system can only be regarded as sanguine, even by its most avid sponsors, if it dovetails with the fate that lies in store for those affected by it. But the aspirations learned in the interest of aggrandizement are widely thwarted by the bureaucratic organizations of work into which our students now move when they "complete" their education. Even more pitiable, however, are those relatively few students who absorb and take seriously the values of realization that are still imbedded in the liberal arts curricula of many colleges; or students whose native talents and inclinations attract them to artistic and intellectual activities that have no other goal but their intrinsic delight. A small proportion of persons attracted to such activities do "succeed" in them —do find a way of fulfilling them in the reality of life beyond their days on the campus. Yet it is an undeniable fact of our society that most of those motivated and educated to the "finer things of life" are forced by economic circumstances to devote their adult years to the "baser things of life." Leaving their finest sensibilities and noblest dreams at the campus gates, these students have little choice but to demean themselves in the grasping ignobility of activities that are most likely to find favor and subsidy in our materialistic world.

Yes, the passage from school to work is usually an unpleasant and frustrating one in our society. For the students—the majority —who have learned to crave aggrandizement, their progress in the post-educational world generally is slower and less exalted than they have been taught to desire. But for the students—the minority—who have yearned for realization, the environment of work is generally not only lacking in gratification for the expression of their values but also plainly hostile to those values. It is, therefore, the ironic outcome of our educational system that it sows disillusion in proportion to its effectiveness in inculcating either its major values or its minor ones.

A humane society would not educate its youth to despair. Instead, educated in the values of realization and equipped to express them, they would find no cleavage between what they wished to do in life and the opportunities to do it. The whole point of such a society would be to create an environment conducive to the expression of the values of realization. A child interested in, capable at, and educated for painting, sculpture, musical composition, scientific research, or any other field would have a societal outlet for his educated predilection. He would be able to maintain his education over the span of a lifetime, and to immerse himself in the exercise of his chosen field even as he continued to be a student. Since there would be no contradiction in being simultaneously a student of a field and an accomplished worker in it, each person would be able to integrate learning and doing, growing and creating in a way that is not possible for most people in our society.

Further, since purely economic considerations would not conspire to thwart the fulfillment of either the values of realization or the skills learned to express them, no person need languish for lack of an appropriate outlet for his creative work. For example, all painters who wished to exhibit their work would have actual *and* equal opportunities to do so, just as all writers who wished to publish their work would be accorded actual *and* equal opportunities for publication. All artists who desired it, would be exhibited; and all writers who desired it would be published. Public preferences for this artist's paintings and that writer's books might well emerge, occasioning the more extensive exhibition or publication of the works in question. But since none of these works would have any commercial value, the additional showings and editions would not result in the financial gain and special recognition of a few creative persons and the impoverishment and total obscurity of the rest.

Neither objects of art nor books would be sold. Rather, after being exhibited, objects of art would be returned to their creators, who would then decide upon their disposition—keeping them, giving them to particular persons or permitting them to circulate upon request. The artist, having expressed himself in a work, would be delighted to let it convey his pleasure to all who might wish to share it; and he would thus participate enthusiastically in any plan, such as the reproduction of his work in prints, that might permit the greatest possible number of his fellows to view his work. Certainly, the creative mood would be generous rather than retentive in such a society; the focus of the artist would be upon the realization of the work in progress and not upon any quantity or quality of aggrandizement that he might attain from the finished product.

A similar spirit would animate the writer, whose products could circulate through libraries. Nor would the inventor and scientist be motivated by any self-centered desire to receive special compensation for their discoveries. Again, as in the case of the arts, the motivations of these persons would be toward the unfolding of their intellectual capacities and the giving of the yield of those capacities to others.

It may be too much to expect, even in a humane society, that competence and excellence would not stir some envy among those who see themselves as less masterful than others in their chosen field of endeavor. Yet such potentially destructive reactions would be minimized—not only by the fact that *everyone* in a particular field would be allowed and encouraged to contribute to it in reality but also by the cooperative attitudes induced by unequivocal education in the value of humanitarianism. Just as education would help the individual to learn the humane values of his society as well as the means of their realization, so would the educational *process* itself be a chief expression of those values. In fact, the student would be fulfilling those values in his very devotion to study, in the inherent enjoyment that he experienced from the development and exercise of his creative powers, in the utilization of his knowledge for the social good, and in the application of the wisdom he gleaned from his years of work to the education of others.

The last point ought particularly to be stressed, since we are so habituated to think of educators as a cadre of specialists set apart from "laymen," on the one hand, and "students," on the other. True, the very young require a good deal of tutelage from their elders, during which the exchange of ideas may not be entirely mutual. Yet even young children may have much to teach their mentors—if only the latter would let them. Similarly, the young can do much to instruct themselves and each other—if only the adequate facilities and social conditions for such instruction were given to them. For example, recent developments in self-instructional devices may open up enormous possibilities for the initiative of young students; and the establishment of a genuinely democratic atmosphere within the classroom would encourage children to communicate creatively and constructively with each other. Education would be founded upon the precepts of equalitarianism; and it surely would do everything it could to banish coercion and authoritarianism from the instruction. It might well be, especially for the youngest children, that specially trained and self-selected adults would take on "teaching" as their chosen sphere for fulfilling their intellectual and humanitarian values. But these "educators" would serve principally as catalysts and sources of inspiration.

As children develop, they become more and more capable of independent inquiry into subjects of their interest, and of defining and articulating these interests. Education would reflect and honor these developments. The "teacher" would stop being a teacher in the authoritative and authoritarian connotations that now infuse that word. Conversely, "students" would stop being students in the submissive and dependent senses with which we presently employ that word. It would be understood that the "students" would be increasingly able to inform not only themselves but also their "teacher"; and that the "teacher" would be able to learn from as well as to inform his "students."

The education of *adults* might be handled by a rotating group of persons, who have an inclination to play that role and who feel sufficiently competent in their fields of work to preside over a gathering of peers. In this connection, the term "preside" is used advisedly; for the education of peers is obviously not a task that one among them can presume to hand down from above.

Still, it would be foolish to deny that incipient workers in every field might be able to benefit from exposure to the competence and experience of older adults, who have already devoted themselves to the various vocations. Similarly, it would be wasteful in the extreme to neglect the matter of seeking to enlist the help of competent and experienced workers in the education of neophytes. In every area of activity, there would be accomplished adults who would also be actively fulfilling themselves within their chosen fields. Teachers would not, therefore, be cut off from their fields of work, scholarship, and creativity, producing a special class of teachers that are separated from a class of scholars and a class of "doers." Those who chose to participate in teaching would also be able to maintain active involvement in all aspects of study and practice that pertained to their fields. Since the values of the society would create a willingness to give of oneself to others, those same values would make for an abundance of persons who would wish to teach. Each person's enduring desires both to help others to develop their potentials and to develop his own would orient him toward the mutuality of communication—the attitude of giving and receiving—that is the essence of education.

As with other associations of work, schools would be organized on an equalitarian basis. All persons who taught would have an equal voice in formulating the policies of their institutions. There would be no "chain of command"—no principal or assistant principals; no professors or associate professors; no provosts or vice presidents in charge of research. All such invidious distinctions would be meaningless. Responsibility for tasks of coordination— both within a particular educational organization and between such organizations—would be delegated by the teachers to their representatives. These would be elected representatives who, like their counterparts in other organizations of work, would be subject to recall by their electors.

Nor would schools require the whole apparatus of grades and diplomas. Since education would be a lifelong process, in connection with which it would be commonplace for persons of all ages to be students, teachers, and workers *all at the same time,* it could dispense with the multitude of traditional academic hurdles. Youngsters would perceive no ending point to their education—in the same way they would perceive no ending point in their efforts to realize themselves and to contribute to the welfare of their society. Nor would age *per se* necessarily be a barrier to such efforts. Certainly, no group of adults would have any vested interest—either economic or tied to the jealous retention of prestige and power—in excluding anyone from work in their fields. Newcomers to a field of work would be welcomed, whether youthful or aged.

Still, the qualification of competence would have a real place in the educational objectives. Such a society would wish to prepare its members to function as effectively as they can in their fields of work—especially in those activities in which the lives of others are immediately at stake. For example, the practice of medicine would not be entrusted to quacks and sadists; nor the building of bridges to incompetent engineers; nor the construction of skyscrapers to architects whose designs would literally be unable to stand up. Accordingly, some methods for assessing competence would have to be evolved by a number of fields of work. But these modes of assessment need not be linked to such artificial devices as the granting of a degree or the attainment of an age or the spending of a particular amount of time in apprenticeship.

The establishment of standards of competency in certain fields, however vital, would not necessarily induce feelings of exclusiveness, invidious distinction, or personal rejection. The educational curriculum would be a principal resource of preparation for meeting those standards. But the individual could seek to be assessed any time he felt himself to be ready—and not, as is the situation today, only after he completes a packaged curriculum and passes a formal set of academic examinations. If he should be found wanting, that person could continue his educational efforts to prepare himself to meet the standards under consideration. While studying toward that end, he could be working in a field for which he does have adequate competence. His failure to be admitted to a given field of work would not deprive him in any way of sharing as fully as those in that field of every resource in society. Nor would it deprive him of a chance to fulfill himself in a different field. In fact, his failure to demonstrate sufficient aptitude for a particular field might be his best indication that the field is not the one in which he is most likely to find maximal realization or to make the greatest possible contribution to society.

Apart from work that directly involves matters of life and death, the question of minimal competency becomes less urgent. For example, a historian may publish a sloppy paper on an esoteric point of scholarship without immediately jeopardizing anyone's well-being. Even so, the values of a humane society would motivate workers in all fields to do the best work of which they are capable—since work would constitute both its own reward and an offering of all that is good in oneself to others. Although many fields—perhaps most—might not require an assessment of competency for entrance to them, the prevailing norms of excellence would lead people to assess themselves objectively and rigorously, and to refrain from commitments to fields in which they themselves felt disqualified by lack of aptitude.

The community would, therefore, be able to count upon its members to restrain and monitor themselves in accordance with the interests of the common good. This discipline would not be too demanding, actually, since the individual good and the common good would be so closely and functionally inter-related. In contrast with our own society, where the pursuit of his egoistic aspirations automatically pits every man against all others, members of a humane society would be automatically contributing to the welfare of all by committing themselves to study and work that was most congenial to their individual aptitudes. In the fullest application of those aptitudes, they would not only be fulfilling themselves but also assisting in the fulfillment of the aptitudes of others.

The Political System of a Humane Society

The need for a variety of governmental functions would not be met in the name of a Nation or a State. Just as it would carry the value of equalitarianism into all its institutions, so would a humane society safeguard the sanity of its citizens and forgo the State and its bloodthirsty megalomania. Since the concept of the State has always been a leading provocation to madness, its banishment from the human scene would have a salutary effect upon man's mental life; and man would no longer be driven to alienation from himself in a wildly sacrificial effort to merge with the purported grandeur of a Nation. Where men stand on their own feet to cope with the ambiguities and challenges of their future, no group of men would presume to speak for anything but their own opinions and the opinions of those they may represent. Nor would anyone be able to invoke the absolute powers of the State as a pretext for manipulating and exploiting others. No, a humane society would have neither spokesmen nor guardians of the State; neither its self-appointed saviors nor its crusaders; neither its weapons and coercions nor its flags, insignias, and uniforms.

Actually, most of the functions of government—arriving at, coordinating, and implementing public policies—would be the appropriate responsibility of the groups elected to conduct the affairs of the economy and the organizations of work. For recognition of the inherent inseparability of the various institutions of society would lead people to acknowledge that economic issues ought to be decided by the same group—the whole people—upon whom the consequences of those decisions impinge. And since people would regard work as an expression of the values of realization, they would all have an equal and vital responsibility for making the decisions that would create increasingly congenial conditions for their work.

The unit of government would be the face-to-face group of co-workers, who elect persons from their own group not only to represent the views of the group in councils that govern the internal affairs of the plant or store or farm *per se* but also to meet with representatives of other economic organizations in order to make decisions for that entire segment of the society's economy. Expanding upon that principle of representation, representatives of each portion of the economy—manufacturing, distribution, and agriculture—would meet in councils to consider, coordinate, and plan economic policies that concern the entire society. Among the various councils—at both the local and societal level—would be representatives of all the other organizations that do serious work in the society. These organizations would cover the fields of art, education, health, communications, transportation, and all the rest. Many persons would, as has been illustrated in regard to professional workers, be members of more than one such economic organization.

With the councils of government representing the spectrum of economic activities in society, with many members of that council familiar with more than one field of work, and with the invidious distinctions of differential rewards of money, prestige, and power eliminated from work, the deliberations of such councils would take place in an objective and creative atmosphere. Knowing that they are subject to recall by their electors, the representatives would be implicitly discouraged from conveying views that are not truly representative of their groups and from failing to keep their groups informed of their actions and intentions in the councils. Because the values of aggrandizement would receive little reinforcement, members of the councils would not be likely to develop strong desires for power; they would not seek election as representatives in order to pursue insatiable ambitions for power. Moreover, all representatives would be limited to a single term, continuously spreading the levels of responsibility for the decisions of the society throughout the population and further reducing the possibility that a need for power might motivate the actions of those elected.

The governmental system would thus be far more democratic and representative than any that can now be found in the parliaments of Western society. Nor would the governing bodies of a humane society be assailed by competing vested economic interests from without or by partisans of those interests from within. On the other hand, they would not have to worry about meddling in the economy, since they would be, in fact, representatives of the economy.

Of course, people would also have to attend to governmental matters pertaining to daily life in their neighborhood of residence. Such matters as landscaping, playgrounds, and the routing of local traffic could be handled by face-to-face residential units which, like their economic counterparts, would elect representatives to a neighborhood council; and this council, in turn, could elect members to a regional council. It would be the job of such councils to attend to civic projects. The local residents would receive whatever technical aid they might need from the society's local economic councils; and they would receive whatever material resources they needed from the society's central pool of funds, a portion of which would be allocated for this purpose on a prorated basis in terms of the population of the neighborhood.

All the institutions needed to provide essential services to the society as a whole—such as the educational system or the health services—would be organized on the same service-wide basis as organizations of work. The persons directly involved with the provision of these services would assume responsibility for their quality and mode of functioning. They would be obliged to secure the funds necessary for their operation from the governing council that represents the total society. However, those who voluntarily train themselves to offer the various services would enjoy autonomy in decisions concerning the ways in which their skills should be rendered as well as in the planning of innovations in those services. Given their basic consensus of values, it would be possible to discuss and resolve matters of budgetary priority on a rational and selfless plane.

Even with all of society's resources funnelled into the fulfillment of its values of realization, problems of differential allocation to different means of expressing those ends might well arise. However, since none of its occupational groups would gain an egoistic advantage from whatever way these budgetary allocations were resolved, and since almost all members of the society would have membership in more than one group of workers, economic decisions would be reached and implemented without coercion and with a minimal amount of friction.

The political climate would be an entirely free one, in which equalitarianism would nurture the expression and acceptance of all differences of opinion. Similarly, the intellectual and esthetic values would encourage citizens to define and re-define their ideas as fully as possible; to apply as much creative thought as possible to the consideration, formulation, and debate of public issues. With intelligence fully restored to a place of respect and utility, the councils of government—at all levels of representation— would become places for the solving of problems. Such councils would take every possible step to settle differences through the application of the scientific method. Formulating questions concerning the best of alternative means for realizing specific objectives that are consonant with their values, they would, as much as is possible, seek empirical answers. A large part of the actual work of government would, in fact, be the job of scientific research[5] rather than the outcome of subjective debate.

Unlike our present society, a humane society would have no military establishment whatsoever. Warfare and armament would be completely opposed to its major values. Consequently, people would not be burdened by expenditures for arms, civil defense, or any other preparations for military attack or defense. Nor, in their passing roles as representatives of their fellows, would people have access to tangible force by which they could transform representation into dominance. Similarly, assuming that they were to grow into adulthood without having acquired a motive to attain power for its own sake, governmental representatives would not encounter, in their term in office, any palpable instruments of power to tempt them to its exercise.

Certainly, a humane society would be a peaceful one. And just as it would have no place for an armory of death, it would have no need of a diplomatic corps to press "national interests" upon others through means "short of war." Still less would it subsidize networks of spies and counterspies to plague neighboring peoples or any group of its own people.

Since political parties represent rival economic interests or socio-economic classes, there would be no need for political parties with broad, general platforms. On the other hand, expressing their complete freedom of thought, speech, and assembly, members of the society might form into various coalitions—both within the same fields of work and between such fields—to disseminate their divergent ideas on specific issues and to persuade each other of the virtues of their differing policies. However, these coalitions would not be lasting or permanent groups, such as the party coalitions we find in presently existing forms of parliamentary governments, but would be changing and fluid. Individuals in the councils of government would be constantly re-aligning themselves in different coalitions in order to work toward the fulfillment of their goals on each specific issue in its own right.

While a humane society would not disallow the expression and promotion of values and institutions antagonistic to its own, it would naturally attempt to imbue its young with its own value preferences. And since their lives, as adults, would be as fulfilling as the values they learned had led them to expect, it is likely that most people in such a society would freely subscribe to and seek to perpetuate the values of realization.

Law in a Humane Society

Members of this society would be free of motivation to commit crimes. Justice in their dealings with each other would be insured by their devotion to humanitarian and equalitarian values. Not feeling driven to pursue egoistic ambitions, people would literally have nothing to gain by manipulating, swindling, or extorting criteria of aggrandizement from others. Instead, they would have every reason to shun such destructive and unjust behavior, since it is completely contrary to the kind of behavior necessary to express their motives. Relieved of material insecurity, people would experience no fear for their health and safety—no extremity of neglect that might provoke them to abuse others in order to protect themselves. Working on the basis of social and economic equality, they would experience none of the envy and resentment that is evoked by competition and invidious distinction; and that culminates in acts of violence aimed at grasping wealth, prestige, or power from others, or at striking out vengefully against those seen as more successful than oneself.

Therefore, crime would be rare, since it would not reflect, as it does in our own society, the very essence of the society's values and ways of pursuing them. On the contrary, both the dominant system of values and the institutions established for their realization would *inevitably* lead to generosity in human affairs rather than to selfishness. Since generosity is the antithesis of injustice, it follows that crime would have no function.

An elaborate legal structure would be of little use. Whatever legal codes existed would be consistent with the ideals of justice, supporting no hypocritical differentiation between crimes allowed and those disallowed. The law could not become a screen to hide the gross injustices of any particular group. Nor would it serve to endorse the inherent criminality of an unjust economic system. All types of human exploitation would be regarded as unjust, and hence illegal, insofar as they would be proscribed by whatever formal statutes it seemed wise to write. Accordingly, all work for private gain would be a crime, since it runs directly counter to the values of a humane society.

Nor would the penal codes resemble those we have today. Certainly, the notion of meting out punishment in quantitative proportion to the presumed magnitude of a crime would be foreign to the precepts of the society. At the present time, in respect to robbery, for example, such a concept of appropriate punishment merely indicates our reverence for materialism, demonstrating that the extent of our outrage at an act of injustice is directly proportional to the amount of money stolen. What an odd concept of justice—to regard it in terms of a quantity of goods rather than in terms of a quality of human relations! We now follow a similarly quantitative model in assessing the degree of punishment to be given to persons who impose varying degrees of physical injury upon others.

Vindictive punishment would be dropped from the penal codes of a humane society. It would be realized that crime is simply the behavioral enactment of injustice; and that the criminal is someone whose sense of justice—whose adherence to the values of realization—is deficient. In the event that crime might begin to occur with any frequency, the society would recognize that something is seriously amiss—either in the extent to which the values of realization are being taught and accepted or in the ways in which its institutions are functioning to permit the expression of those values. Attempts would be made to locate the *social source* of the symptom, and appropriate steps would be taken to remedy its underlying causes at a societal level, putting the onus of responsibility for criminal *trends* where it rightly belongs.

In dealing with the individuals who have violated its values— the formal articulation of which would constitute such legal statutes as did exist—the society would be entirely oriented toward their moral education and the succor of their victims. It would not react to crime by applying punishment to the person of the criminal. For clearly, *punishment qua punishment* is an act of injustice in its own right—regardless of the party who administers it.

At present, we rationalize our punishment of criminals by holding that we would deserve similar punishment if we committed the same crimes. But since it cannot undo the crime, punishment represents a gratuitous act on the part of the representatives of society who are empowered to apprehend, try, convict, and sentence the criminal. And, what kind of gratuitous act is it? Nothing other than a fresh crime. Thus, in our present order, crime is compounded upon crime, the injustice done by the criminal exacerbated by the injustice done, in turn, to the criminal by the legal arm of society.

Every effort would be made to avoid the addition of the crimes of legalized punishment to the crimes that brought the criminal before the law. Capital punishment would be unknown, and so would be unproductive incarceration in prison. Lacking a fear of punishment, the criminal would not be loath to admit his culpability. True, he would feel guilty for having violated his fellows' values; but he would, at the same time, know that an admission of guilt would never be followed by the commission of a crime against himself.

Every criminal would be studied as a unique individual and an attempt would be made to assess as precisely as possible the causes of his crime. Based upon this careful and individualized study, a panel of experts could then prescribe a program of rehabilitation for him. Such a program could include a wide range of educational and psychological procedures, the selection and application of which would be guided by knowledge of the measures most likely to have the desired rehabilitative effect. In many cases, no special program would be recommended for the criminal, since his crime might be diagnosed, for example, as an isolated fit of passion that would probably never occur again. In any event, given this flexible and non-punitive approach to criminals, prisons could be dispensed with altogether. Even murderers would be returned to the community immediately upon the assessment of the determinants of their crime and upon the formulation of a rehabilitative program for them, should one be deemed necessary.

Nor would the criminals themselves play a small part in these procedures. Their views would be fully taken into account on all matters pertaining to the reasons for their crimes and the way in which they might be helped to avoid further crimes in the future. It would be up to the criminal himself to follow through upon whatever recommendations might be made for his rehabilitation;

these recommendations might involve the help of untrained friends, relatives, and associates as well as professional workers. Parole and other quasi-coercive procedures would be inappropriate. For it would be understood that the prevention of subsequent acts of injustice rests upon the criminal's own freely given adherence to the value of justice.

In such vital matters as the establishment of an individual's guilt and the formulation of constructive plans for his future, responsibility would be delegated to those who were trained in the evaluation of evidence, on the one hand, and the vicissitudes of human behavior, on the other. Such specially trained persons would be asked to deal separately with the establishment of the criminal's guilt and its aftermath. Recognizing that they were neither bludgeons of vengeance nor incipient perpetrators of new crimes in the name of justice, these experts could respond objectively and constructively to the problems brought before them. Even if they were to make gross errors in ascribing guilt to innocent persons, the experts would have done no more injury to those persons than can be caused by temporary embarrassment. Those erroneously accused or found guilty of crimes would suffer no loss of their place in society; and they could soon regain, like those whose guilt is real, the esteem of their fellows by demonstrating their adherence to the values of realization.

There would be no reason to retain our present legal apparatus of trial by jury and sentence by judges. Nor would the kind of police familiar to us be needed. Instead, the "police" would serve to direct the flow of traffic, to act as guides to tourists and those unfamiliar with a particular geographical location, to aid elderly, infirm, or youthful pedestrians, and to minister to those who fall ill or suffer accidents on the street. In the conduct of these functions, the "police" would go about without firearms, clubs, handcuffs, or weapons of any kind. Nor would the manufacture and distribution of pistols, rifles, and other weapons of destruction be allowed. Individuals performing these civic services might adopt, for the convenience of pedestrians, some form of identification—a white carnation, let us say, pinned to a lapel. But they would surely disavow the militaristic uniforms now worn by our police to personify the authority of the State and to inspire terrified obedience to its dictates.

The Social Institutions
of a Humane Society

The economic and political characteristics of a humane society would effectively prevent the formation of invidious socioeconomic groupings within organizations of work and government. For example, with private property abolished, housing would be organized on the same cooperative and democratic basis as manufacturing. No longer restricted by the economics of scarcity and profits, the community of equals could decide what sorts of dwelling places and housing arrangements were appropriate to the furtherance of human potentials. In part, such decisions would rest upon the data of architectural, sociological, and psychological studies of the impact, for instance, of particular sizes of rooms upon families of various compositions and ages. Knowing that the values of realization would stand as the society's constant criteria for evaluating itself, the diverse specialists would orient their research toward the gathering of information relevant to such values. Still, a number of decisions concerning housing arrangements would be automatically fixed by common consent. Certainly, no variety of social discrimination would be permitted; nor would it be difficult for people to put their democratic principles into social practice. Lacking the egoistic motives that are generated by the values of aggrandizement, the population would be freed of the basic impetus toward inter-group prejudice that has made a shambles of our traditional pretensions to social democracy. Since people would have no inclination to pursue aggrandizement, they would have no need to derive a vicarious sense of superiority from keeping any of their fellows in an inferior social position.

Social life would, therefore, be liberated from the constraints of prejudice, discrimination, segregation, and special privilege. All facilities of the society would be genuinely public—no invidious restrictions being attached to their use. All persons would have equal social standing with and access to each other. Both class and caste distinctions would be as unthinkable in informal social relations as within all formal organizations. Companionship, friendship, love, and marriage would be freed of racial and ethnic prejudice, the insecurity of economic competition, and the snobbery of egoism. Relieved of the destructive effects of invidious distinction, those relationships could be more harmonious and fulfilling than it is now possible for us to imagine.

Surely, love would be among the most important beneficiaries. And the institution of marriage could truly be established and maintained on the basis of love. For there would be no reason but love to pick one marital partner or another; the choice of a mate would be determined by one's affection rather than any extraneous consideration, such as religion, skin color, or socio-economic status. Not being threatened by the very concept of "inter-marriage," couples in a humane society would let their spontaneous and personal feelings—unblocked and uncensored by prejudice—guide them to each other.

Having married, a couple would have the time, the energy, and the disposition to keep their love alive. Neither husband nor wife would be driven toward aggrandizement—in the pursuit of which married couples in our society exhaust their energies or seek to extract self-seeking adulation from each other. Already oriented toward generosity by their fundamental values, married couples would willingly give each other love; and they would be able to spend as much time as they wished in expressing that love, for no one would have to do long, hard, and debilitating work. If one chose to work long and hard at some mode of realization, it would truly be a labor of love which—far from dampening or squelching the love of his mate—should keep his morale, zest, and confidence at a high level, his ardor bubbling and effervescent. If a couple wanted to withdraw from most of their occupational activities, they could do so without jeopardizing their economic security or that of their children. Apart from their commitment to brief stints at services that had to be performed by all in order to conduct the economy and safeguard the health of the community, the couple would have the option of doing whatever they wished to do together.

Parents would not be reluctant to rear their own children, or to have the offspring of their love reared by others. The competition between the sexes having disappeared as fully as that among the sexes, neither men nor women would feel abashed about spending time at home with their children. Women would not experience any conflict of roles, since society would not be dominated by males any more than it would be by white-skinned or dark-skinned persons; and since invidious distinction would have no institutional support in terms of differentials in external reward, motherhood would not be implicitly denigrated as a major role for women who chose it. On the contrary, all the values of society would lead its citizens to feel sincerely that the care of life itself—exemplified by the care and rearing of its newborn members—is as worth while an activity as any that takes place within it. Marriage would be a totally voluntary commitment between man and wife; the notion of "sanctifying" their marriage in the "eyes" of God—or "legalizing" it in the "name" of the State—would seem absurd. For the subservience of love and equality to concepts of aggrandizement, whether they be religious or nationalistic in content, would be regarded with abhorrence by persons who would see in the values of aggrandizement the seeds of injustice and insanity among men.

Men and women would accept complete responsibility for the contract and conduct of their marriage. Nor would they require the coercion of religious or legal prohibitions to remain attached and loyal to each other and to their children. Such attachment and loyalty would have every chance to be strengthened naturally during the marriage, since the couple, having married for love, would not be obliged to neglect that love in pursuit of egoistic ambitions.

Still, it is conceivable that married couples, even in a humane society, might wish to part at some time after their marriage. In such cases, the parting would be carried out under conditions of minimal stress to all concerned. There would be no complex legal machinery to adjudicate these partings. Couples would not have to get a divorce or legal separation or annulment in order to terminate their marriage. Just as they married without such legal sanctions, so would they be able to do without them in regard to ending their marriage. Since neither property nor possessions would be at issue, incompatible couples would not have to worry about safeguarding any economic prerogatives. Being able to obtain whatever material help they needed, they would have no economic incentives for marriage and no economic fears of divorce. Finally, ample provision would be made for the care and rearing of children of broken marriages.

It is difficult, under such circumstances, to imagine the occurrence of outright desertion, cases in which one of the marital partners precipitously abandoned his family or the yet more extreme case of both parents abandoning their children. Because of both their values and their economic security, couples would, in cases of incompatibility, be motivated to make the most wholesome arrangements possible for the rearing of their children following their parting. But for those children for whom such arrangements could not be made by their parents, service organizations would find adequate surrogates and facilities.

Neither illegitimacy nor poverty could blight the lives of children in a humane society. All children would be equally legitimate, the legitimacy of a relationship between man and woman being no longer a question for external agents to decide; and every family would be established within a context of equal access by all members to the material resources of their society. Hence, even in instances of broken families, children would not be scarred by anything except the disruption of the break itself—which, of course, may still be a considerably upsetting experience in its own right.

Although it is impossible to predict the exact form of family life in such a society, it is likely that marriage would be monogamous, since the general conditions of life would permit the development of deep and intense relationships. Lacking the concept of property and the motivation for acquisitiveness, marital partners could regard each other as equals rather than as possessions. Since possessiveness would not intrude upon their marriage, husband and wife might feel free, like the Polar Eskimos of our time, to share their spouses, even sexually, with others. Or, if a shortage of males or females should exist, whatever form of polygamy seemed best suited to meet the sociological realities might well be countenanced.

The acceptance of sexual drives as one of the intrinsic characteristics of mankind would be basic to the society; it would do as much to facilitate the gratification of the sexual needs of its members as it would to insure their health and survival. At the same time, there would be recognition of the relationship between sex and affection; and, far from teaching its youth to separate sex from love, a humane society would give them every encouragement to integrate the two. Boys and girls would be free to associate with each other intimately, from earliest childhood onward. Nor would they be in any way discouraged from relating to each other sexually. Education in sex, procreation, venereal disease, and similar topics, still largely withheld from our own children, would be given to every child. Techniques of contraception would be readily available to all, insuring that no unwanted children are brought into the society. Similarly, abortion would be provided—upon request and without penalty to physician or patient—to any woman who conceived a child she did not wish to bear.

The society would work unsparingly toward the prevention of illness and infirmity. Still, such instances of social pathology that remained would command the humane attention of the people; and whatever new and unforeseen disturbance might arise would soon become the object of a similar regard.

Having ceased to react to the commission of a crime with the fresh crime of legalized punishment, the people would also refrain from responding to insanity by alienating the individual—already alienated from himself—from society. Once again, as in the case of crime, the conditions of life would minimize the possibility of individuals becoming alienated from themselves. If alienation from oneself did occur, it would be treated in the same way undertaken to treat crime. Individuals so alienated would not be sequestered behind the walls of an asylum. Instead, they would be referred to specially qualified panels of experts, who would recommend the mode of rehabilitation deemed most likely to implant in the individual a greater adherence to the values of realization—to restore him to himself.

In keeping with the equalitarian spirit, both the individual's appearance before such a panel as well as his actions upon their recommendations would be unquestionably voluntary; and he would suffer no loss of his place in society if he chose not to avail himself of the services of those experts or if he failed to apply their recommendations. He would undoubtedly feel a good deal of informal social pressure from his family, friends, and colleagues to seek and apply the help available—especially since, in the matter of applying the panel's recommendations, persons closely related to and associated with the alienated person would frequently be called upon by the panel for assistance.

But a panel might find, after careful examination, that the alienated behavior in question is an isolated instance, not likely to be repeated in the future; and that the individual manifesting the behavior needs no special help. Or, the panel might determine that the behavior under consideration was provoked by a particular physiological deficiency or ailment rather than by a lack of commitment to the values of realization. In such cases, the panel would, naturally, prescribe whatever medical treatment the prevailing state of knowledge indicated to be most effective in remedying the illness. (The same contingency might arise in regard to crimes that represent uncontrollable outbursts caused by an anomolous physiological state—such as crimes committed during epileptic periods that are not accompanied by full-blown seizures.[6])

Both insanity and crime would be generally regarded, unless

shown to have a specific and demonstrable physical basis, as reflecting defects in the moral education of the individuals concerned. It follows that the moral re-education of those individuals would be the objective of the recommendations aimed at increasing a sense of justice among the criminals and a sense of adequacy among the insane. At the same time, that re-education would be conducted in an atmosphere of concern for the welfare of the individual. Widespread insanity would be interpreted in the same way as widespread crime, namely, as a societal failure in the transmission and maintenance of the values of realization. Hence, any large-scale incidence of insanity would be approached at a social and preventive level rather than solely from the vantage point of ameliorating the condition of the individuals already insane.

10

Society with Tears

HAVING HAD a lovely sojourn in the imaginary world of a humane society, it is time for us to return to the bitter disquiet of the here and now. Admittedly, anyone who has a flair for fantasies of Utopia may react with acute dismay to the intrusion of harsh and unkempt reality upon the pristine elegance of his untried ideals. Yet the social critic should feel obligated, both by the presumption of his criticism of the present society and out of respect for his conceptions of a better one, to carry his thoughts to their practical implications as well as their logical conclusions.

Unquestionably, the task of making constructive suggestions for dealing with the destructiveness of our society might be very much facilitated if we could locate a technologically advanced society whose basic values and institutions were, in actuality, demonstrably more humane than our own. For we could then mark out such a society as a viable example that would be worthy of our emulation.

It is true that several existing societies, both similar to and different from our own, follow certain institutional practices whose adoption by us would improve the lot of our most downtrodden citizens. But even if we assume the most charitable and sympathetic of attitudes in evaluating modern societies, we must regretfully assert that none of them—as a total configuration of values and institutions—comes any closer than America to being a suitable place for human habitation.

Why is this so? Why are none of the technologically advanced societies of the world really fit for people to live in? Their principal drawback, it must be sadly acknowledged, is their lack of humanity. Not a single one of them is free of dehumanizing aspirations for aggrandizement. Instead, every one of them places the values and vehicles of aggrandizement far above those of realization. And wherever one has the heart to explore, one will find concerted assaults upon justice and sanity in human affairs. Wherever we may choose to listen, we hear a din of exhortation to superhumanity, a mad clamor of promptings to grandiosity. It is not surprising, therefore, that daily life in modern societies throughout the world is replete with injustice and alienation, albeit that their manifest forms may differ somewhat from society to society.

Nowhere is it presently sufficient for man to be man. Everywhere he is urged to strive to become something beyond himself, beyond anything he could actually be. And the most prominent incitements to aggrandizement are still the three concepts that have befouled the history of mankind: property, God, and the State.

Of course, the relative influence of each of these concepts varies among the different societies, reflecting the vicissitudes of their particular histories as well as the nature of their contemporaneous economic and political systems. For example, among the capitalistic democracies of the West, property tends to be a more influential concept than either God or the State; and the citizens of those societies are more likely to aspire to limitless aggrandizement through the accumulation and consumption of wealth than through religious or nationalistic activities.

Among these capitalistic democracies, however, there are considerable differences in the status of their religious institutions vis-à-vis their economic and political ones; and, in those countries, such as Italy, that have a very homogeneous population of adherents to the same Church, religion may play a very important role as an alternative road to aggrandizement. In the case of Italy, the very presence of the Pope and the center of Catholicism cannot fail to impress many Italians with the possibility of attaining glory through a vicarious merger with God.

The State, however, appears to be the most ubiquitous of the three conceptual inducements to aggrandizement. Regardless of its economy and its religious institutions, regardless of its social history and its present political system, every modern society invokes nationalism as a call to the glorification of its citizens. In America as in Russia, in China as in France, in Poland as in Cuba, the citizenry is daily and steadily infected with the delusion—no less dangerous to themselves than to others—that they are as great or small as their nation; that, as the power of their nation expands or contracts, so does their individual worth. Thus, individuals of all nations are implicitly denigrated at the same time that they are offered psychological coalescence with the State as a means of self-aggrandizement. Yes, the maddening voice of nationalism sounds exactly the same in Washington as in Moscow, in Peking as in Paris. From every capital, that voice extols the status quo, whatever it may happen to be. From every capital, it breeds hysteria, so befuddling the people that many of them seem quite ready to rip or blast their fellow men to pieces if they happen to live in another nation that the voice condemns as inferior or threatening to their own.

As might well be expected, the voice of nationalism speaks, primarily, on behalf of the oligarchical elites that control the economic and political institutions of the various societies, the available means by which aggrandizement can be pursued. And it is these elites who most desire to retain and augment their appropriated pre-eminence; to be celebrated as the grandest of the grand; to be accepted, by their fellow citizens, as the proper proprietors of their society.

In openly totalitarian societies, a single oligarchy controls all the institutions of society, manipulating them as it deems expedient to the continuance of its supremacy. But even in our society, as in other capitalistic democracies, the dispersion of the media of aggrandizement throughout the population is very unequal, being increasingly concentrated into the hands of those who run our bureaucratic *and* totalitarian organizations of work. Nor do our corporate oligarchs hesitate to influence the course of the country's political affairs. On the contrary, such influence, toward which they can apply the enormous resources of their economic domains, is very formidable; it heralds an ominous development that may rapidly erase the differences that still obtain between our version of democracy and other versions of totalitarianism.

Having bemoaned the precedence accorded by all modern societies to the values of aggrandizement, can we discover among them any in which the values of realization receive greater support than they do in our own?

That question is most readily answered in the negative with regard to fascistic societies. In those societies, as exemplified by contemporary Spain,[1] the debasement of the majority of men is diligently and deliberately sustained by a self-glorifying minority. Standing on the shoulders of the unopposed Falange party, within whose ranks the power of all the country's institutions is cemented into a totalitarian monolith, is the Spanish dictator, Franco. And from that position of absolute authority he directs his political cohorts in the systematic robbery of their fellow citizens, stealing their freedom of thought and expression as well as their goods; adding economic injury to political insult by taking the wealth that others have produced. And, as if that were not enough, Franco and his henchmen directly enforce their whims through methods of terror and surveillance, which make captive animals of their human subjects. Although they are given leave to exist, the hapless people of Spain need not feel gratitude for the mercy of their rulers. For whom would there be to dominate in a nation without people? And who would fatten the lords of the land if not the oppressed? No, fascism, from whose pernicious effects the world suffered so bitterly in the first half of this century, provides no comfort at all to the values of realization.

In general, the capitalistic democracies of Europe so closely resemble the essential features of our own society that we can scarcely expect to find in them institutional supports to the values of realization that are lacking here. Nevertheless, the presence of socialistic parties in Great Britain and the Scandinavian countries, for example, has helped to advance some areas of social legislation[2] further than they have been advanced in America. These countries have paid more genuine and effective heed to the distress of those most obviously victimized by the inherent ruthlessness of capitalism: the aged, the ill, and the unemployed.

Still, ever since the administration of Franklin D. Roosevelt, our government has sponsored and passed measures aimed at helping those most damaged by the operation of our economy. Few luminaries of either of our political parties would now be publicly willing to propose the abolition of the system of social security that was introduced during the days of the New Deal. And while our legislators may act more slowly on these matters and may be more reluctant to condone the assumption of responsibility by the government for economic planning, they have already demonstrated their inclination to pass "welfare" legislation when sizeable blocks of their constituents demand economic relief. For example, the financial support[3] that our government has for years been giving to farmers is probably unparalleled anywhere in the world.

Nevertheless, economic "reforms" in our society, as in the capitalistic societies of Europe, are not meant to be institutional alternatives to the basic economic system. On the contrary, such reforms are undertaken in order to preserve capitalism by softening its most severe blows and by placating those who might become most hostile toward it. By thus attempting to keep their economic systems intact, the capitalistic democracies implicitly demonstrate their fundamental preference for the values of aggrandizement, together with all of the institutional bulwarks and manifestations of those values. Great Britain and the Scandinavian countries maintain not only the inhumanity of private enterprise but also the megalomaniacal baggage and retinue of royalty. And it may not be impossible to conjecture why, despite their admirable progress in the field of legislation for the welfare of those in the lowest ranks of invidious distinction, Denmark and Sweden are afflicted by great rates[4] of alcoholism and suicide. While the people of those countries may not want for material security and palliatives, they may still be in need of meaningful ends to which they can dedicate their lives. And since such ends can only be provided by a society that is itself committed to the values of realization, their absence creates a demoralizing vacuum that may be as onerous for people to bear as extreme material privation.

Well, then, what about communism? Is it merely an accident of history that communism has arisen as the chief societal competitor of capitalistic democracy? Or have the communistic societies made such strong institutional commitments to the values of realization that they have enlisted the allegiance and excited the sympathy of their massive populations?

It must be said, at once, that none of the existing communistic societies can be properly regarded as a perfect prototype of that system, any more than we or any of the Western democracies can be put forward as the ideal representation of capitalism. The actual functioning of any politico-economic system reflects the imprint of local exigencies as well as the outcome of internal and international struggles for power. The leaders of China and the Soviet Union, for example, have recently engaged in mutual castigation[5] for the deviations that each has accused the other of committing in the application of Marxist-Leninist principles, of which they both claim to be indisputable paragons.

Nevertheless, since the Soviet Union is still regarded—and regards itself—as our principal adversary in the competition for the minds of the "neutral" peoples of the world, it seems fitting to take Russia as our example of a communistic society, and to ask how the values of realization fare under the Soviet regime.

A first and objective glance indicates that the virtues of Soviet society, in regard to the values of realization, cannot be perfunctorily dismissed. For there is no doubt that the Soviet economy is based upon a more humane ethic than our own—that is, upon the elimination of interpersonal exploitation for material gain. By seeking to destroy the profit system, the Soviet Union has done much, within its borders, to vitiate materialism as a tool of personal aggrandizement. More, it has branded the pursuit of private financial profit a high crime—according it the severest of all its legal forms of punishment, death itself.[6] Naturally, the application of capital punishment to the crime of profiteering involves the commission of a new and horrible injustice. Still, the very labeling of profit-seeking as a crime is an act of truthfulness that has not been loudly voiced in the world since the Christian complaints against usury in the Middle Ages.

The Soviet Union's concern for justice in its economic affairs does not stop with its strictures against greed. It has undertaken to guarantee the economic security of all its citizens—providing them, however humbly placed in the economy, with employment, vacations, medical care, and pensions in old age. The government attends to the universal education of all its citizens, granting free higher education to its gifted students. The government also assumes responsibility for the construction of suitable living quarters and facilities of transportation for its citizens, albeit that adequate housing is still in short supply. Finally, the government takes on the task of long-range economic planning for the entire society, distributing its available material resources and manpower in such a way as to insure the ample production not only of capital goods but also of consumer goods and agricultural produce.[7]

It cannot be doubted that, in the economic sphere, the socialism of Soviet society represents a marked departure from our own, taking much more seriously than we do the matter of realizing justice in the economic relations among its citizens. And yet, having paused to recover our breath from the enthusiasm of a first impression, we take a second and longer look at Soviet economics. And we note that, alas, the revolution inspired by Marx has yet to come. Judged in terms of the Czarist era, justice in economic affairs has advanced remarkably. But the sad fact is that real, glaring, and harmful inequities in the structure of the economy continue to persist. Neither property nor invidious distinction have disappeared from the scene. Instead, the present proprietor of the material resources of Soviet society is the Communist Party. And while no class of capitalists exists there to accumulate and dispose of the society's wealth, the oligarchical elite of the Communist Party have appropriated for themselves the prerogatives formerly exercised by capitalists and their political representatives.

Similarly, the entire Soviet economy, no less than our own, is organized into bureaucratic structures of work, each standing as a personification of their system of invidious distinction. Various jobs within those structures are differentially rewarded with differentials in pay, prestige, and power. These external differences in the rewards given to persons who perform different economic functions contribute to the crystallization of socio-economic groupings that are every bit as indicative of different degrees of aggrandizement as similar groupings are in our society.

It matters not that the Soviet Union gives relatively greater material reward to the scientist than we do; or that the prima ballerina receives relatively more money and kudos than her opposite number here; or that, although the personnel of Soviet economic organizations are scaled in a hierarchy of invidious distinction, no able-bodied person is allowed to languish in humiliating unemployment. All of these comparisons cannot undo the principal point at issue; namely, that the Soviet Union, despite its substitution of a socialistic economy for a capitalistic one, has failed to eliminate from the functioning of its economy the values of aggrandizement and the invidious distinctions of hierarchical organization that both manifest and support those values. Yes, even as the Soviet economy purports to represent a genuine revolution in the practice of economic justice—in the equalitarian and humanitarian conduct of economic relationships—it contrives to establish, in a somewhat new guise, the essence of the invidious distinctions that the Russian Revolution aimed to banish. While certain aspects of its economic practices do introduce greater justice into economic affairs than is true of our economy, the overall structure and functioning of the Soviet economy is such as to perpetuate and give precedence to the incentives and media of aggrandizement.

Looking still further into the psychological implications of its economic practices, one can see that the pursuit of aggrandizement is likely to be as great a preoccupation in Soviet society as it is in our own. Admittedly, the Soviet citizen is not enjoined, as is the American citizen, to aggrandize himself through the accumulation of private profit. However, it is clear to any Soviet child that some types of work are more amply rewarded—financially as well as in terms of social acclaim and personal power—than other types of work. And, since he has been inculcated with these values at home and in school, he is likely, no less than his American peer, to aspire to grandeur through vocational attainment. Competition[8] for the socially and economically favored positions is, therefore, bound to be as keen in Soviet society as in ours; and so is the competition for upward mobility within the bureaucratic structures of work.

Whatever incentives for megalomania may be lacking in its economy, the Soviet Union more than fully supplies in its political affairs. The monolithic political party loses few opportunities to incite the Russian people to identification with the grandiosity of the Soviet State. Controlling all media of communication, the Communist Party sings lyrical and endless hymns to the glories and might and incomparability of the Soviet Union, cajoling all viewers, listeners, and readers to share psychologically in the superhuman transcendence of "their" State. At the same time, the Party can blot out any criticism of the State—in the final analysis, themselves—that they feel might sully the image of omnipotence they are seeking to project and to have absorbed into the mentality of their subjects.

One could give many specific instances of egoistic glorification in which the Soviet leaders have been wont to indulge, thereby currying the adulation of their people and inviting vicarious self-glorification on their part. However, there can be no more striking example of this dual process than the annual parade in Red Square on May Day, when the current dictator and his immediate ruling clique stand on Lenin's tomb high above the awed multitude in Red Square. Below them, the deadly weapons of the Soviet Armed Forces pass in review—tanks, guns, and rockets. Overhead, the fighting jets of the Soviet Air Force boom through the sky in precise formations. And on the buildings in the vicinity and borne aloft by the fervid crowd are huge portraits of Marx, Engels, Lenin, and other heroes of the Soviet Valhalla—portraits much bigger than life, much bigger than men.

Of course, all countries have their nationalistic orgies; and the leaders of all nations have a weakness for glorifying themselves and their kind, constantly reminding their citizens how blessed they are to have such great men to control their destiny. But the universal quality of nationalism makes it no less virulent wherever it takes root. And it surely has taken root as firmly in Soviet society as in any other on earth.

While the concept of the State looms excessively large in the Soviet Union, beclouding the humanitarian cast of its economy, the concept of God plays a very minor role in inciting the people toward aggrandizement. The Soviet regime opposes the institution of religion on ideological grounds, since belief in God is alien to the naturalistic precepts of Marxian philosophy. By stressing the reasonableness of atheism, the leaders of Soviet society have taken a position that is consistent with the values of realization. However, the Communist Party has virtually idolized itself, and the doctrines of Marx, Engels, and Lenin are taught and upheld as if they were Holy Writ. It is difficult to say, therefore, to what extent the coldness of the regime's attitude toward the Church represents a rivalry of aggrandizement—the State and its officers versus God and His—and to what extent it represents genuine adherence to the values of realization.

We may obtain some insight into this question by examining the attitude of the leadership toward the creative arts. Unfortunately, there is little doubt that the Soviet oligarchy sets its own wishes[9] above those of the individual creator, demanding that the artist and the writer devote themselves to the glorification of the status quo, thus implicitly glorifying the communist leaders themselves. But such an attitude toward creativity goes directly against the humane objectives of esthetic and intellectual activity. For those activities, to fulfill their humane function, must emanate freely and spontaneously from the creator; must express his uniqueness, his capacities, his sensibilities—whatever they may be, however they may strike someone else. By squelching or restricting freedom of creative expression, the Soviet leaders again reveal a readiness to set the values of realization aside in favor of their own aggrandizement.

To be sure, Soviet society is complicated and fluid, as is our own. It has changed markedly in the past—from an "idealistic" phase of Lenin's rule to its present movement toward "liberalism" and its repudiation of the authoritarian extremes of the Stalinist days. No doubt Soviet society, like ours, will continue to change. Its recent rivalry with China seems to be a sign of such change; and it is already not at all bizarre to imagine that the Soviet Union and the United States will one day be bosom allies against a commonly feared pretender to international power from the Orient. Nor, for that matter, is it outlandish to imagine the gradual introduction of private enterprise in the Soviet Union, together with a gradual easing of the Communist Party's totalitarian controls; and to imagine, conversely, a gradual trend toward economic planning and the monopolization of power by an oligarchical clique in our society—both eventualities preparing the ground for an ideological as well as an opportunistic rapprochement between the Soviet Union and America.

But holding our imagination in abeyance, for the moment, let us attempt to draw some general conclusions about the status of the values of realization in Soviet society. In particular, do those values receive more support, all things considered, in Soviet society than in our own?

Actually, the matter appears to be a virtual deadlock, as is the balance of destructive power that now lies poised between the two societies. Clearly, in the economic realm, the Soviet society puts the values of realization much more conscientiously into practice than we do. True, its bureaucratic hierarchies of work are based upon invidious distinctions of salary, prestige, and power. But these distinctions are not nearly as grossly apparent as those that separate the various socio-economic groupings in our own society. In contrast with us, the Russians have sought to cleanse themselves of the *intrinsic* egoism and injustice of capitalism, as well as the noxious effects of its operation. Although property and the economic exploitation of man by man have passed from individual proprietors to rulers of the State, the Soviet leaders tend to use their proprietorship not so much for the financial as for the political exploitation of their subjects; the currency of aggrandizement with which they expand their concepts of self tends to be power rather than money. Yet, just because they have such a monopoly of power, the Soviet leaders can engage in very long-range economic planning; and they can enforce their plans throughout the whole of society. Thus, the Soviet government can make more adequate and effective arrangements for gratifying the basic physical and material needs of *all* its people than we have yet been able to do for *all* of ours.

Whereas the Soviet economy seems to give fuller expression than ours to the values of realization, our political system still gives those values much more real support than does theirs. The totalitarian control of Soviet life that rests in the hands of the Communist Party is, in itself, a slur upon those values. Admittedly, our organizations of work are totalitarian, as are those in the Soviet Union—small comfort to Americans and Russians alike! But we still enjoy vastly more freedom of expression in political affairs than do the Russians. For all its flaws, our parliamentary system is obviously more answerable and responsive to the popular will than is the Presidium[10] of the Communist Party. For all their underlying communality of ideology, our political parties continue to offer more choices among aternative policies than does the single and unopposed Communist Party. For all their conformity to our dominant values and institutions, our media of communication do present a greater diversity of opinions than is found in similar media in the Soviet Union. For all of our neglect and vulgarization of art and the intellect, our artists, writers, and intellectuals are infinitely freer to express the uniqueness of their thoughts and feelings than are their colleagues in the Soviet Union. For all the oppressive zeal of the late Senator Joseph R. McCarthy and the continuing un-American committees of Congress, we have never confined thousands of people to camps[11] of slave labor for the "crime" of political deviation from the views of the government in power.

Where starvation is literal and rampant, however, the majority of men are understandably more likely to be attracted to economic justice than to be repelled by political injustice. It is for this simple reason that the hungry people of Asia and Latin America—or, wherever masses of hungry people still exist—are more likely to find greater appeal in Marxian ideology than in the ideology of democratic capitalism. But Marxism extends an additional and psychological offering to the economically disadvantaged and dispossessed. In a curious way, this special source of appeal is analogous to one held forth in the Gospels to potential Christians. For just as Christianity promises the poor a better chance of entering the gates of heaven than the rich, so does Marxism promise the proletariat the kingdom of the earth. Indeed, Marx charged the proletariat with the salvation of all mankind, holding that it is the historic mission of the workers to install a classless society in which life would be better than it is for anyone under capitalism.[12]

Marx saw the "dictatorship of the proletariat"[13] as a passing phase in the eventual attainment of ideal communism, a condition in which the State would have "withered away,"[14] along with all remnants of invidious distinctions of salary, prestige, and power. Under these ideal circumstances, cooperation among people in all spheres of life would be freely and gladly given, each person being sufficiently liberated from all the noxious values of the old and abolished capitalistic order to be entrusted to treat each other decently without external coercion or incentive. Their material problems having been solved by the rational and social application of technology and science, people in the ideally communistic society could then devote themselves primarily to the unfolding of their human capacities rather than to the problems of production and distribution. It would then finally be possible to practice, in reality, the ideal of permitting each member of society to take whatever material resources he needed from it.[15]

Actually, many of Marx's conceptions of an ideal social order dovetail with those appropriate to a humane society. In fact, on *humane* grounds, it would be exceedingly difficult for a person of *any* economic persuasion whatsoever to argue that Marx's ultimate vision of peace, brotherhood, freedom, material abundance, mutual aid, and creative purposefulness among men is not eminently desirable.[16] Yet it is most paradoxical that Marx provided the rationale for the very institution, dictatorship, which has thus far been the biggest obstacle in the actual fulfillment of his social dream. For this dictatorship, together with the means—violent revolution—which brought it into being, is diametrically opposed to the means that would be consonant with Marx's conception of an ideal social order. Putting the Soviet dilemma into our terminology, while Marx envisioned a humane alternative to the beastliness of capitalism, he advocated, as a way of attaining the new society, means that reflect and support the values of aggrandizement rather than those of realization. For he encouraged members of the working class to seize a monopoly of power and to impose their will forcibly upon all elements in society.

Unquestionably, Marx put forth some impressive arguments[17] for these tactics. Principally, he held that the favored classes would not voluntarily give up their economic prerogatives—even if they were logically convinced of the injustice of the class system. Assuming, therefore, that most of the bourgeoisie would desire to retain their vested economic interests in capitalistic society, Marx reasoned that the proletariat would have to take the matter of societal change into their own hands if they ever wished to end their victimization by capitalism. They would have to exercise absolute power in the new society for an indefinite period of time —an epoch long enough to people the land with an overwhelming majority of citizens that supported its values and institutions; long enough to secure the new society against external attack from encircling and hostile capitalistic countries; long enough to purge society of dissident groups of people whose values were still bourgeois and whose inner loyalty was still given over to the deposed capitalistic regime.

Marx personally helped to lay the groundwork for a political organization[18] that was to evolve into the spearhead of the Russian Revolution. Of course, following that Revolution, leadership in the Soviet Communist Party has changed hands several times. But the Party itself can always harken back to Marx for a justification for whatever lengths of absolutism and terror it sees fit to impose upon the Russian people. For did not Marx say that the representatives of the proletariat had the exclusive responsibility for furthering the aims of the revolution? And was it not up to their discretion to say when and in what ways the Soviet people were ready to be entrusted with a bit of "withering" of the power of the State?

Under the theory of the "dictatorship of the proletariat," it has been possible for the leaders of the Soviet Communist Party to rationalize not only the bloody disposition of the pre-revolutionary Russian regime but also the "liquidations," imprisonments, and tortures that they have inflicted upon all those who opposed, or were alleged to oppose, whatever plans, policies, or programs the dictatorship promulgated on behalf of its guardianship of communism.

Similarly, drawing upon his concept of historical materialism,[19] Marx gave the leaders of Soviet society persuasive theoretical reasons for extending the system of invidious economic distinctions into the post-revolutionary era. He pointed out that every society, however novel its economic principles, inevitably continues to reflect the influence of the society that preceded it; and that every revolutionary change would have to accommodate attitudes that had been formed in the overthrown society. Thus, Marx claimed that the wage system was a necessary transitional device; that, since people were used to the incentive of differential wages, it would be necessary to continue that practice until the time came when the State had "withered away" and conditions were right for the institution of a completely equitable economy.[20]

From Lenin[21] onward, the leaders of the "dictatorship of the proletariat" had on hand a set of systematic ideological justifications for their totalitarian proprietorship as well as for its perpetuation; a carte blanche bequeathed to them by Marx himself. Yet it is—or seemingly should be—perfectly apparent to anyone who has the slightest feeling for human psychology, that means and ends must be coordinated if the ends are to be properly served; that just as the intrinsic selfishness of capitalistic economics cannot possibly fail to promote the values of aggrandizement, coercion, murder, and dictatorship cannot advance the cause of the values of realization. He who snuffs out the life of another in the name of humanitarianism is playing a macabre joke on the value he purports to uphold. And he who proclaims that he is pointing the way to equalitarianism by subordinating millions upon millions of people to his absolute will is deluding himself to a grotesque extreme. No, the values of realization are not furthered by methods appropriate to the pursuit of aggrandizement. This fact is just as true in America as in Russia; just as valid in a socialistic economy as in a capitalistic one. Nor is it a matter of the ancient question of the ends justifying the means. Such a question immediately suggests stupidity or maliciousness on the part of the person who asks it. For ends are always expressed in the means used to further them.

Values, after all, are abstract concepts which, however, have specific implications for the kinds of concrete actions that are appropriate to their conceptual properties. And it is quite possible to say which concrete actions reflect which abstract values. Admittedly, human beings tend to attach benevolent motives to even the most despicable of their actions. However, our most reliable guide to the values that underlie an act is the act itself, and not the reasons given for it by the behaving person. Willful murder, therefore, connotes a contempt for human life—for the value of humanitarianism—regardless of the pretext given for it. He who murders deliberately—whether he be killing for avowedly selfless reasons or selfish ones, whether in the name of the values of realization or those of aggrandizement—is debasing the values of human life. And he who enslaves others—whether expressly to spare unborn generations from the coils of an unjust society or to exploit contemporaries for his own glorification—is raising himself above his brethren, showing contempt for the value of equalitarianism.

Perhaps the leaders of the Russian Revolution, even as the leaders of the American Revolution, were so intoxicated by the righteousness of their cause that they could scarcely be troubled to think through the long-range implications of their actions. Moreover, the world had not yet witnessed the holocaust of Nazism, the fantastic extremes to which human destruction and enslavement could be ideologically rationalized. But those of us who survived World War II have had more than a passing glimpse into the burning pit that can be dug and lit by an excess of presumption. And those of us for whom the words Hiroshima and Nagasaki conjure up the cauldron of all cauldrons are more than a little wary of noble pronouncements that are not matched by humane deeds.

In spite of the cold war of words that America and the Soviet Union have been conducting with each other since the time when they were military allies, each of those societies has about the same number, if different, of virtues and vices—insofar as the values of realization are concerned. Our government, in the name of the democratic values for which it professes to stand, might well take some lessons from the Russians concerning economic justice. But the Russian people would similarly benefit if their leaders, on behalf of helping to advance Marx's ideal of democratic communism, took some lessons from us in political and intellectual freedom.

Interestingly, it does seem that internal and international pressures are inducing both countries to move somewhat in these directions—toward greater economic justice here and greater political freedom there—albeit that such movements are not necessarily the result of mutual and deliberate emulation. Moreover, owing to the technology of automation, both countries will be increasingly confronted by exactly the same problems, and they may well decide upon a common mode of coping with them.

Prospects for the Future of Our Society

Since other modern societies give the values of realization no more support than does ours, it follows that we have as good a chance to evolve a humane society here as may obtain anywhere else in the real world. However, our society is not simply marking time, waiting for proponents of those values to make up their minds about how to change it. On the contrary, we are now caught up in the most important technological development of our era—automation; a development that, depending upon how we deal with it, can result either in our further degradation or in the evolution of a more humane society.

The application of automation[22] by industry has already had telling effects, and it has stirred ominous warnings[23] about the millions of workers threatened with permanent joblessness. To meet the challenge of automation, we shall be steadily obliged to shorten the working week, periodically scaling it downward as automated production becomes more widespread and efficient. And, assuming that we wish all possible workers to be employed, we shall soon reach a point at which, technically speaking, most "full-time" workers are, in fact, unemployed most of the time. We may even wish to adopt the principle of a guaranteed yearly wage.[24] Under that sort of agreement, many workers might spend whole weeks or months in idleness during the course of the year.

But what are the "full-time" workers of the era of automation to do in their "leisure" time? How will it be possible for them to feel that they are continually aggrandizing themselves when they are deprived of the usual means of achievement and accomplishment? Nor will the workers be the only ones faced with this dilemma. For as automation is introduced into management, the managers, too, will be confronted with the problem of how to pursue aggrandizement during the actually non-managing preponderance of their managerial "week." How will it be possible, therefore, for the oligarchies of industry and labor to provide tens of millions of essentially idle employees with the feeling that they are making continual progress in pursuing their limitless and egoistic ambitions? When active work itself ceases to be a viable means of pursuing aggrandizement, what will take its place?

Automation and the Spectre of Totalitarianism

If attempts are made to cope with these problems without changing either the dominant values of our society or the hierarchical and oligarchical structure of the organizations that personify these values, our future may be dismal indeed. For the almost irresistible trend would be toward a dictatorship—possibly a quite genteel one—in which the oligarchies of industry and labor would join forces and use their consolidated super-organization to pre-empt all of the effective political power of the country; in a word, to control that biggest of all our big organizations, the government.

But how could such a dictatorship arise? Theoretically, our economy has been independent of our political institutions. In the economic sphere, various oligarchies in the community have competed with each other—business with business, labor with labor, and business with labor. The role of the government, elected to represent the interests of the public-as-a-whole, has been to mediate between disputing vested interests and to maintain some semblance of a balance of forces in the economy. When economic conditions have been so bad as to create widespread unemployment and hunger, the government has initiated measures aimed at stimulating the economy. Our government has, in fact, become a major consumer, granting to American corporate enterprises vast sums for public works and military equipment. Still, it is *supposed* to be a neutral and detached observer of the economic scene, stepping in to patch up a bit here, inject a bit of cash there and arbitrate impartially between the competing oligarchies of capital and labor.

But the oligarchies that control our organizations of work do not hesitate to wield as much political influence as they can through every possible channel: by lobbying for legislative favor, by participation in and contributions to political campaigns, and by the dissemination of propaganda. In general, the wealth commanded by the oligarchies of industry has given them considerable advantages over those of labor in regard to the matter of securing the election of legislators and the passage of legislation that is congenial to their special interests.

Organized labor has also been somewhat effective in this respect, having available to it the monthly dues of millions of workers. On the other hand, since the largest of union organizations, the AFL-CIO, is guided by an economic philosophy that accepts the legitimacy of the capitalistic status quo, the economic disputes between the oligarchies of labor and industry are amenable to easy resolution; and the oligarchs of each group may well and often find themselves supporting the political careers of the same men. As the most affluent unions grow even more affluent by investing the dues of the workers they represent in the enterprises run by their industrial counterparts (one already hesitates to employ the word "antagonists" here for fear of its inappropriate usage), they may find themselves in an increasingly anomalous position. The boundaries between union and company have already begun to blur;[25] and the officials of the union may eventually find themselves called upon to sit on boards of directors of the industrial organizations in which their union is a major shareholder. When this happens on a widespread scale, the stage will have been set for the kind of political alliance between capital and labor that characterizes fascism; namely, state capitalism. At that time, it may behoove the oligarchies of capital-labor to cement their joint control of society by appropriating its political power as well as its economic resources. From that point, the step from democracy to totalitarianism is a small one. Indeed, such a coalition of industrial and labor oligarchies could produce a *de facto* totalitarian society within a *de jure* democratic one. Even at this juncture in our history, one cannot help but feel that our "two party" political system rests upon rather spurious distinctions of ideology; and that the choice among candidates presented by those parties often is a meaningless one.

Perhaps the clearest actual difference between the parties today lies in the oligarchies that support them rather than in their philosophies. Organized labor is in the Democratic camp, while organized capital usually has been in the Republican one. But if organized labor merged financially, if not organizationally, with organized capital, the differences in the sociological composition of the political parties would cease, in effect, to exist. Assuming a monopoly of power, the ruling oligarchical elite could then proceed to stupefy the nation systematically, releasing sufficient material wealth in the form of salaries for its quasi-employed population of underlings. And, in this way, the people could endlessly titillate their egoistic needs through the purchase and consumption of goods and services.

At the same time, by making readily available abundant supplies of soporifics and other drugs, the dictatorial oligarchy could give their subjects quick, sure, and easy methods of quelling boredom and inner distress. Inasmuch as some of the drugs would be able—as ones already on hand are known to do—to induce a great variety of intriguing hallucinations,[26] people could find their passivity not only painless but also diverting.

If baubles and palliatives proved insufficient to appease egoism and to dissipate boredom, the totalitarian rulers could keep the people preoccupied with international rivalries; concern with such rivalries could also incite nationalism, which has always served as one of the major channels of aggrandizement in the history of men. The proprietors of the State could strive to keep this channel of aggrandizement constantly before the eyes and ears of their subjects, exhorting them by inflammatory propaganda to identify with and preserve the reputed grandeur of "their" country against its covetous and menacing "inferiors" from abroad.

Naturally, purported threats from within as well as those from without could be used by the dictatorship to underscore its indispensability, to gain fearful respect for its military might, and to legitimize the prevailing economic and political status quo. And the dictatorship could, if it were felt necessary by it, keep the basically unemployed population in arms and in uniforms, prepared to fight "their" foreign "enemies," while ferreting out, arresting, guarding, and punishing "their" domestic "enemies." Under such circumstances, the dictatorship would be far from genteel. It might be as bloody as the most horrendous ones that have defaced the earth.

Still, it does seem quite possible to conceive of a genteel dictatorship, which could maintain its totalitarian rule even in the absence of international tensions; even, indeed, on an international basis. For "world government," assuming that it brings military peace in its wake, need not necessarily be dedicated to and established on behalf of the values of realization. On the contrary, it might more readily come into being as a tool of the values of aggrandizement, since those values are the most influential ones in each of the separate societies that would enter into the consolidation of national States.

Thus, it is conceivable to have both world government *and*

world peace *without* any basic change in either the set of values or the hierarchies of invidious distinction that now characterize and oppress the people of *all* societies in the world. Unless this possibility is fully recognized, unless we realize that an international order could suffer as badly as our present national order from the values of aggrandizement, we might not help ourselves very much by effecting a mammoth coalescence of individual States. True, in an international order, nationalism *per se* could no longer be used as a conceptual inducement to aggrandizement or as a device for maintaining dictatorial control over a specific territory. But to bring about such a global unification of political entities without altering either the basic values or the systems of invidious distinction that now prevail in each and every one of them, might simply insure the establishment of a genteel dictatorship on a worldwide scope.

Some might argue that a genteel dictatorship—be it national or global—is preferable to a crude one. To choose between the two seems, however, to be a matter of sophistic hair-splitting. In fact, a genteel dictatorship may be more effectively corrupting than a crude one. For where dictators show their megalomaniacal faces and openly seek to oppress, one can at least identify the instigators of one's torment. And if one has to die in protesting against the dictatorship, one at least knows whom to oppose. But in the kind of genteel dictatorship that it is now, most unfortunately, possible to envision, the dictators could function facelessly and subtly, employing the same kind of tactics of institutionalized propaganda and social control as are now used by the oligarchies that run our organizations of work; and, these genteel dictators could have us prancing or bemused, like so many docile monkeys.

Automation and the Opportunity for Realization

Fortunately, we have a real and most worthy alternative to such a chilling prospect; an alternative that is as easy to articulate as it may be difficult to implement. Quite simply, we can give the values of realization priority over those of aggrandizement; and we can alter our economic and political institutions in ways that are consistent with those values. Utilizing the potentially liberating effects of automation, we can take some major strides toward a humane society.

It is apparent that the liberating potentials of automation concern the release of human beings from their traditional bondage to monotonous or back-breaking labor. Accordingly, automation creates the viable possibility, perhaps the *first* viable one in the history of mankind, for thinking about men as creators rather than producers; for taking the adequate provision of men's material needs for granted as a technological plausibility and for regarding work primarily as a creative outlet for the unique potentials of man rather than as an imperative for his physical survival. By making it possible to view work independently of material necessity, to which its mechanical efficiency can attend, automation implicitly stimulates all of us to think of the kinds of work that would be inherently fulfilling; that men would wish to do of their own accord, and not because they are required to do it for extrinsic reasons.

Instead of fearing the arrival of automation, we ought to be grateful for it and to adapt it to the service of our humanity. To receive it in this optimistic spirit, however, we must first stop thinking in terms of self-centered economic prerogatives and begin planning for it rationally and generously.

Using automation as our lever, we should, first of all, press unrelentingly for economic justice. Surely, if automation can eliminate the indignities of stupefying labor, there can be no further excuse for the employment of men as drays and drudges. Surely, if automation can eliminate the bite of material deprivation, there is no excuse for man to suffer from poverty. We are now in a position not only to demand justice in our economy but also to utilize automation as a means of insuring it. Our government, still theoretically responsible for heeding the public will, is the institution most likely to translate public demands for justice into action.

Accordingly, we should petition our governmental representatives to view the development of automation as an aspect of the extension of justice. We should impel them through every possible means of exhortation to take an unambiguous stand on this matter.

Specifically, an unequivocal stand in favor of economic justice requires much more than legislative reforms that, for example, provide a more adequate dole for the "technologically unemployed." It requires nothing less than direct, deliberate, and purposeful intervention into the economy, transforming it from a capitalistic one into a cooperative one. Unopposed by such forthright intervention, the oligarchies of industry may well be content to continue to amass profits even as their use of automation permits them to discharge steadily mounting numbers of employees. Our government must function as more than an almshouse that caters to the corporate oligarchies; that collects and barely mollifies the millions of men set adrift by those oligarchies. Representing the people, the government must once and for all drop the pretense of being a neutral arbiter among competing vested interests and speak out in the interests of the humanity of its citizens—the only interests it ought to worry about protecting.

The government already intervenes profoundly in our economic life—subsidizing agriculture as well as a host of industries that produce for the "national defense." Although it may attach some conditions to the use of those funds—for example, the quality of the arms it purchases or the number of acres that must lie fallow for a given amount of financial support—the government has thus far imposed few stipulations that bear upon the economic justice of those employed by its subsidized corporate enterprises and agricultural entrepreneurs. However, in regard to its contracts, the government does ask[27] contractors to agree formally that they will not refuse employment to anyone on the basis of race, creed, or color. Having established this principle of intervention on behalf of justice for its citizens, the government has no reason, *in principle*, to balk at taking further steps to safeguard the humanity of the people. Indeed, it has *every* reason, in principle, to see to it that justice is done in economic affairs as well as in political affairs.

Consequently, we must encourage the representatives of government not only to acknowledge their responsibilities in regard to economic justice but also to act upon them. Legislatively speaking, such action would involve the passage of laws designed to eliminate private profit and invidious distinction from the entire economy. For only if the irrationalities of profit and invidious distinction are thus eliminated can automation be humanely applied and its fruits equitably distributed.

Ultimately, the demands of justice can be completely satisfied only under the kinds of democratic conditions that would obtain in the economy of a humane society. In urging legislation on behalf of economic justice, we should take great pains in specifying the changes that might truly increase the democracy of work—and not merely lead to an exchange of masters, the functionaries of the State for the oligarchs of industry. We must make sure that legislation in these and all the other relevant areas actually does work toward the "withering away" of the power of the State as well as the power of the oligarchs against whose hegemony we seek the government's intervention.

Obviously, it will not be easy to ask the government for intervention and, at the same time, require that its help be given in such a way as to have the ultimate effect of reducing its powers rather than of augmenting them. And yet, have not various propertied interests succeeded in making just such compacts with the government—albeit in furthering the values of aggrandizement rather than those of realization? During World War II, for example, the government often absorbed the entire cost of construction of new facilities for private corporations engaged in producing arms. When the war was over, however, such corporations retained those facilities and were free to use them for the production of whatever goods they wished to sell to the public. Therefore, a precedent has been established, in principle, for the kind of governmental intervention that, in effect, renders the aided party relatively stronger than it was before the government's intervention took place. That same principle could be just as logically applied to the nature of governmental intervention on behalf of the values of realization—that is, to further the humane interests of the people.

While working for economic justice, we must not fail to demand political and social justice as well. For if automation can give all men the time to educate themselves and to dwell upon the problems of their existence, there is no excuse for any group of men to hold themselves forth as specially qualified to determine the fate of their fellows. As in the case of economic justice, these demands may be most appropriately and effectively made via governmental channels, by pressing our elected representatives for legislation aimed at removing particular injustices and at widening the scope of political and social democracy. Certainly, we should require "the representatives of the people" to take legislative stands that leave no doubt about their commitment to the humanity of the people they represent. Legislation in favor of the granting of full civil rights to all the people would be consonant with such a commitment. But much more would have to be done along these lines before we begin to approach the level of political and social justice that should be found in a humane society.

As the humane application of automation unshackles us from the constraints involved in the specialization and division of labor, it makes education in the values of realization a very practical possibility. Such education is desirable not only as the chief underpinning of a humane society but also as the best way of preparing children to enjoy the time of adulthood that automation frees them to use as they please. In fact, there can be no better preventive against boredom than the continual cultivation and expression of one's creative capacities—both as a source of intrinsic joy and as a joy to others.

Anticipating the increase in unfettered time that automation will grant to adults—even within our existing social order—we should begin at once to make drastic alterations in the educational curricula of our schools. Specifically, we should turn away from narrowly vocational education, whose raison d'être has been the preparation of the young for the filling of highly specialized slots in a bureaucratic economy. Instead, looking forward to the time when that economy will be both less bureaucratic and less dependent upon human specialists and cogs, we should work toward a rebirth of the liberal arts and humanities; toward the development of a curriculum which, from youth through old age, will be oriented toward assisting the creative growth of men rather than toward the arrest of that growth early in life and the relegation of men to permanent occupational stalls.

In former times, the liberal arts curriculum was a luxury that only aristocrats could afford. Destined to be gentlemen of leisure, children of the aristocracy were given an education that would prepare them for the economic freedom of their adulthood. Such children could devote their adult years to an interesting avocation —or, perhaps, to several such avocations. And, if they were more seriously disposed, the moneyed gentry could apply the broad vistas of their educational background to the practical arts of statecraft or to some other realm of worldly affairs that involved the making of decisions whose effects might impinge upon all of their countrymen.

But the intelligent and just use of automation would bring about precisely the same conditions of adult freedom for *all persons* in society—not merely for a specially privileged class. And the liberal arts curriculum—with its emphasis upon intellectual breadth and historical perspective, with its explicit dedication to the creative development of the person *qua* person—would help our youth to approach their freedom with constructive zest; to look forward to it rather than to shun its ambiguities or to flee its challenges. Being educated, at the same time, in the values of humanitarianism, our youth would not regard service to their fellow men as a matter of *noblesse oblige* but, instead, as an opportunity to express their deepest values.

A *Humane Credo for Political Action*

As much as we might desire a speedy transition to a humane society, we cannot, in the name of the values of realization, propose an armed revolt against the institutions that presently uphold the values of aggrandizement in our society. For a revolutionary uprising, even if it could recruit a sufficient number of firebrands to vouchsafe it success, would surely require bloodshed—followed, in all likelihood, by an indefinite period of totalitarian rule by those who seize power. But both planful murder and dictatorship are contrary to the values of realization; and, because of their implicit arrogance, both of them reek with the excesses of aggrandizement.

The megalomania of dictatorship needs no further elucidation. But why is it that willful murder is the most extreme of all manifestations of megalomania? The answer is plain enough: such murder is an *irrevocable* assertion of the superiority of the killer's life over that of his victim. And it is just because this assertion is final and irreversible that it is the greatest of all injustices—no matter what its pretext; no matter how condemnatory its provocation; no matter how worthy the cause that presumes to justify it. Thus, premeditated murder can *never* be sanctioned on behalf of justice and humanity, since it is the supreme act of injustice and inhumanity.

To say that any *idea* about how life should be lived is more valuable than *life* itself not only reveals a failure of thought but also paves the way for slaughter. For it is obvious that life precedes ideas; and that ideas are meaningless without life. The newborn babe does not emerge from the womb with militant opinions about what is best for himself and others. Nor can corpses put into action the principles of living on whose behalf they were slain. Certainly, when the guillotine falls, it ends the controversy between executioner and victim. But it does not resolve the questions about life that each of them had sought to answer in a different way.

Life transcends all ideologies, all programs, all systems. And there cannot possibly be any idea that is preferable to human life, the source and the objective and the proving ground of all ideas. One might suppose that the precedence of life over ideas would have been recognized by all learned metaphysicians, if not by all untutored laymen. Yet even Camus, whose humane conscience permeated the ideological camps of the 1940's and 1950's like a head-clearing wind, rationalized his own homicidal actions on ideological grounds. Explaining his underground combat against the Nazis during their occupation of France, Camus said: "Paris is fighting today so that France may speak up tomorrow. The people are under arms tonight because they hope for justice for tomorrow."[28]

But Camus would have been more faithful to his own anguished quest for uncompromising ethical truth if he had held that no ideology—however false and bestial or honest and humane—is worth the life of a single person; and that, in shooting Nazis, he was destroying, not injustice, but human beings. And while Camus, in protesting the inhumanity of the Nazis, would no doubt have been forced, by their murderous reaction to his protest, to kill in self-defense, he ought to have recognized that, at the moment he squeezed the trigger, he was defending his life and not his concepts about life.

But it may be vehemently objected that men would never have been able to advance or preserve the values of realization if they had not been ready to take the lives of adversaries who opposed those values; if they had not been prepared, for the sake of those values, to sacrifice their own lives. To such an objection, one can only reply that history is not a controlled experiment, and that we do not know how societies might have developed if all men had renounced violence as a means of producing social change. Certainly, under such circumstances, the minds of every generation of men would not have been blighted, nor their hearts benumbed, by the assumption that murder was always possible if other forms of political action appeared to be too slow or ineffectual.

Ironically, the nuclear era seems, at last, to have put all ideological conflicts between "atomic" nations into a humane perspective—one in which the potential human cost of war is so great as to overshadow whatever competing principles may be at issue; one in which it is no longer possible to think of war without envisioning oneself strewn among the dead that would litter the land within moments after the onset of hostilities. Yet, while a balance of terror has increased the readiness of atomic nations to negotiate peacefully on differences that, in pre-atomic times, they might have attempted to settle in bloody combat, no such humanizing balance of power prevails among competing groups within those and other countries.

In the case of Soviet-American relationships, it is now possible for each side not only to register its discontents with the other but also to expect that its complaints will be respectfully considered and that serious attempts at redress and compromise will be undertaken. Within those countries, however, there exists the possibility that violence may still be employed—either as a means of protest on the part of people who differ ideologically from the oligarchies in power or as a means to which those oligarchies may resort in suppressing such protests.

Certainly, in our own society, the protests of the Negro people against their continuing degradation may not always be as peaceful as they have been thus far. Both Negro and white groups may one day become impatient with each other—the Negroes striking out vengefully for the justice that is rightly theirs; the whites striking back to enforce their long-held, if unfair, prerogatives.

But what would we have the Negroes do? Renounce protest? Resign themselves to injustice? Certainly not. And yet, how is it possible to protest without running the risk of incurring, if not inflicting, violence? Without running the risk of suicide, if not murder?

This last question raises to consciousness the three agonies that cannot be avoided by all who seek to aid the cause of justice. First, if our protest against injustice is made with a promise in advance that we shall not defend our lives from the anger of those against whom we complain, we may, in effect, be committing suicide. For if those who resent our demands for justice are sufficiently unjust, they may attempt to still us by resorting to the most heinous of all injustices, murder. Second, if we set out to murder them, we destroy not only our adversaries but also our own cause, having proven ourselves unable to act in accordance with our professed values. Third, if we seek to avoid the slightest possibility of incurring suicide or committing murder by shunning protest altogether—retiring to the silent underground of our private thoughts—we abet the forces of inhumanity by default. For an unheard voice cannot give pause to injustice.

It would be fairly simple to find a way out of these agonies by concluding that suicide is ethically preferable to murder. However, such a conclusion would be both logically and ethically insupportable. For if we assume that all human life is equally valuable, one's own life is as worthy of preservation as that of anyone else. Therefore, suicide is as monstrous an act of injustice as willful murder; and knowingly to invite the murder of oneself is as morally reprehensible as knowingly to murder another person.

It is for this reason—because suicide and homicide are equally impossible from a humanitarian viewpoint—that many conscientious humanitarians may be tempted to avoid becoming embroiled in ideological struggles that may result in violence. It is for this reason, too, that many such persons may balk at the tactics of "passive resistance"—if the passivity of the resisters is such as to allow themselves, if it should come to that, to be decimated without making any attempt to disarm or subdue those who attack them.

But complete withdrawal from protest against injustice, as we have seen, is a tacit acceptance of the values of aggrandizement; and the resistance of a passivity unto suicide is active complicity in injustice. Indeed, the martyr and the assassin are psychologically identical. For the martyr simply murders himself rather than someone else; and the grandiosity behind the taking of his own life is just as mad as that which motivates the assassin to kill another. Thus, under conditions that force a weaker party to petition justice from a stronger one, the possibility of assassination or suicide will necessarily exist unless *both* sides are committed to the *unconditional* renunciation of violence. But it may be argued that the stronger party might readily accede to such an agreement, since he would still be retaining his position of strength; and since his greater strength would still give him the power to deny to the weaker party his claims for justice.

And yet, what do we mean by "strength," in political terms, if not access to the powers of physical coercion? There can scarcely be any doubt that a renunciation of those powers would facilitate a humane dialogue between groups that feel themselves inequitably treated and those against whom they protest. Even a minority can appeal to the conscience of a majority—if the majority is obligated to confront its conscience, having voluntarily agreed that it cannot dispense with such a confrontation merely by calling out the militia and routing the protestors.

There have been some recent indications that the Congress of the United States may be ready to honor some of the protests that have emanated not only from the injustices of caste but also from the injustices of class. Nevertheless, the evolution of a more humane society will no doubt continue to be slow at best— perhaps excruciatingly slow for those whose need for social and economic justice is most acute. No doubt, too, such persons—as well as those more socially and economically advantaged persons who wish to see the values of realization replace those of aggrandizement—will find themselves wishing to speed that evolution. And so they should. For the protestations of millions of people cannot fail to impress Congress with the desirability of enacting more humane economic, political, and social laws—however much that legislation may be regarded by the Congressmen as a grudging consolation to those most hurt by our social order.

Massive protests against injustice serve to prick the conscience of large groups of Americans who might otherwise grow overly complacent with the status quo and overly acceptant of the degree to which the nation's democratic ideology, to which most of them subscribe, is discrepant from the actual inequities that deform the daily lives of millions of their fellow—but often unseen—citizens. For example, the dramatic and widespread Negro protests in favor of integration in every sphere of life have engaged the active support of many, many white Americans who might otherwise have evaded the discomfort of taking an unequivocal and public stand on that issue.

Yes, on behalf of the values of realization, we should protest injustice and press for the kinds of changes that would move us in the direction of a humane society. And, in these protests, we must take care to avoid both suicide and murder. Our protests, therefore, should be peaceful; and we should use only non-violent means of expressing the values in which we believe.

But to give up revolutionary violence—to give up offensive murder—is not to give up defense against murder; that is, the renunciation of murder cannot be a suicide-pact, lest we merely trade our own lives for others. We must protest and yet defend our lives as much as we would the lives of those whom our protests, insofar as they reached fruition, would protect, preserve, and benefit. If those against whose inequitable and inhumane practices we protest turn upon us with the intent to kill, we must attempt to disarm them. And if, in that kind of a struggle to save our lives, we kill our attackers, we should mourn for ourselves as well as for them—mourn for the senselessness of a human condition that thrusts us into such an impossible, yet such an inescapable, plight.

So, it appears that a genuinely humane position on political action for societal change would involve neither murder in the interest of revolutionary change nor suicide in the interest of evolutionary change nor a retreat from the field of action. Instead, to seek a humane society is to live out its values in one's political activity as well as in one's other activities. In the political sphere, this means bearing witness to the injustice of our dominant values and institutions. It means protesting against those values and institutions and attempting in every peaceful way possible to replace them with the values of realization and with institutions appropriate to the expression of those values. It means pressing for these changes without committing murder or suicide. And, finally, it means risking safety and security while, at the same time, being prepared to defend life—one's own no less than one's fellows'—against the presumptive onslaughts of a declared murderer.

This is not a simple formula for action; nor does it envision any political party, either one now in existence or one to form at some future date, as the sole champion of humanity. We must be prepared to work patiently with a variety of groups and organizations for changes that would be consonant with the values of realization. True, political murder has traditionally been employed by men throughout the world as the hoped-for instrument of a swift transformation from Hell to Heaven. Knowing, however, that Heaven has never been thus achieved—that not even decency can be thus achieved—we have little to lose in a strategy of firmness and forbearance. Surely, if we ever get a humane society, it will not be served up to us at the end of a sword. And if we honestly desire a humane society, we shall seek to realize it through means that express its values.

Notes

CHAPTER 1   AGGRANDIZEMENT VS. REALIZATION

1. For a small indication of the plethora of cultural differences in values that may be found in the world, see the empirical study by C. Morris, *Varieties of Human Value*. Chicago: University of Chicago Press, 1956.

2. Much of the analysis presented in this chapter is either abstracted or revised from an unpublished paper: I. Sarnoff, "Juvenile delinquency and the social psychology of limitless aspiration." Western Reserve University, School of Applied Social Sciences, 1961. A number of the central ideas in that early paper, it should be noted, have since been drastically modified or discarded in accordance with the further development of my thoughts on the topic.

3. In respect to the dominant place of these values on the American scene, little seems to have changed in the past 135 years. As Alexis de Tocqueville observed about us in his classic commentaries: "The spirit of gain is always on the stretch, and the human mind, constantly diverted from the pleasures of imagination and the labours of the intellect, is there swayed by no impulse but the pursuit of wealth . . ." (*Democracy in America*. New York: Schocken, 1961, Vol. II, p. 41); "All are constantly seeking to acquire property, power and reputation . . ." (Vol. II, p. 290).

4. Irving Sarnoff, *Personality Dynamics and Development*. New York: Wiley, 1962, p. 142.

5. *Ibid.*, p. 145.

6. The general ideal of unending progress, which may be linked to any specific value, seems to have gathered momentum in the history of Western society since the Middle Ages. It has been argued convincingly, however, that this ideal did not become a salient facet of European philosophy until the seventeenth century. (See J. B. Bury, *The Idea of Progress*. New York: Dover, 1955.)

7. L. Kohlberg, "The development of children's orientations toward a moral order: I. Sequence in the development of moral thought." *Vita Humana*, 1963, Vol. VI, pp. 11-33.

8. David Riesman, *The Lonely Crowd*. New Haven: Yale University Press, 1950.

9. Sigmund Freud, *A General Introduction to Psychoanalysis*. New York: Permabooks, 1958.

10. J. Piaget, *The Language and Thought of the Child*. New York: Meridian, 1955.

11. See, for example: O. Fenichel, *The Psychoanalytic Theory of Neurosis*. New York: Norton, 1945, pp. 278-84; and S. Freud, "Character and anal eroticism." In *Collected Papers*, Vol. II. London: Hogarth, 1949, pp. 45-50.

12. Sigmund Freud, Two encyclopaedia articles: (a) "Psychoanalysis"; (b) "The libido theory." In *Collected Papers*, Vol. V. London: Hogarth, 1950, pp. 107-35.

CHAPTER 2 IMAGES FOR THE AMERICAN DREAM

1. For a highly documented history of the development of the Hebrew concept of monotheism, see: T. J. Meek, *Hebrew Origins*. New York: Harper, 1960, Chapter III.

2. Meek (*ibid.*, p. 228) has said of the Hebrew evolution of monotheism: "With them . . . religion became a matter of the heart and of righteous living rather than mere ritualistic practice."

3. In his speculative account of the origin of Hebraic monotheism (*Moses and Monotheism*. London: Hogarth, 1951), Freud holds that the concept arose in Egypt during the reign of Amenhotep IV, who came into power about 1375 B.C.; and that its dissemination served the Pharaoh's desire to impose unity upon the diverse sections of his empire.

4. In the opening page of *The Iliad* (New York: Bantam, 1960, p. 35), the literary stature of which remains undiminished after two thousand years, Homer seriously poses this question about the antagonists in the Trojan War: "Which one of the gods, then, set them to angry quarreling?"

5. Sigmund Freud, *The Future of an Illusion*. London: Hogarth, 1949.

6. P. A. Kropotkin, *Ethics: Origin and Development*. New York: Tudor, 1947.

7. *Ibid.*, p. 118.

8. The following works are, perhaps, the best-known attempts to draw a psychological relationship between the theology of Protestantism and the economics of capitalism: E. Fromm, *Escape from Freedom*. New York: Farrar and Rinehart, 1941; R. H. Tawney, *Religion*

and the Rise of Capitalism. New York: Penguin, 1947; and M. Weber, *The Protestant Ethic and the Spirit of Capitalism.* London: Allen and Unwin, 1948.

9. J. Burkhardt, *The Civilization of the Renaissance in Italy.* New York: Mentor, 1960.

10. See, for example, the role of Catholic monks in the history of medieval literature: W. P. Ker, *The Dark Ages.* New York: Mentor, 1958.

11. For detailed examples of the artistic patronage of the Popes of the Renaissance, see: H. S. Lucas, *The Renaissance and the Reformation.* New York: Harper, 1934, Parts IV and V; and H. Daniel-Rops, *The Protestant Reformation.* New York: Dutton, 1961, Chapter IV.

12. R. S. Lopez, "Hard times and investment in culture." In *The Renaissance: Six Essays.* New York: Harper, 1962, pp. 29-54.

13. For example, according to Daniel-Rops (*op. cit.,* p. 261): "Raphael, during his brief career in Rome, was treated as a prince, fawned upon and flattered by all and sundry, even by Pope Leo X, who talked of making him a cardinal."

14. Perhaps the most famous of these was Benvenuto Cellini, also a sculptor of great renown, whose autobiography is almost a caricature of self-glorification—and a documentary record of the many and different ways by which exceptionally talented men of the Renaissance were glorified by their contemporaries. (See *The Autobiography of Benvenuto Cellini.* New York: Washington Square Press, 1963.)

15. See W. K. Ferguson, "Toward the modern state." In *The Renaissance: Six Essays, op. cit.,* pp. 1-28; and H. Pirenne, *A History of Europe* Vol. II. New York: Anchor, 1956, Book III.

16. See Pirenne, *op. cit.;* also Daniel-Rops, *op. cit.,* Chapter VII; and Lucas, *op. cit.,* Book II.

17. "Every individual is continually exerting himself to find out the most advantageous employment for whatever capital he can demand. It is his own advantage, indeed, and not that of society, which he has in view. But the study of his own advantage naturally or rather necessarily, leads him to prefer that employment which is most advantageous to society." (Adam Smith, *An Inquiry into the Causes of the Wealth of Nations,* Vol. II. Oxford: Clarendon Press, 1880, p. 26.)

18. For example, Smith (*ibid.,* Vol. I, p. 85) uses purely economic reasons in seeking to persuade entrepreneurs to shun slavery: "The wear and tear of a slave, it has been said, is at the expense of his master; but that of a free servant is at his own expense. The wear and tear of the latter, however, is, in reality, as much at the expense of his master as that of the former. The wages paid to journeymen and

servants of every kind must be such as may enable them, one with another, to continue the race of journeymen and servants, according as the increasing, diminishing, or stationary demand of the society may happen to require. But though the wear and tear of a free servant be equally at the expense of his master, it generally costs him much less than that of the slave. The fund destined for replacing or repairing, if I may say so, the wear and tear of the slave, is commonly managed by a negligent master or careless overseer. That destined for performing the same office with regard to the free man, is managed by the free man himself. The disorders which generally prevail in the economy of the rich, naturally introduce themselves into the management of the former: the strict frugality and parsimonious attention of the poor as naturally establish themselves in that of the latter. Under such different management, the same purpose must require very different degrees of expense to execute it. It appears, accordingly, from the experience of all ages and nations, I, believe, that the work done by freemen comes cheaper in the end than that performed by slaves. . . ."

19. H. Pirenne, *Medieval Cities*. New York: Anchor, 1956, p. 82.

CHAPTER 3   FROM FRONTIER TO OLIGARCHY

1. "Immigration in the eighteenth century was almost wholly economic in motive. The reports of free land and free opportunity in America penetrated to remote hamlets of Great Britain, and more slowly to the continent, and drew hither a rude influx of the dispossessed and disinherited of Europe." (V. L. Parrington, *Main Currents in American Thought*, Vol. I. New York: Harvest, 1961, p. 135.) Another commentator on the early American scene has, in fact, attributed the failure of the Dutch to become a more important power in the New World to their reluctance to accommodate the economic motives of the immigrants who settled in their territory. "Although the Dutch were shrewd businessmen, they failed to capitalize on the greatest of all impulses toward the colonization of America—the desire of the underprivileged people of Europe to secure a piece of land which they could call their own." (R. B. Morris, "Why the Dutch failed." In E. S. Miers [ed.], *The American Story*. Great Neck, N.Y.: Channel Press, 1956, pp. 41-42.)

2. "It became sinful to spend freely, just as it was sinful not to be forever at work, except on the Sabbath; and when the catch of fish or slaves was good, God had smiled on one of his saints." (J. T. Adams, *The Epic of America*. Boston: Little, Brown, 1932, p. 58.) An excel-

lent statement summarizing the impact of Puritanism on the economic history of America may be found in Parrington, *op. cit.*, p. 272.

3. Concerning those who emerged victorious as the "steel kings," "railway magnates" and "Napoleons of finance," it has been said: "Arising in most cases from obscure origins, and unhindered by moral scruples, they were fired by a passionate will to succeed. They conceived themselves as above the law though always willing to hide behind it." (A. M. Schlesinger, *Political and Social Growth of the American People: 1865-1940.* New York: Macmillan, 1941, p. 129.)

4. See R. Presthus, *The Organizational Society.* New York: Knopf, 1962, Chapter III.

5. See W. Miller, *A New History of the United States.* New York: Braziller, 1958, Chapter XI.

6. Schlesinger, *op. cit.*, pp. 127-42.

7. For data on and references to the extent of interlocking directorship in American corporations, see: C. W. Mills, *The Power Elite.* New York: Oxford University Press, 1959, pp. 383-84.

8. J. K. Galbraith, *American Capitalism.* Boston: Houghton Mifflin, 1956, Chapter IV.

9. *Ibid.*, p. 42.

10. Presthus, *op. cit.*, p. 80.

11. Adams, *op. cit.*, p. 38.

12. It has been estimated that half the European immigrants who came to America in the eighteenth century entered the country "under some form of 'white servitude' . . . The institution of white servitude survived the Revolution. George Washington was ordering the purchase of servants for his Virginia plantation in 1784; while in Pennsylvania as late as 1793 it was held that tampering with the indenture system would bring severe social and economic dislocations." (Miller, *op. cit.*, pp. 70-71.)

13. S. Rezneck, "The influence of depression upon American opinion, 1857-1859." *The Journal of Economic History*, 1942, Vol. II, p. 4.

14. Schlesinger, *op. cit.*, p. 523.

15. Schlesinger (*ibid.*, p. 149) quotes the United States Bureau of Labor as reporting that almost 24,000 lockouts and strikes occurred in this country between 1881 and 1900.

16. It is true that Eugene V. Debs, the candidate of the Socialist Party for the Presidency of the United States in the election of 1920, polled 919,799 votes—and that while serving a sentence in a Federal penitentiary (S. Holbrook, *Dreamers of the American Dream.* New York: Doubleday, 1957, p. 334). But even if we wished to assume,

with unjustified rashness, that each of those votes was registered by a member of the working class, we would still be obliged to conclude that the overwhelming majority of workers voted for one of the adherents of capitalism who ran against Debs: Warren Harding and James M. Cox.

17. *Ibid.*, p. 337.

18. Presthus, *op. cit.*, p. 81.

19. Actually, the percentage of unionized workers has been shrinking, slightly, relative to the total number of workers in the labor force. In 1956, the percentage of unionized workers was 24.8 per cent, the highest figure since the beginning of the labor movement in America. But by 1960, it had declined to 23.3 per cent (*Statistical Abstract of the United States.* Washington: United States Department of Commerce, 1963, p. 250). This trend probably reflects, in large measure, the much more rapid rate in the growth of "white collar" jobs as compared with "blue collar" jobs. (See Presthus, *op. cit.*, p. 78.)

20. Indeed, the constitutions of our most populous unions appear only rarely to acknowledge the right of members to form groups in opposition to the policies of their leaders. (See C. Argyris, *Integrating the Individual and the Organization.* New York: Wiley, 1964, p. 62.)

21. Presthus, *op. cit.*, p. 50. See also C. W. Mills, *The New Men of Power.* New York: Harcourt, Brace, 1948, pp. 64-67.

22. See, for example: A. H. Raskin, "Union discrimination is hard to erase." *The New York Times*, May 10, 1964, Section IV, p. 5.

23. See E. Reid, *Mafia.* New York: Random House, 1962; and E. Perlmutter, "Mafia wields sinister power." *The New York Times*, September 29, 1963, Section IV, p. 5.

24. Presthus, *op. cit.*, p. 11.

25. *Ibid.*, p. 79.

26. *Ibid.*, pp. 10, 79.

27. *Ibid.*, p. 78.

28. For examples of the lengths to which workers may go in coercing each other to produce less than they are physically able to do, see: G. Homans, *The Human Group.* New York: Harcourt, Brace, 1950, pp. 60-61.

CHAPTER 4   THE TYRANNY OF CLASS AND CASTE

1. Mills, *The Power Elite, op. cit.*, p. 260.

2. See, for example: A. B. Hollingshead, *Elmtown's Youth.* New York: Wiley, 1949; and W. L. Warner and P. S. Lunt, *The Social Life*

of a Modern Community, Vol. I. New Haven: Yale University Press, 1941.

3. For a review and discussion of investigations that demonstrate this point, see: Argyris, *op. cit.*, Chapter IV, and Presthus, *op. cit.*, Chapter VII.

4. A. J. Mayer and P. Hauser, "Class differentials in expectation of life at birth." In R. Bendix and S. M. Lipset (eds.), *Class, Status and Power*. Glencoe, Ill.: Free Press, 1953, pp. 281-83.

5. See Argyris, *op. cit.*, and Presthus, *op. cit.*

6. To savor the nuances of these differences in definitions of class, see: Bendix and Lipset, *op. cit.*, Part I.

7. Presthus, *op. cit.*, p. 206.

8. W. P. Reuther, "First things first." Santa Barbara, Calif.: The Fund for the Republic, p. 4.

9. Mills, *The Power Elite*, *op. cit.*, Chapters VIII, IX, and X.

10. *Ibid.*, p. 262, Presthus, *op. cit.*, p. 50; and, A. H. Raskin, "Hoffa shaping a teamster colossus." *The New York Times*, November 11, 1963, Section IV, p. 5.

11. Mills, *The Power Elite*, *op.cit.*, Chapter VI.

12. Presthus, *op. cit.*, Chapter VI.

13. Mills, *The Power Elite*, *op. cit.*, Chapter V.

14. D. R. Miller and G. E. Swanson, *The Changing American Parent*. New York: Wiley, 1958.

15. Clearly, the unemployed would fall into the group of Americans whose poverty, in the midst of the affluence of their fellow citizens, has moved Michael Harrington to call them *The Other America* (Baltimore: Penguin, 1963). Harrington estimates that between 40 and 50 million people in this country may still be properly classified as poor, with all the physical and psychological handicaps that follow from low income. Obviously, Harrington's figures include not only the unemployed and their families but also poorly paid employees and their families.

16. L. E. Lomax, *The Negro Revolt*. New York: Signet, 1963, p. 27.

17. T. Dobzhansky, *Mankind Evolving*. New Haven: Yale University Press, 1962, p. 269.

18. W. M. Young, Jr., "Racial discrimination." In N. E. Cohen (ed.), *Social Work and Social Problems*. New York: National Association of Social Workers, 1964, p. 347.

19. Civil rights bill—V. *The New York Times*, May 8, 1964, p. 32.

20. T. F. Pettigrew, A *Profile of the Negro American*. Princeton: Van Nostrand, 1964, p. 71.

21. Dobzhansky, *op. cit.*, p. 286 .

22. Young, *op. cit.*

23. It has been noted that in the United States slavery operated as a more drastic exclusion of the individual slave from the rest of society than it did elsewhere. "In the slave system of the United States—so finely circumscribed and so clearly self-contained—virtually all avenues of recourse for the slave, all lines of communication to society at large, originated and ended with the master." (S. M. Elkins, *Slavery*. New York: Grosset and Dunlap, 1963, p. 63.)

24. Indeed, the Constitution of the United States did not even deign to regard slaves as whole persons—for purposes of either taxation or representation. Instead, referring to them euphemistically as "other persons," Article 1, Section 2 ruled, by implication, that Negro slaves were only three-fifths as human as whites. By contrast, that same Section equates indentured servants, "those bound to service for a term of years," with "free persons."

25. See S. Lubell, *White and Black: Test of a Nation*. New York: Harper & Row, 1964, Chapter II.

26. W. M. Young, Jr., *To Be Equal*. New York: McGraw-Hill, 1964, p. 155.

27. *Ibid.*

28. R. K. Plumb, "Harvard finds U. S. trailing other nations in infant care, life expectancy." *The New York Times*, November 26, 1963, p. 45.

29. S. M. Willhelm and E. H. Powell "Who needs the Negro?" *Trans-action*, September/October 1964, pp. 4-5.

30. Young, "Racial discrimination," *op. cit.*, p. 346.

31. Pettigrew, *op. cit.*, pp. 16-17.

32. For extensive reviews of these studies, see: *Ibid.*; and T. F. Pettigrew and D. C. Thompson (eds.), "Negro American personality." *The Journal of Social Issues*, April, 1964 (entire number).

33. Lomax, *op. cit.*, p. 224.

34. *Ibid.*, p. 225.

35. Young, *To Be Equal*, *op. cit.*, pp. 217-18.

36. *Ibid.*, p. 219.

37. N. Glazer, "The Negroes." In N. Glazer and D. P. Moynihan, *Beyond the Melting Pot*. Cambridge, Mass.: The M.I.T. Press, 1963, pp. 51-52.

38. *Ibid.*, p. 84.

39. In Nazi Germany, needless to say, Jews were totally and fatally expelled from the caste of the self-styled "master race."

40. Lubell, *op. cit.*, p. 192.

41. *Ibid.*

42. *Ibid.*

43. C. E. Silberman, *Crisis in Black and White*. New York: Random House, 1964, Chapter X.

44. N. Hentoff, *The New Equality*. New York: Viking, 1964, Chapter XII.

45. R. P. Warren, "Five books on the race crisis." *The New York Review*, October 8, 1964, pp. 7-9.

46. M. L. King, Jr., *Why We Can't Wait*. New York: Signet, 1964, Chapter VIII.

47. Silberman, *op. cit.*, p. 289.

48. *Ibid.*, p. 290.

49. For Negroes who seek housing in a predominantly white neighborhood or building, the process of locating, purchasing, or renting a place can also become a nightmare of anxiety, uncertainty, humiliation, and harassment.

50. For detailed accounts of the history and ideology of the Black Muslims, see: E. C. Lincoln, *The Black Muslims in America*. Boston: Beacon, 1961; and L. E. Lomax, *When the Word Is Given*. Cleveland: World, 1963.

51. Chief among these organizations are: the National Association for the Advancement of Colored People (NAACP), the Urban League, the Congress of Racial Equality (CORE), the Southern Christian Leadership Conference (SCLC) and the Student Non-Violent Coordinating Committee (SNCC).

52. See, for example: King, *op. cit.*; and Young, *To Be Equal*, *op. cit.*

53. Most white supporters of the Negro Revolution would agree, in general, with this way of defining and combating the injustice of caste. For they, too, are inclined to accept the values and institutions of our present society as the appropriate context for making and evaluating recommendations aimed at reducing or eliminating the inequities of caste. And while they may differ with each other over the relative merits of specific remedial measures, their prescriptions are not designed—any more than those of the Negro leaders of the "revolution"—to bring about *basic* alterations in the societal status quo.

54. See the previously cited works by Young.

55. Lubell, *op. cit.*, p. 141.

56. Willhelm and Powell (*op. cit.*) have remarked, with laudable frankness, that the inhumane application of automation could result in the *permanent* unemployment of those Negroes who are presently unemployed in numbers far outweighing the proportion of Negroes in the American population. Naturally, such an application of automation would also enlarge the ranks of the unemployed, both Negro and white. However, it is entirely possible to prevent these dire prospects by gearing our technology to the best interests of our humanity. For specific suggestions about how this could be done, see Chapters IX and X of this book.

57. When Lubell (*op. cit.*, p. 193) laments that "full 'freedom' is beyond the reach of any of us," he is seeking to apologize for the odious limitations upon freedom maintained by our present society. However, we have the option of working to bring much fuller freedom than we now have within the reach of all of us. Yet this option might not suggest itself spontaneously to Lubell or any writer who discusses the Negro's struggle against caste within a context that assumes the basic values and structure of our society to be either good or inviolable.

58. For example, as King (*op. cit.*, p. 124) has sadly reported, the National Council of the largest of all American labor unions, the AFL-CIO, voted against joining the greatest single demonstration for civil rights ever held in this country—the March on Washington of August 28, 1963.

59. As Hentoff (*op. cit.*, p. 220) has reminded us, "while there are proportionately more Negro than white poor, at least 75 per cent of *all* the poor are white."

CHAPTER 5   THE CONFORMITY OF EGOISM

1. See L. I. Pearlin and M. Rosenberg, "Propaganda techniques in institutional advertising." *Public Opinion Quarterly*, 1952, Vol. XVI, pp. 5-26.

2. For a review of empirical studies that underscore not only this realization but also its damaging effects on the morale of workers, see: Argyris, *op. cit.*, Chapter IV.

3. Throughout the whole of his magnum opus (*Capital*. New York: Modern Library, 1939), Karl Marx tends to give his readers the impression that all capitalists exploit their employees with untroubled gusto, reveling with unspoiled delight in the prerogatives of their class. P. J. Proudhon, the "father" of the anarchist movement that

flowered in the nineteenth century, conveys much the same tone in his classic condemnation of private property. (*What Is Property?* New York: Humboldt, 1898.)

4. Mills, *The Power Elite, op. cit.*

5. Marx, for example, conjures this horrendous and inhuman image of the capitalist: "Capital is dead labor, that vampire-like, only lives by sucking living labor, and lives the more, the more it sucks." (*Capital, op. cit.*, p. 257.)

6. See Mills, *The Power Elite, op. cit.*, Chapter V.

7. "Some industrial and business concerns assign vice presidents to serve on agency boards and welfare federation committees, not as an expression of their humanitarian commitment, but rather for the sake of good public relations or so that they may guide decision-making." (A. Blum, "Values and aspirations as a focus for treatment." *In Social Work Practice.* New York: Columbia University Press, 1963, p. 36.)

8. See Mills, *The Power Elite, op. cit.*, Chapter X.

9. For the deficiencies of the parliamentary system in regard to the matter of truly representing the wishes of all the people, see the criticisms raised by the following spokesmen of diverse ideological persuasions: M. Bakunin, *Marxism, Freedom and the State.* London: Freedom Press, 1950; G. D. H. Cole, *Guild Socialism.* New York: Stokes, 1920; and K. Marx, *The Eighteenth Brumaire of Louis Bonaparte.* New York: New York Labor News Company, 1951.

10. Mills, *The Power Elite, op. cit.*, pp. 400-402.

11. For discussions of the psychology of duplicity in the context of life in contemporary organizations of work, see: A. Green, "Duplicity: Yesterday, today, and tomorrow." *Psychiatry*, 1943, Vol. VI, pp. 411-24; and I. Sarnoff, *Personality Dynamics and Development, op. cit.*, Chapter XIV, pp. 446-48.

12. Presthus, *op. cit.*, Chapter VI.

13. Mills, *op. cit.*, Chapter VI.

14. See V. Packard, *The Status Seekers.* New York: McKay, 1959; and W. H. Whyte, Jr., *The Organization Man.* New York: Simon and Schuster, 1956.

15. A portrait of the "marketing personality" may be found in E. Fromm, *Man for Himself.* New York: Rinehart, 1947, pp. 67-81.

16. See Miller and Swanson, *op. cit.*

17. Riesman, *op. cit.*

18. See Argyris, *op. cit.*

19. See, for example: R. H. Guest, "Work careers and aspirations of automobile workers." *Administrative Science Review*, Vol. XIX,

1954, pp. 155-63; A. Kornhauser, "Mental health of factory workers: a Detroit study." *Human Organization*, 1962, Vol. XXI, pp. 43-46; and H. Swados, "The myth of the happy worker." In M. R. Stein, *et al.* (eds.), *Identity and Anxiety*. Glencoe, Ill.: Free Press, pp. 198-204.

20. Presthus, *op. cit.*, Chapter VII.

21. *Ibid.*, Chapter VIII.

22. From 1945 through 1962, credit buying in America soared from $5,700,000,000 to $63,500,000,000; and debts on mortgages which were taken out primarily for the construction of private homes increased almost tenfold, from 1945 through 1962, going from $27,000,000,000 to $210,900,000,000. ("Why debt is a growing worry." *U. S. News and World Report*, August 26, 1963, pp. 90-91.)

23. The volume of these bills seems to be crushing a rapidly increasing number of Americans. Whereas 22,933 employees voluntarily filed cases of personal bankruptcy in 1950, 46,163 such cases were filed in 1955, 89,639 in 1960 and 120,742 in 1962 (*Statistical Abstract of the United States*, 1963, p. 508).

24. K. Marx and F. Engels, *Literature and Art*. New York: International Publishers, 1947, p. 33.

25. A. B. Hollingshead and F. C. Redlich, *Social Class and Mental Illness*. New York: Wiley, 1958, Chapter VIII.

26. E. Durkheim, *Suicide*. Glencoe, Ill.: Free Press, 1951, Chapter V.

27. "Such specialization encourages total recall of an artist by an easily identifiable tag—the 'mailboxes man' or the 'blue dots man.' Individuality is ready-made in ways acceptable to a new semi-educated public." B. O'Doherty, "The corruption of individuality." *The New York Times*, June 23, 1963, Section II, p. 15.

28. In 1950, 11,022 new books and new editions were published, of which 1,907 or 17 per cent were in the category of fiction (*Statistical Abstract of the United States*, 1963, p. 527). In 1963, by contrast, 25,784 new books and editions were published, of which 3,124 or only 12 per cent were in the category of fiction ("1963: Subject analysis of American book title output." *Publishers' Weekly*, January 20, 1964, p. 59).

29. Among the most popular of these recent collaborations have been: E. Burdick, and H. Wheeler, *Fail-Safe*. New York: McGraw-Hill, 1962; F. Knebel and C. W. Bailey, *Seven Days in May*. New York: Harper, 1962; and W. J. Lederer and E. Burdick, *The Ugly American*. New York: Norton, 1958.

CHAPTER 6   INJUSTICE, CRIME, AND DELINQUENCY

1. Indeed, the very extremity of the means used by burglars, extortionists, swindlers, forgers, and other flagrant criminals to obtain money indicates the degree of their commitment to the leading value of our society.

2. Proudhon, *op. cit.*, p. 183.

3. See, for example: "Crime in U.S.—Is it getting out of hand?" *U. S. News and World Report*, August 26, 1963, pp. 38-43.

4. For empirical studies of the relationship between frustration and aggression, see: J. Dollard, L. W. Doob, N. E. Miller, O. H. Mowrer, and R. R. Sears, *Frustration and Aggression*. New Haven: Yale University Press, 1939.

5. *U. S. News and World Report, op. cit.*

6. Proudhon, *op. cit.*, p. 263.

7. *Ibid.*, p. 265.

8. *U. S. News and World Report, op. cit.*

9. M. Rosenberg, "Social class, values and juvenile delinquency." Unpublished M. A. thesis. Western Reserve University, School of Applied Social Sciences, 1962, pp. 3-4. The references mentioned by Rosenberg are, in their order of presentation: E. H. Sutherland and D. Cressey, *Principles of Criminology*. Philadelphia: Lippincott, 1955, p. 120; J. S. Wallerstein and C. J. Wyle, "Our law-abiding law breakers." *Probation*, 1947, Vol. XXV, pp. 107-12; A. L. Porterfield, *Youth in Trouble*. Fort Worth: Leo Potishman Foundation, 1946, pp. 37-41; and I. F. Nye, J. F. Short, and V. J. Olson, "Socio-economic status and delinquent behavior." *American Journal of Sociology*, 1958, Vol. LXIII, pp. 381-89.

10. Much of the remaining material in this chapter is either abstracted or revised from: I. Sarnoff, "Juvenile delinquency and the social psychology of limitless aspiration," *op. cit.*

11. The figures cited in this paragraph are taken from *U. S. News and World Report, op. cit.*

12. S. Grafton, "The tense generation." *Look*, August 27, 1963, pp. 18-23.

13. "In fact, during periods of economic prosperity, delinquency increases, whereas during periods of economic depression and recession it decreases. (During the depression of the '30s, delinquency rates dropped sharply. They picked up during World War II, declined during the post-war recession, and have been steadily mounting since the prosperous period of 1958.)

"In addition, the relationship between poverty, lower-class standards, slums and delinquency is not substantiated by statistics from other countries. Sweden, for example, an almost entirely middle-class country, has one of the highest delinquency rates in the world. . . . Turkey, on the other hand, a rather poor and underprivileged country, by our standards, has one of the lowest delinquency rates in the world. Another country whose delinquency rates are beginning to mount is Israel, which just ten years ago was a relatively poor country struggling to provide its people with a minimum level of subsistence. Today, as Israel's prosperity continues to expand, so also does her delinquency rate." (Rosenberg, *op. cit.*, pp. 1-2. As his source for the trend described in the first paragraph of this note, Rosenberg cites: H. M. Shulman. *Juvenile Delinquency in American Society*. New York: Harper, 1961; the reference cited for the trends reported in the second paragraph is: R. Tunley, *Kids, Crime and Chaos*. New York: Harper, 1962.)

14. R. H. Bohlke, "Social mobility, stratification inconsistency and middle class delinquency." *Social Problems*, 1961, Vol. VIII, pp. 351-63.

15. Mills, *The Power Elite, op. cit.*, Chapter III.

16. J. B. Conant, "Social dynamite in our large cities." *Children*, 1961, Vol. VIII, pp. 160-69.

17. "Juvenile delinquency: the scope of the problem." Attachment to the testimony of the Secretary, on behalf of H. R. 7178. Washington: United States Department of Health, Education and Welfare, 1961, p. 13.

18. "Report to the Congress on juvenile delinquency." Washington: Children's Bureau, United States Department of Health, Education and Welfare, 1960, p. 32.

19. R. A. Cloward and L. E. Ohlin, *Delinquency and Opportunity*. Glencoe, Ill.: Free Press, 1960.

CHAPTER 7   SANITY AND LOVE BESIEGED

1. See *Facts on the Major Killing and Crippling Diseases in the United States Today*. New York: The National Health Education Committee, Inc., 1961.

2. G. Gurin, J. Veroff, and Sheila Feld, *Americans View Their Mental Health*. New York: Basic Books, 1960, p. 38.

3. See, for example, Fenichel, *op. cit.*, Chapter XVI.

4. Clara Thompson, "Changing concepts of homosexuality in psychoanalysis." *Psychiatry*, 1947, Vol. X, pp. 183-89.

5. For detailed descriptions of individuals who have been so diagnosed, see: H. Cleckley, *The Mask of Sanity*. St. Louis: Mosby, 1955.

6. *Ibid.*, p. 424.

7. Gurin, Veroff, and Feld, *op. cit.*, p. 402.

8. According to the National Council on Alcoholism, reporting the most recent estimates released by experts in that field, 5,015,000 Americans were alcoholics as of 1956. (See "Facts and figures." New York: National Council on Alcoholism, 1963, p. 2.) Surely, we have no reason to believe that the prevalence of alcoholism has since diminished.

9. The function of psychotherapy as a formal and institutionalized antidote for loneliness has been examined in a recent book by W. Schofield, *Psychotherapy: The Purchase of Friendship*. Englewood Cliffs, N.J.: Prentice-Hall, 1964.

10. The psychological meaning of the contrast between American affability and European "reserve" has been explored in a penetrating essay by Kurt Lewin, whose insights lent so much substance to contemporary social psychology. See K. Lewin, *Resolving Social Conflicts*. New York: Harper, 1948, pp. 3-33.

11. W. F. Ogburn and C. Tibbetts, "The family and its functions." In R. Freedman, *et. al.* (eds.), *Principles of Sociology*. New York: Holt, 1956, pp. 421-32.

12. *The World Almanac* 1964. New York: *New York World-Telegram*, 1964, p. 310.

CHAPTER 8   PALLIATIVES IN PURGATORY

1. So pervasive is this mistaken faith that President Lyndon Johnson, striving to evoke the deepest possible sense of unity among the American people on the day we buried his assassinated predecessor, made the following declaration: "We think that where a capitalist can put up a dollar, we can get a return on it. A manager can get up early to work and with money and men he can build a better mousetrap. A laborer who is worthy of his hire stands a chance of getting attention and maybe a little profit-sharing system, and the highest minimum wages of any nation in the world." (*The New York Times*, November 26, 1963, p. 13.)

2. See, for example, another portion of President Johnson's statement, *ibid.*

3. R. Gardner, "A judge tells how to deal with 'under-age hoods.' " *U. S. News and World Report*, August 26, 1963, pp. 44-45.

4. See, for example, some of the statements reported by James Reston in *The New York Times*, November 25, 1963, p. 5.

5. As of 1962, 90 per cent of the households in the United States had at least one television set (*Statistical Abstract of the United States, op. cit.*, p. 523). In that same year, the number of hours of television usage per day in homes containing sets averaged somewhat over 5 hours. (C. S. Aaronson [ed.], *International Television Almanac*. New York: Quigley Publications, 1963, 28a.)

6. For an amusing commentary upon the viewing habits of television's post-midnight "regulars," see: Dorothy Ferenbaugh, "Bedside manner." *The New York Times*, May 17, 1964, Section II, p. 17.

7. See Note 8 of Chapter VII above for the figures on alcoholism that dramatize this need.

8. Furthermore, the use of tranquilizers has been rising annually, the number of prescriptions going up over the past five years: 1959—65,395,000; 1960—68,695,000; 1961—71,783,000; 1962—76,590,000; and 1963—85,113,000 (All of these figures, and the one cited in the text for 1963, were taken from the magazine *American Druggist*: March 16, 1964, p. 14; April 1, 1963, p. 8; March 19, 1962, p. 8, and August 7, 1961, p. 8.)

9. See N. E. Miller, "Some recent studies of conflict behavior and drugs." *American Psychologist*, 1961, Vol. XVI, pp. 12-24.

10. See, for example: B. Bursten and J. M. R. Delgado, "Positive reinforcement induced by intracerebral stimulation in the monkey." *Journal of Comparative and Physiological Psychology*, 1960, Vol. LIII, pp. 128-37; J. Olds, "Self-stimulation experiments and differentiated reward systems." In H. H. Jasper, *et al.* (eds.), *Reticular Formation of the Brain*. Boston: Little, Brown, 1958, pp. 671-87.

11. See J. M. R. Delgado, "Emotional behavior in animals and humans." In "Explorations in the physiology of emotions." *Psychiatric Research Reports*, 1960, No. 12, pp. 259-66.

12. See S. Garattini and V. Ghetti (eds.), *Psychotropic Drugs*. Princeton, N.J.: Van Nostrand, 1958.

13. The Police Department of New York City has estimated that 40 per cent of the addicts known to it are 25 years of age or less; and that youths under 20 years of age constitute 14 per cent of the total number of known addicts. (*Second Interim Report of the State of New York: Joint Legislative Committe on Narcotic Study*, Legislative Document, 1958, No. 16, p. 23.)

14. *Prevention and Control of Narcotics addiction*. Washington: United States Treasury Department, Bureau of Narcotics, 1962, p. 8.

15. It has been pointed out that the official figure, based upon addicts listed in police reports, may be a gross underestimate of the number of Americans who, while illicitly using narcotics as their major palliative, manage to remain undetected by the agents of law enforcement. (See R. D. Schwartz's book review of W. B. Eldridge, *Narcotics and the Law: A Critique of the American Experiment in Narcotic Drug Control*. In the *Harvard Law Review*, 1963, Vol. LXXVII, p. 193.)

16. See L. B. Kalinowsky and P. H. Hoch, *Shock Treatments and Other Somatic Procedures in Psychiatry*. New York: Grune and Stratton, 1946.

17. See, for example: W. J. Freeman and J. W. Watts *Psychosurgery*. Springfield, Ill.: Thomas, 1942; N. D. C. Lewis, C. Landis, and H. E. King (eds.), *Studies in Topectomy*. New York: Grune and Stratton, 1956; and Mary F. Robinson and W. Freeman, *Psychosurgery and the Self*. New York: Grune and Stratton, 1954.

18. For a theoretical discussion of this concept, see: R. K. Merton, *Social Theory and Social Structure*. Glencoe, Ill.: Free Press, 1949, Chapter VII.

19. One may obtain a feeling for the variety and extent of these "side effects" by browsing through advertisements that drug companies address to psychiatrists who are likely to have severely distraught patients under their care. While each company emphasizes the purportedly benevolent effects of its particular brand of tranquilizer, it also devotes some space to the unpleasant consequences its product has been known to induce. (See, for example, any recent issue of *Mental Hospitals*, an official publication of the American Psychiatric Association.)

20. See "Johnson signs fund bill for mental health program." *The New York Times*, February 11, 1964, p. 14.

21. For portents of future developments in the "treatment" of disturbed individuals, witness these glowing reports: "The tranquilizing drugs . . . have, over the past five years, revolutionized the care of state mental hospital patients and brought about a sustained annual reduction in state hospital populations. . . . In some states where more intense application of the drugs has occurred, reductions have far exceeded the national average." (*Facts on the Major Killing and Crippling Diseases in the United States Today, op. cit.*, pp. 15-16, 19.)

22. Sigmund Freud, "The future prospects of psychoanalytic therapy." *Collected Papers*, Vol. II. London: Hogarth, 1949, pp. 285-96.

23. A sampling of some of these methods is contained in: D. H. Ford and H. B. Urban, *Systems of Psychotherapy: A Comparative Study*. New York: Wiley, 1963.

24. For an introductory glimpse of some of the problems attendant upon the scientific evaluation of the effects of psychotherapy, see: H. H. Strupp, "Patient-doctor relationships: The psychotherapist in the therapeutic process." In A. Bachrach (ed.), *Experimental Foundations of Clinical Psychology* New York: Basic Books, 1962, pp. 576-615.

25. One cannot devise a method of changing the behavior of individuals without making a host of assumptions—implicit, if not explicit—about the general determinants and principles of human behavior. In the case of most psychotherapies, the approach to behavioral change has been via attempts to alter crucial aspects of the individual's personality, an abstract and hypothetical construction that is inferred from overt behavior and that is presumed to give rise to that behavior.

26. The late Robert Lindner noted that much of his psychotherapeutic caseload was composed of persons who had previously been considered—and had considered themselves—"cured" after a lengthy course of psychoanalytic treatment. (*Prescription for Rebellion.* New York: Rinehart, 1952, Chapter IV.)

27. Freudian theory or one of its neo-Freudian modifications. For evaluative reviews of these theories, see: Ruth Monroe, *Schools of Psychoanalytic Thought.* New York: Dryden, 1955; and C. S. Hall and G. Lindzey, *Theories of Personality.* New York: Wiley, 1957, Chapters II, III, and IV.

28. Speaking of the "arrogant and unbridled egoists" whose demented foibles are socially acclaimed, however much they may cause others to suffer, Ruth Benedict has put this paradox well: "They are not described in our manuals of psychiatry because they are supported by every tenet of our civilization." (Ruth Benedict, *Patterns of Culture.* New York: Mentor, 1951, p. 256.)

CHAPTER 9   MUSINGS ON UTOPIA

1. It must be admitted that a humane society could not hope to exist save on an international basis. Nations committed to aggrandizement could scarcely be expected to look kindly upon such an anomaly in their midst. Indeed, a single country that sought to live by humane

principles would be as vulnerable to extinction by the inhumane world from without as have been those idealistic microcosms which, in the course of American history, have succumbed to the encroachments of a surrounding society hostile to their values. (See Holbrook, *op. cit.*, Parts I and II, for examples of the destructive pressures brought to bear upon a variety of isolated communal experiments that have been attempted by dedicated minorities.)

2. This conception is neither a starry-eyed impracticality nor a self-deluding flattery. On the contrary, we cannot reasonably look forward to any fate better than the one we set in store for ourselves.

3. Proudhon, *op. cit.*, gives a compelling discussion of the justice of this position.

4. K. Marx, *Critique of the Gotha Programme.* New York: International Publishers, 1933, p. 10.

5. Of course, scientific research cannot determine the objectives of a society, since these are, exclusively, a reflection of the values held by the people of that society. However, the scientific method can be very usefully employed in developing the technical means that are most consonant with a society's ends. (See Sarnoff, *Personality Dynamics and Development, op. cit.*, Chapters I and XVII, for a further consideration of the relationship between values and science.)

6. J. M. Nielsen, *A Textbook of Clinical Neurology.* New York: Hoeber, 1947, pp. 503-4.

CHAPTER 10   SOCIETY WITH TEARS

1. See S. G. Payne, *Falange; a History of Spanish Fascism.* Stanford, Calif.: Stanford University Press, 1961.

2. See, for example: W. A. Robson (ed.), *Social Security.* London: Allen and Unwin, 1945; *Social Sweden.* Stockholm: Social Welfare Board, 1952; and Socialt Tidsskrift (eds.), *Social Denmark.* London: Allen and Unwin, 1946.

3. See D. C. Blaisdell, *Government and Agriculture; The Growth of Federal Farm Aid.* New York: Farrar and Rinehart, 1940; and G. C. Fite, *George N. Peek and the Fight for Farm Parity.* Norman, Okla.: University of Oklahoma Press, 1954.

4. See Fromm, *The Sane Society, op cit.*, pp. 8-9.

5. See, for example: E. Crankshaw, *The New Cold War, Moscow v. Pekin.* Baltimore: Penguin, 1963; and D. S. Zagoria, *The Sino-Soviet Conflict, 1959-1961.* Princeton: Princeton University Press, 1962.

6. See, for example: "Soviets condemn 2 to die for reducing meat-

pie fat." *The New York Times*, February 6, 1964, p. 7; and "8 shot in Soviet charges of embezzling and bribery." *The New York Times*, April 18, 1964, p. 10.

7. Examples of the Soviet provisions for the economic security and welfare of its citizens may be found in: I. R. Levine, *Main Street, U.S.S.R.* New York, Doubleday, 1959.

8. For manifestations of the competition among Soviet youth in the pursuit of the values of aggrandizement, see: A Kassoff, "Now the angry young Ivans." *The New York Times*, November 19, 1961, Section VI, p. 22.

9. See, for example: Levine, *op. cit.*, pp. 376-81; and "Soviet paper asks rein on writers." *The New York Times*, December 1, 1963, Section I, p. 32.

10. "The peasant, the soldier, the worker, the artist, and the scientist play their roles in accordance with a web of decisions that ultimately originate in, or are approved by, the Presidium (formerly the Politburo), the highest organ of the Communist Party, of the Soviet Union." (B. Moore, *Terror and Progress USSR*. Cambridge: Harvard University Press, 1954, p. 3.)

11. For a first-hand description of life in these camps by one of the many Soviet citizens who were imprisoned in them, see: A. Solzhenitsyn, *One Day in the Life of Ivan Denisovich*. New York: Dutton, 1963.

12. The following quotations illustrate the missionary flavor of the exhortations that Marx and Engels addressed to the members of the working class: "Proletarians have nothing of their own to safeguard; it is their business to destroy all pre-existent private proprietary securities and private proprietary safeguards." (K. Marx and F. Engels, *The Communist Manifesto*. New York: International Publishers, 1930, p. 40.) " . . . This revolution is necessary, therefore, not only because the ruling class cannot be overthrown in any other way, but also because the class *overthrowing* it can only in a revolution succeed in ridding itself of all the muck of the ages and become fitted to found society anew." (K. Marx and F. Engels, *The German Ideology*. London: Lawrence and Wishart, 1938, p. 69.) "The working class, in the course of its development, will substitute for the old civil society an association which will exclude classes and their antagonism, and there will be no more political power properly so-called, since political power is precisely the official expression of antagonism in civil society." (K. Marx, *The Poverty of Philosophy*. London: Lawrence and Wishart, 1956, p. 174.)

13. "Between capitalist and communist society lies the period of the revolutionary transformation of the one into the other. There corresponds to this also a political transition period in which the state can be nothing but *the revolutionary dictatorship of the proletariat.*" (Marx, *Critique of the Gotha Programme, op. cit.,* p. 18.)

14. "State interference in social relations, becomes, in one sphere after another, superfluous and then dies of itself. In the place of the government over persons, steps the administration of things and the management of the processes of production. The State is not 'abolished'; *it withers away.*" (F. Engels, *Anti-Dühring.* Chicago: Kerr, 1935, p. 292.)

15. Marx, *Critique of the Gotha Programme, op. cit.,* p. 10.

16. Surely, few humanitarians could take exception with Marx (*ibid.,* p. 10) over the desirability of a society in which "the enslaving subordination of individuals under division of labour, and therewith also the antithesis between mental and physical labour, has vanished"; in which "labour, from a mere means of life, has itself become a prime necessity of life"; in which "the productive forces have also increased with the all-round development of the individual. . . ."

17. Reference has already been made to major sources containing such arguments: Marx, *ibid.;* Marx and Engels, *The Communist Manifesto, op. cit.;* and Marx and Engels, *The German Ideology, op. cit.* Marx further sought to bolster his theoretical views on this matter in a detailed post mortem of the short-lived Paris Commune of 1871. (See *The Civil War in France.* London: Martin, 1933.)

18. See D. Ryazanoff's introduction to *The Communist Manifesto, op. cit.,* pp. 1-24, for an account of Marx's role in the formulation of the earliest international organization of workers opposed to capitalism.

19. For a detailed statement of this concept, see: Marx and Engels, *The German Ideology, op. cit.*

20. See *Critique of the Gotha Programme, op. cit.,* pp. 8-10, for Marx's exposition of the points summarized in this paragraph.

21. In fact, Lenin, who put Marxian theory into practice as leader of the Russian Revolution, prepared himself and his followers for the installation of the "dictatorship of the proletariat" by writing a small book on the relationship between the state and revolution. In that tract, he reiterated the views of Marx and Engels, implicitly invoking their authority for the actions he was about to undertake. (See V. I. Lenin, *The State and Revolution.* Moscow: Foreign Languages Publishing House, 1947.)

22. For an appreciation of the variety of ways in which automation has already been applied in our economy, see: D. N. Michael, *Cybernation: The Silent Revolution*. Santa Barbara, Calif.: The Fund for the Republic, 1962; and W. Buckingham, *Automation: Its Impact on Business and People*. New York: Mentor, 1963.

23. See, for example: Michael, *ibid.*, pp. 14-24; and "Automation called major cause in loss of 40,000 jobs a week." *The New York Times* October 4, 1963, p. 1.

24. Recently, just such a proposal was put forward by a group composed of well-known persons in a variety of fields, the Ad Hoc Committee on the Triple Revolution. (See J. D. Pomfret, "Guaranteed income asked for all, employed or not." *The New York Times*, March 23, 1964, p. 1.)

25. In *The New Men of Power* (*op. cit.*, p. 223), Mills reports that, as far back as 1946, a poll of the "mass public" revealed 42 per cent of the people to be in favor of requiring all corporations "to put a union representative on their board of directors."

26. See H. K. Beecher, "Psychotomimetic drugs." *Journal of Chronic Diseases*, 1958, Vol. VIII, pp. 253-85.

27. See, for example: "Equal job rights." *Business Week*, March 11, 1961, p. 120; and W. H. Speck, "Enforcement of nondiscrimination requirements for government contract work." *Columbia Law Review*, 1963, Vol. LXIII, pp. 243-65.

28. A. Camus, *Resistance, Rebellion and Death*. New York: Knopf, 1961, p. 36.

Index

AFL-CIO, 70-71, 274
Alcoholism, 202-3, 206
Alienation, in bureaucracy, 137
  and insanity, 177-83
  and the values of aggrandizement,
    181-2
Alinsky, S., 101
Ambivalents, 137
Apartheid, 95
Apathy, and conformity, 132-22, 137
  and the idle rich, 142-143
  among Negroes, 101
Automation, and degradation, 272
  and dictatorship, 273
  and education, 282
  and fulfillment, 278
  in a humane society, 223
  and limitless aspirations, 273
  and management, 273
  and proposals for social change,
    278, 281
  and unemployment, 88, 135, 273
  and the values of realization, 272

Baldwin, James, 98
Black Muslims, 104
Bohlke, R. H., 167-8
British Labour Party, 69
Buddha, 41
Bureaucracy, and class, 81
  and crime, 71
  and labor unions, 71
  and organizations of work, 66, 71-
    73, 115
  and the values of aggrandizement,
    73
Business cycle, 67-8

Calvinism, 43, 104
Capitalism, and aggrandizement, 53-6
  and crime, 159-61

and Protestantism, 43-44
relationship to Church and State, 53
Caste, and aggrandizement, 96, 109
  and barriers to the values of realiza-
    tion, 96
  and crime, 161
  effects on Negroes, 97-102, 104
  effects on non-whites, 94
  effects on whites, 94
  and juvenile delinquency, 171
  mortality rates of Negroes and
    whites, 97
  and prejudice, 100
  proposals for the elimination of,
    103, 105-8
  socio-economic bases, 109
Catholicism, and aggrandizement, 47
  and megalomania, 41, 45
  and nationalism, 50-1
Christ, 39-42, 44, 48
Christianity, and egoism, 48
  and megalomania, 39-41
Civil Rights Act of 1964, 95
Civil Rights Movement, 105, 108, 110
Class, and aggrandizement, 78
  and bureaucracy, 81
  and caste, 91
  categories of, 77-87
  and crime, 161, 163-4
  effects on non-whites, 112
  effects on whites, 112
  and the hierarchy of invidious dis-
    tinction, 87-8
  and the industrial revolution, 78
  and juvenile delinquency, 164-5
  and mental illness, 141
  mortality rates of highest and low-
    est, 77
  and social discontent, 197
  in the Soviet Union, 262-3
  stability of, 79, 87-8

Cleckly, H., 180
Cloward, R., 175-6
Cognitive development, and values, 22
Communism, and nationalism, 51
    and the values of realization, 260-1
Communist Party, 69, 262-7, 269
Conformity, and apathy, 132-3, 137
    and child-rearing, 132
    and creative artists, 152-4
    and the idle rich, 139
    and interpersonal skills, 130, 132
    and managers, 127-32
    and oligarchs, 126
    organizational coercions for, 116
    organizational incentives for, 116
    and other-directed personalities, 132
    and the professional class, 144-5
    and the working class, 135
    and the unemployed workers, 155
Crime, and capitalism, 159-61
    and caste, 161
    and class, 161, 163-4
    and insanity, 179, 183
    rates of, 163
    treatment of in American society, 159-60, 212-14, 216
    treatment of in a humane society, 244-8

da Vinci, Leonardo, 45
Delinquency, see Juvenile delinquency
Democracy, in a humane society, 222-243
    and nationalism, 51
Democratic Party, 275
Discrimination, see Caste, Prejudice, and Racism
Dictatorship of the proletariat, Marx's doctrine of, 269-70
Divorce, effects on children, 187
    rates of, 187
    and the values of aggrandizement, 186-8, 190, 192
Domestic Marshall Plan, 105
Durkheim, E., 142-3

Economic competition, and American history, 62-4

and juvenile delinquency, 166
and the self-employed entrepreneur, 151
Economic consolidation, and agriculture, 66
    and bureaucracy, 66
    and distribution, 65
    and industrial growth, 64
    and industrial relations, 68
    and labor unions, 70-1
    and oligarchy, 69
    and production, 65
    and the self-employed entrepreneur, 149-50
Education, and bureaucracy, 231
    and class, 231
    in a humane society, 228-38
    and the values of aggrandizement, 232
    and the values of realization, 228-238, 281-2
Egoism, see Megalomania and the Values of aggrandizement
Ellison, Ralph, 98
Employees, categories of, 71-2
    percentage in labor force, 71-2
Engels, F., 264
Equalitarian values, definition of, 19-20
Esthetic values, definition of, 20-1

Falange party, 258
Fascism, and nationalism, 51
    Spanish, 258
Franco, Francisco, 258
Freud, Sigmund, 27, 30-1, 39, 217-18

Galbraith, J. K., 65
Gambling, motives for, 208, 210
    and the stock market, 211-12
    and the values of aggrandizement, 209, 212
Glazer, N., 100-1
Gompers, Samuel, 69, 71
Green, W., 71

Hentoff, Nat, 101
Hierarchy of invidious distinction, 77, 85, 87, 90, 107, 117, 134, 248, 262, 270, 280

Hierarchy *(continued)*
  elimination in a humane society, 248
  proposals for elimination of, 280
  in the Soviet Union, 262, 270
  see also Caste, Class, and Bureaucracy
Homestead Act of 1862, 62
Housing, and caste, 96
  in a humane society, 248
Humane society, artists in, 227-8, 233-234
  automation in, 223
  conditions of work in, 224-5
  economic system of, 222-38
  education in, 228-38
  and international economic organizations, 226-7
  law in, 243-8
  marriage in, 249-52
  political system of, 239-43
  social institutions of, 248-53
  standards of competence in, 237-8
  treatment of crime in, 244-8
  treatment of insanity in, 253-4
  and the values of realization, 220-2, 226, 228-38, 243, 249-50
Humanitarian values, definition of, 19
Hutcheson, W., 71

Idle Rich, class definition of, 85
  psychological problems of, 141
Indentured servants, 67, 89, 90
Indifferents, 137
Insanity, and crime, 179, 183
  definition of in American society, 177-9
  rates of, 179
  treatment of in American society, 212-16
  treatment of in a humane society, 253-4
  and the values of aggrandizement, 177, 183
Integration, in housing, 103
  in public education, 103
Intellectual values, definition of, 20-1

Judaism, and megalomania, 39-40
  and monotheism, 37-9

Juvenile delinquency, and caste, 170-1
  and class, 164-6
  and competition, 166, 172
  and lack of commitment to values, 174
  and limitless aspirations, 165-6, 168
  and opportunity, 175-6
  proposals for prevention of, 175-6
  and prosperity, 167
  rates of, 164, 173
  and relative deprivation, 167
  and social hypocrisy, 173
  and the values of aggrandizement, 165, 169-70, 173
  and the values of realization, 173-174, 176

Kennedy, John F., 198-9
King, Martin Luther, Jr., 102, 108
Kropotkin, P. A., 40-1

Labor, relations with industry, 135
Labor unions, bureaucracy in, 71
  development of, 69-70
  economic consolidation of, 70-1
  and oligarchy, 275
  and political influence, 274
  and the status quo, 134-5, 274
Law, and crime, 163
  enforcement among classes, 163-4
  functions of in American society, 160
  in a humane society, 243-8
Lenin, V. I., 260, 264-5, 270
Leo X, Pope, 46
Limitless aspirations, and class, 77
  and juvenile delinquency, 165-6, 168
  and lack of love, 184-5
  and loneliness, 184-5
  and the values of aggrandizement, 26
  and the values of realization, 26, 221-2
Lomax, L. E., 99-100
Love, in a humane society, 249-50, 252
  and the values of aggrandizement, 186-9, 191
  and the values of realization, 192
Lubell, S., 101

Managers, class definition of, 82-3
  and oligarchs, 83
  psychological problems of, 126-33
  required personality traits, 128-9
Marriage, in a humane society, 249-52
  and the values of aggrandizement, 186-92
  and the values of realization, 192
Marx, Karl, 139, 143, 260-1, 264, 267-70, 272
Marxism, and development of labor unions, 69
  and dictatorship, 267-70
  and proposals for elimination of caste, 105
  and Soviet-Chinese competition, 260
  and the values of aggrandizement, 268
  and the values of realization, 268
Mass media, and propaganda, 115
  and public opinion, 201
  and the status quo, 202
Material wealth as a value, definition of, 16-18
McCarthy, Joseph R., 267
Megalomania, effects on marriage, 192
  and nationalism, 48-52
  and religion, 36-41, 45, 49
  and royalty, 260
  and the values of aggrandizement, 35-6
Mental illness, see Insanity
Mills, C. W., 81, 83, 85, 118, 123, 126, 168
Modern societies, aggrandizement in, 256-7
Monopolies, see Economic consolidation
Monotheism, and the ancient Hebrews, 37-9
  Christian compared to Judaic, 42
  concept of, 37
  and megalomania, 36-40, 49
Mortality rates, comparisons between castes, 97
  comparisons between classes, 77
Motives, physiologically derived, 15
  socially learned, 16
  and values, 16, 20, 22

Narcotics, incentives for use, 206
  rates of use, 205
Nationalism, and megalomania, 48-52
  and oligarchy, 257
  and the status quo, 257
  and the values of aggrandizement, 276
Negro Revolution, 105-8, 110
Nye, I. F., 164

Ohlin, L., 175-6
Oligarchs, alliance of corporate and labor, 275
  class definition of, 84
  corporate, 81, 83, 115-6
  governmental, 81
  labor, 71, 82
  military, 81
  passive, 85
  and political influence, 121-3, 274
  psychological problems of, 118-20
  required personality traits, 126
Oligarchy, means of perpetuation, 125
  and dictatorship, 275
  and economic consolidation, 69
Oligopoly, among labor unions, 71
  in industry, 66
Olson, V. J., 164
Organizations of work, basic characteristics of in America, 66, 71-3, 81, 85, 115
  see also Bureaucracy and Hierarchy of invidious distinction

Palliatives for social discontent, alcohol, 202-3
  brain surgery, 215
  chemical, 202-6
  consumption of material goods, 206-7
  electric shock therapy, 215
  gambling, 208-12
  hallucinatory drugs, 204-5, 276
  hedonic drugs, 204-5
  ideological, 197-201
  and the mass media, 200-1
  mental health professions, 217-19
  mental hospitals, 213-16
  narcotics, 202-6

Palliatives (*continued*)
prisons, 213-16
psychiatric clinics, 216
psychotherapy, 217-19
television, 200-1
tranquilizers, 202-16
Perfectibility, concept of, 24
Piaget, J., 27
Polytheism, 36
Power as a value, definition of, 16-18
Prejudice, and caste, 100-1
effects on Negroes, 95
Presthus, R., 83, 126, 137
Prestige as a value, definition of, 16-18
Private property, absence of in a humane society, 222
and crime, 159-62
Professional class, definition of, 86
and private practice, 146-8
Progress, and the values of aggrandizement, 25-6, 75
and the values of realization, 25-6
Proposals for social change, elimination of capitalism, 280
elimination of caste, 102, 111
elimination of class, 111-12
elimination of invidious distinction, 280
governmental intervention for economic justice, 279-80
governmental intervention for political justice, 281
governmental intervention for social justice, 281
and the liberal arts curriculum, 282
and non-violence, 287-8
and passive resistance, 286
and political action, 283-8
and the prevention of juvenile delinquency, 175-6
and values of realization, 278, 283, 288-9
Protestantism, and aggrandizement, 44, 47
and capitalism, 43-4, 60
and nationalism, 50-1
Proudhon, P. J., 159-60, 162, 211
Psychotherapy, effects of, 219

and lack of love, 184
and the values of aggrandizement, 218

Racism, 88-9, 93, 104, 109
Reformation, 43-4, 46, 49-52
Renaissance, 44-9
Republican party, 275
Roosevelt, Franklin D., 259

Self-concept, formation of, 22-6
functions of, 22-3
and motives, 22
and values, 23-4
and the values of aggrandizement, 24-6, 47
and the values of realization, 25-6
Self-employed class, and aggrandizement, 86-7
definition of, 85-6
psychological problems of, 143-51
Short, J. F., Jr., 164
Silberman, C., 101
Slavery, 67, 89, 91, 95-6
Smith, Adam, 52
Social change, *see* Proposals for social change
Social Security, 259
Socialist Party, 69
Soviet-Chinese competition, 260, 265
Soviet Union, class in, 262-3
Communist Party in, 262-7
constraints on freedom in, 265-7
economy of, 261-6
education in, 261
hierarchy of invidious distinction in, 262, 270
megalomania in, 263-4
nationalism in, 263-4
oligarchy in, 262-3, 265
religion in, 264
values of aggrandizement in, 262-3, 265, 267
values of realization in, 260-1, 266
Stalin, Josef, 265
State capitalism, 275
State religion, 50
Supreme Court ruling of 1954 against public school segregation, 103
Sutherland, E. H., 163-4

Thompson, Clara, 180
Tranquilizers, physiological effects, 203-4
  psychological effects, 203-4
  rates of use, 203
  use in mental hospitals, 216

Upward-mobiles, 126, 137
Unemployed workers, class definition of, 85
  and conformity, 155
  psychological problems of, 86, 155-157
Unemployment, and alcoholism, 156
  and crime, 156
  and drug addiction, 157
  psychological effects, 155-7
  rates among Negroes and whites, 91
  technological, 109
Urban League, 99

Values, American hierarchy of, 16
  and behavior, 24, 271
  and child-rearing, 31
  and cognitive development, 22
  conflicts of creative artists, 152-4
  conflicts of professionals, 145-8
  and motives, 16, 20, 22-6
  and ontogenetic development, 26
  and social institutions, 32-3
Values of aggrandizement, and the American Dream, 34-6
  and American frontier life, 61-2
  and bureaucracy, 73
  and caste, 92, 94, 96
  and civil rights, 105
  and crime, 158, 161-2, 168
  definition of, 16-18
  effects on attitudes toward education, 131
  effects on child-rearing, 196
  effects on education, 171-2
  effects on the idle rich, 140, 142
  effects on love, 186-9, 191
  effects on managerial class, 127, 130
  effects on marriage, 186-92

effects on non-professional entrepreneurs, 149-50
  effects on oligarchs, 117-24
  effects on public morality, 199
  effects on the self-employed, 144-5
  effects on working class, 133-6, 138
  effects on unemployed workers, 154-156
  and injustice, 158
  and insanity, 177, 183
  and juvenile delinquency, 158, 165, 169-70, 175, 176
  and the psychopathic personality, 180
  and social discontent, 197
Values of realization, and automation, 272
  and communism, 260-1
  definition of, 19-21
  and education, 228-38, 281-2
  in a humane society, 220-2, 226, 228-38, 243, 249-50
  and the idea of progress, 25-6
  and the idle rich, 140-1
  and limitless aspirations, 26, 221-2
  and love, 192
  and marriage, 192
  and Marxism, 268
  and the prevention of juvenile delinquency, 173-4, 176
  and proposals for social change, 278, 288-9
  and the Renaissance, 145
  and the self-concept, 25-6
  in the Soviet Union, 260-1, 266

Wallerstein, J. S., 164
Warren, R. P., 102
Washington, Booker T., 95
Welfare legislation, 259-60
White backlash, 108, 110
Workers, class definition of, 83-4
  psychological problems of, 133-8
World government, and the values of aggrandizement, 276-7
Wright, Richard, 98
Wyle, C. J., 164

Young, W. M., Jr., 99-100, 105